WRITING OUT LOUD

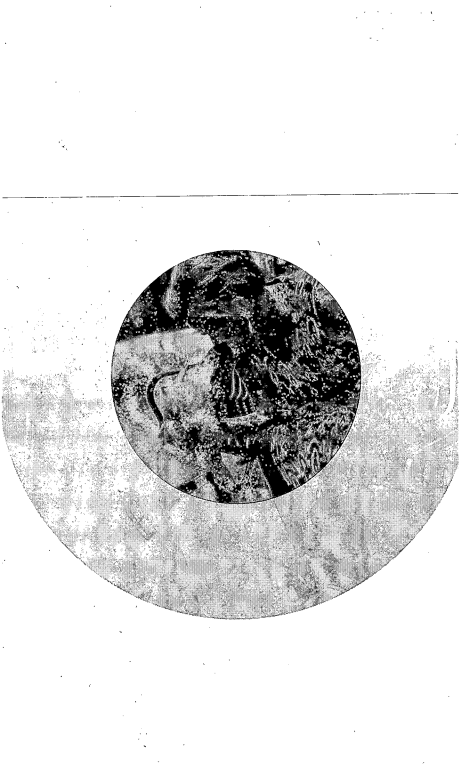

Writing Out Loud

what a blind teacher learned from
leading a memoir class for seniors

Beth Finke

 Golden Alley Press
Emmaus, Pennsylvania

This work is based on real events. Sure, some names have been changed, some events have been compressed, some dialogue has been recreated, but really, so many colorful characters have passed through my unconventional life that I didn't have to bother making anything up. Oh, and writers excerpted in this memoir have given me permission to share their stories.

Golden Alley Press
37 South 6th Street
Emmaus, Pennsylvania 18049

www.goldenalleypress.com

Golden Alley Press books may be purchased for educational, business, or sales promotional use. For information please contact the publisher.

▉▤ Printed in the United States of America

Writing Out Loud / Beth Finke. -1st ed.

Library of Congress Control Number: 2017940779

ISBN 978-0-9984429-2-1   *print*
ISBN 978-0-9984429-3-8   *ebook*

Front cover photograph: © Bill Healy, www.billhealymedia.com

Back cover photograph: © Kaitlin McCall

Cover design: Michael S. Sayre

*To all you lively writers who share your stories
in my writing classes.*

Contents

CONTENTS

CONTENTS

CONTENTS

PREFACE

I HAD TO laugh. The woman who wrote a favorable review of *Long Time, No See* in the *Chicago Tribune* back in 2003 had written three memoirs. I loved her review, but who would think enough of themselves to write more than one memoir?

Well, the laugh is on me.

Writing my first book gave me permission to work through losing my sight. I came to realize that going blind was like going through a second adolescence. I felt uncertain of myself. I wanted to be accepted. I wanted people to like me. And I was afraid I'd never fit in. There was a lot to overcome, both internally and externally.

So in the end, *Long Time, No See* was about surviving. I'd made it. My husband had made it. Our marriage survived. Our family was intact. As a fledgling writer, I was about to soar.

But I soon learned that living blind is a lot different from becoming blind. Take employment, for example. When I lost my sight, I lost my job. This was a problem because, for lots of reasons, I needed to work. So I was primed and ready when the fateful phone call that you're going to read about came in 2004.

My original intention for this manuscript was to collect favorite writing prompts I've assigned over the years, write my own 500-word essays on those topics, and compile them into a book to prove to my writers that it can be done. But my editor is far more lenient with word count than I am and has lifted my self-imposed word limit. And just like it so often goes with the writers in my memoir classes, as I wrote, the crux of my story emerged. Having these older writers in my life is a gift. I need to write about them. So here it is, my second memoir: *Writing Out Loud*, a story about what all of us can learn...when we listen.

Beth Finke
Chicago, Illinois
April 2017

WRITING OUT LOUD

1

The Brown Envelope

LIKE SO MANY other rules, I learned this one the hard way: if you're far from the phone, and you can't see, never rush to answer it. I pick up on the fifth ring.

It's the commissioner of Mayor Daley's Department on Aging. Daley? Mayor Richard Daley? Mayor of Chicago? We've only lived here a year. Does she have the right number?

She goes on. She heard me give a presentation the weekend before about my memoir, *Long Time, No See*. "Have any interest in leading memoir-writing classes for senior citizens?"

Me, teach? I loved school when I was a kid. I respect good teachers. My sister Marilee is one of them, so was my mother-in-law. I like to think I stay open to possibilities, but I respect the teaching profession too much to take this lightly. I've never led a class in anything. And writing a memoir doesn't qualify me to teach memoir writing.

The silence stretches between us, save the click, click, click of my Seeing Eye® dog's paws heading my way across the hardwood floor. Hanni thinks I'm standing there waiting for her.

The commissioner finally breaks in. "Need some time to think about it?" she asks, offering to discuss it over lunch. Where do the people who work for the Daley machine eat lunch, I wonder? I accept her invite.

After small talk and egg salad sandwiches at a Chicago Loop diner, the commissioner pulls something out of her bag.

"I have the application right here," she says, drumming her fingers on what I guess is a big brown envelope.

"It's already filled out. You'll do great!"

2

Getting There

MY SEEING EYE dog, Hanni, and I do a few trial runs from our Printers Row neighborhood to the Chicago Cultural Center before the first day of class. It's only been a year since we moved here from Urbana, Illinois in 2003, and it is important to me to find my way to class on my own. Blindness affects my every move, but out there in the streets of Chicago I'm not really worried about getting hit by a car or accosted by a ne'er-do-well. I'm far more concerned about people staring at me. Delusions of grandeur? Maybe, but I'm convinced they're out there, and I don't want them to catch me making a mistake.

So Hanni guides me downtown on this beautiful October day to the Chicago Cultural Center, the neo-classical landmark building that was originally the Chicago Public Library. From when I could still see, I remember its green-veined marble walls, mosaic tiles, magnificent staircases, and Tiffany glass dome. And now Hanni will be guiding me through the Cultural Center's magnificent mahogany doors every week.

I'd written a short description for the eight-week class for my husband Mike to format. The flyer identifies me as an NPR contributor and author of a memoir called *Long Time, No See*, but it doesn't come right out and advertise that the woman teaching the class is blind. I'd dropped the flyer off at the front desk during one of my test runs and volunteers readily agreed to make copies and plaster it all over the walls. "Here's a class for anyone who's been told, 'You should write a book!'" it reads. "'Me, Myself, and I,' taught by Beth Finke...." Was I really going to pull this off, leading a memoir class for the City of Chicago?

On our way to the first day of class, Hanni looks ahead, makes a split-second decision, and darts left. Holding tight to her harness, I sidestep along with her. My shoulders breeze by something as we needle our way down Michigan Avenue. A tree? A lamppost? A person? Without being able to see, I have no idea what we missed. I'm just glad we missed it.

"That dog isn't looking where he's going!" a random voice calls out from behind me. But what does the voice know? That's just the way Hanni works. She's quick on her feet. A proud graduate of The Seeing Eye, class of December, 2001, Hanni – her name rhymes with Bonnie – was taught to make quick decisions. She has to. That's the only way we can avoid collisions with pedestrians. With cars pulling out of parking garages. With taxis turning right on red. With delivery trucks rushing out of blind alleys.

The trip is less than a mile from our apartment. Commuting by foot and paw, we sail down Michigan Avenue. Weaving through the lunch crowd, we are right on time. Until we run into this guy.

Okay, "run into" is not a phrase a blind writer should use flippantly. We don't actually run into him. More like he interrupts our progress by calling out to us.

"Beth! Hello! How you doan?" My confusion is obvious. An accent. South American? African?

"It's Herman!" he finally announces. The "h" is silent. Air-Mann. Like Thomas Mann, only different. Now I remember – a friend's roommate married Air-Mann after we graduated from college. A few weeks earlier we'd gotten reacquainted with the couple at a party. Otherwise I'm sure he never would have recognized me on Michigan Avenue. I could see when I was in college. Now I travel by dog.

I thrust my hand out, hoping he'll know to give it a shake. He does.

"Where you goan?" he asks.

I tell him I'm teaching a writing class. "At the Cultural Center," my voice rings out. Loud enough for everyone passing by to overhear, I hope. I like the picture. An accomplished teacher with her Seeing Eye dog, on her way to class. She's stopping on Michigan Avenue for a bit, talking to a handsome foreigner. I really have no idea what Air-Mann looks like now, but I picture him handsome. Why think otherwise?

"It's my first day. Class starts at 1:30," I continue, turning my head towards the next intersection. A bit of body language I still remember from my seeing days, meant to let Air-Mann know I need to get going.

But Air-Mann doesn't notice. He wants to chat. About that nice party. About where he is working now. About what time he'll be meeting his wife after work tonight.

Last time I looked in the mirror, I was slim, trim, and 26 years old. But maybe body language has changed some since 1985, too? Air-man isn't reading my signals. I want to be at class very early today. I want to be seated, my dog arranged underneath me, all set and looking like I have my act together if any students actually arrive. But here's the problem. I want to look like a woman with her act together on Michigan Avenue, too. Interrupting Air-Mann, telling him right out loud that I need to get going, that would expose me for what I am: an anxious amateur. With 40 whole minutes to travel two measly blocks, I am still nervous about getting there on time.

So I don't interrupt Air-Mann. Hanni does, though. Bored, she eases herself down to the pavement in a move that is deliberately slow, yet dramatic enough to jiggle her harness and draw Air-Mann's attention. I love that dog.

"Lying down on the job!" I joke, picking up her harness handle. "We'd better get going."

3

Eyebrows Up

"HELLO?" NO ANSWER.

The classroom is empty when Hanni and I arrive. High ceilings echo our movement, making the room feel bigger than it is. But Hanni and I have practiced this. We thread our way to a seat at the table. I fish my memoir, *Long Time, No See*, out of my backpack and plunk it on the table. With any luck, it has landed face up. A published book might lend me some credibility with these senior citizens.

I poke the button on my talking watch. "It's one-seventeen-p-m." Class begins at 1:30. I should have brought Braille to read. Books on tape don't work at times like this – headphones prevent me from hearing what's going on around me. I need to be aware if, by some miracle, a senior shows up.

A copy machine whirrs in a nearby office. Footsteps tread past my room. Time trickles. No, it's more annoying than that. It drips, like water from a broken faucet.

The vacant room comes as no surprise. Who would sign up for a writing class taught by someone who didn't know how to teach?

I press my watch again. "It's one-twenty-three-p.m." Still just me and Hanni. I bend down to pet her, and just as I place my hand behind my head to avoid bumping it on the way up, the miracle happens. Seniors start showing up for class. All at once. At first I'm startled by their arrival. Then I'm surprised at how happy I feel. Apparently they actually believed the stuff they read on those posters.

"My name is Beth," I say, as chairs shuffle around. Have they noticed the dog under the table? Do they know I can't see them? I don't know.

"Is this the writing class?" one of them asks. I sense skepticism.

My sister Marilee learned at a teaching seminar that if you talk with your eyebrows up you sound more positive. I decide to give eyebrows-up a try. Throwing out a laugh, I say, "This is it! This is the writing class!"

Eyebrows-up works. The students stay.

I ask them to introduce themselves. They have great names. Minerva. Lita. Ida. Hannelore. Tom is the only man, and he has brought his wife along. Why? I don't ask. I'm just glad they are all here.

By asking them to tell me a little bit about themselves, I learn that these senior citizens have grown up on the South Side, in the suburbs, in St. Louis. One has a master's degree. Another never finished high school. A third completed her associate's degree at age 72. When Louise introduces herself,

I have a little trouble understanding her. The puzzled look on my face forces her to explain.

"My tooth ith mything," she says. She hadn't been able to get an appointment with a dentist before today, and she didn't want to miss the first class.

"Ooòoh. Does it hurt?" I ask.

"No, it juth lookth terrible!" she says, all her sibilant sounds lingering longer than they should. "I'm holding a Kleenecth in front of my mouth while I talk," she explains. I remind her that I won't even notice how she looks. "I'm sure no one else here will mind, either." The class reassures her they won't. Louise puts the Kleenex back in her purse.

A retired postal worker, Louise had gone to college in her 60s and studied theater. "I want to be an actreth!" she announces. We would soon learn that Louise does indeed have a sense for the dramatic.

Missing teeth aside, one thing all of the students have in common? They are all writers. Some have taken other writing classes. One woman retired from a career in journalism and PR, for Pete's sake.

Act professional, I tell myself. Don't let on. But I know I'm sunk. I thought I had one – and only one – chance of getting away with this sham: the students all had to be naïve beginners. But not this group.

Deep breath. Eyebrows up again.

My plan for our first meeting is to show them how to dictate their memories into a tape recorder. The method had worked for me when I recorded the rough draft of my own memoir from a hospital bed years ago, when I'd spent months after my 26th birthday undergoing surgeries in a vain attempt to save my eyesight. A hospital social worker suggested I record an audio journal, which I later transcribed with my talking computer. Those tapes eventually led to *Long Time, No See*. So I knew it could work for my seniors.

I'd brought special five-minute-per-side tapes for them. "All you have to do is go home, sit down with a recorder, and talk about what it was like getting to school in the winter. What did you wear? How long was the walk? Who did you walk with? Where was the school?

"Let yourself go off on tangents at first," I say. "What do you think of when you remember those cold days? Long underwear? Mittens? The smell of your wet socks drying on the radiator?" If the tape runs out, I tell them they should turn it around and start over again. "Keep doing this until you finally get it down to five minutes," I say, pointing out that one easy way to accomplish this would be to devote the entire essay to one specific thing. "You'll be amazed what all can be said about long underwear."

I have it all worked out. My writers will bring their tapes back to the next class. I'll take the cassettes home, type up what I hear, bring the papers back, and hand them out. "Look! You all wrote something!" I'll say.

I finish telling them about my great idea, and the room falls quiet. They are riveted, I'm sure, by the thought of recording their stories.

But I'm wrong. They are simply being polite. The silence stretches between us, and then, suddenly, they erupt in protest. "Our other writing teacher told us never to use cassette tapes.

He said we should only write!"

I surrender. "Forget the tapes. Don't talk about your walks to school," I tell them. "Write about them instead."

They fiddle with bags and briefcases. Nothing has been said about class being over, but everyone is ready to leave. I'm about to stand up and give Hanni the "outside!" command when I feel a gentle tap on my wrist.

"It's Minerva," she says. "I'll take one of those cassettes." I want to reach out and hug her, but in an attempt to maintain my professional image, I reach for my backpack instead. Digging through my stuff, I find a tape and hand it in her direction.

"Do you need a recorder, too?" I ask, willing to lend mine to this woman with the sweet, dignified voice.

"No thank you," she says, unzipping her handbag and sliding the cassette inside. "I have one."

4

Around the World with Sylvia

BACK HOME, I start typing each student's name into my talking computer. "L-i-t-a," I type, my computer parroting the letters as I punch the keys. "Radio soap opera actress." I do my best to list the names in the order they'd been sitting around the table. Alice likes dogs. Olga writes poetry. Minerva took a cassette. Hannelore has a German accent. Writing all this down helps me remember their names. And just before Hanni and I head out for the second class, I listen to the list of names once more.

As my writers file in, they sit in the exact seats they'd been in the week before. That list I made? Priceless! I wow them by calling each one by name when it is their turn to read aloud.

They are a good audience. Writers clap and cheer after each and every story. No one critiques, no one talks about plot or character development. One comments on having had a similar experience walking to school back in the day, another asks exactly where it was that the essay reader had grown up. "Oh, yeah!" they laugh, recognizing the crossroads. "Remember the Regal Theater? Wasn't that near your school?"

The class is right to applaud each essay. The stories are fascinating. A week before, I had no idea what background each student came from, what color skin they had, how old they were. Now their school stories tell all. Minerva, an 86-year-old African-American, grew up on the South Side, long before Brown v. Board of Education. Hannelore grew up in Germany and graduated from school there before World War II. Alice couldn't remember any special stories about getting to school on cold days, so she wrote a simple story about her childhood on Chicago's West Side instead.

I make no comments on structure, grammar, point of view. I just clap along with everyone else.

Is this all there is to it? Just figure out a subject for them to write about, assign things I want to hear about, then let them read? I can do this.

"For next week, write about a travel fiasco you've experienced," I tell them, suggesting they do their best to remember exactly how they felt at the moment their journey began to unravel. "Instead of just saying you were tired, or you were angry at your husband or whatever, show your readers how you reacted." I suggest they end their essays with how they feel about that vacation now.

STUDENTS SHOW UP to our next class with travel stories about misplaced airline tickets, botched hotel reservations, incompetent tour guides. These seniors are survivors. Rather than thinking of their travel trials as crushing, they find them amusing.

The stories are entertaining, and as a bonus, one of them – about a flat tire – serves as a brilliant example of one of my so-called theories of good memoir writing. Stories are more interesting if aspects of life – rationing during World War II, for example – sneak into an essay. Georgia's grandchildren might never pick up a "How World War II Affected Us at Home" essay. But they – and maybe their grandchildren, too – will love her flat-tire-beach story. And they'll learn a lot about life during wartime, like how rubber was hard to come by.

The students enjoy hearing each other's tales, clapping and cheering just like the week before. Growing more comfortable with each other, they ask their fellow writers for more details and brainstorm on how some might expand their written ideas. I am delighted, and starting to think maybe, just maybe, I am actually qualified to lead this class after all.

But then comes Sylvia's turn to read.

Sylvia had the great fortune to travel around the world with her husband after they retired. A trip around the world is, by nature, rife with fiasco. Sylvia wants to tell us about everything that went wrong on their trip. Everything.

"Our first stop was in Los Angeles. When we got to LAX, which is the airport in Los Angeles, we phoned our daughter Laurel, Laurel is our youngest daughter. We have four children, and they all got together to help us afford this wonderful trip on which we were about to embark."

From there Sylvia gives us the name of each of her children, how old each one is, where each one lives now, what each one does for a living. Sylvia has a gift: she can read and read without ever looking up or needing a breath. We hear about how many times she and her husband phoned Laurel, how they worried, tried again. And again. And again. Finally they realized they'd been dialing the wrong number. They still laugh about it now.

I figure that is the end of the story. I am wrong.

"We landed in Hawaii. The travel brochure had said, quote, Hawaii is by far the most beautiful place you will ever lay eyes on, end of quote. And, quote, once you arrive you will never want to leave, end of quote. The brochure was correct. Hawaii is the most beautiful place I have ever seen in my entire life. Dick and I have returned to the Aloha State many, many times and have never been disappointed. On that first trip we were very surprised when a Hawaiian woman in a colorful muumuu met us in the airport and placed a lei over Dick's shoulders. When she put one over my head, though, the flowers caught on my glasses. My glasses flew to the floor! I was worried. What would I do if my glasses had broken? Lucky for me, they were okay. We still laugh to think about it now."

Sylvia continues with stories of hairdos ruined in humidity, gestures misunderstood by people who couldn't speak English, rickshaw drivers overcharging them in Asia. Her grammar is flawless, her punctuation perfect. The essay should have been riveting.

And indeed, the non-stop reading does leave Sylvia's audience...breathless. Chairs creak. Papers rustle. A woman harrumphs. I hear it all. Sylvia does not. She just keeps reading.

I can feel the other students looking to me for help here. It isn't their job to stop her, it is mine. I am there to lead the class. I need to step in, show some leadership.

But I am a coward, sitting silently, hoping for a miracle. I assure myself I won't have to interrupt her – and everyone will still like me and think I am nice. Sylvia will come to the end of her essay on her own. Any minute now.

But the miracle doesn't come. Each time her essay nears a natural conclusion, a new travel fiasco erupts.

Sylvia drones on. I keep quiet, and my silence starts making me mad. Angry at myself, really. I don't have the guts to stop her. I am letting down the other students.

Never one to readily admit fault, I cook up reasons to blame Sylvia. She is a bad person, forcing me to do something a good person like me shouldn't have to do: interrupt a senior citizen. She is self-centered. She never pauses for a reaction from others, and even I can tell she never looks up from her paper. She is insensitive. Any decent person would show more respect to their fellow students.

Self-righteous now, I continue building my case. A decent person would not gloat about money and luxuries on a retirement trip. And half the students in the class are widows. Does she have to mention her husband, her husband, her husband? And her superiority over the Asian people she mentions in the story, those people who "couldn't speak English."

"Stop!" I blurt out. My voice is high-pitched, childish. Grasping for more composure, I take a breath, start again, apologize for interrupting. "I am sorry, Sylvia. But you have gone on a bit too long."

Sylvia is stunned, as if she's been snapped out of a trance. Disappointed, too. "I didn't even get to Australia yet," she says. "That's the best part of the story."

The interruption is far too late. I have managed to hurt Sylvia's feelings, disappoint the rest of the class, and personally feel like a shit. The delayed interruption also means that some students won't have time to read at all today. We need to vacate promptly; "Spanish for Seniors" meets in our room at 2:30.

"Those of you who didn't get to read today, bring your travel essays again next week. I promise you'll go first," I say. "And for next week, write about your fathers." They must be wondering why they should bother. They'll never get to read their essays anyway.

One student doesn't know much about her father. He worked all the time. "It's not like today," she says. "My grandson even changes diapers," another student chimes in.

"Write about that, then," I say. "Write about how things have changed for fathers."

I hear a protest. "I don't want to write about my father. I want to write about my son." Everyone sounds miffed. I sense a small rebellion brewing. "Go ahead and write about your son," I say, scrambling for Hanni's harness handle to lead me out of there. "That'll be fine."

A student catches up with me on the way out. "I'm Georgia. You're too nice in class," she says, grabbing my arm to slow me down. "When I signed up for this class I was hoping for some helpful criticism. No one is going to learn anything if you don't critique."

"I know," I tell her. She is right.

"Do you want me to play bad cop?" she offers. "I'm happy to play bad cop to your good cop."

I'm not sure I like that idea, but I thank her for the offer.

"Maybe you should teach the class," I say, hoping she might actually take me up on the suggestion.

Oh, no!" she laughs. "I'm retired."

5

Memory Walk

HANNI'S TAIL DOESN'T wag once during our walk home down Michigan Avenue. "You are an idiot," I say. I am talking to myself. I never talk to myself. "Why did you agree to do this? You have no idea what you are doing in that class. How can you face them next week?"

Hanni's shoulders are slumped when I take her harness off, giving her permission to "empty" at her favorite tree. Poor Hanni. She must think I am talking to her. Wasn't it bad enough that I had just disappointed a bunch of senior citizens? Now I am letting my Seeing Eye dog down, too.

A bowl of dog food, a romp with a squeak toy, and one belly rub later, and all my scolding on the way home has been forgiven. Hanni guides me around on errands the next morning as if nothing has happened. Seeing Eye dogs are forgiving, thank goodness. Courageous, too. And smart. But MapQuest they ain't. I don't get up in the morning, say, "Hanni, library!" and expect her to lead me there. I have to know where we're going, how many blocks it is, when to turn and when to stay straight. Hanni's job is to pull me forward until we get to the end of a block. She waits there while I listen to traffic. I'm the one who determines it's our turn to go. Depending on our destination, I command either "forward," "left," or "right." She looks both ways, confirming it's safe to proceed, and we're off.

Chicago street crossings can be intense, but the sidewalks in between are surprisingly easy. Especially the north-south ones downtown, where the sidewalks are wide and aren't interrupted by alleys or entryways to parking garages.

On my walk north on Michigan Avenue to our next class, I am able to do something I never could do when using a white cane: daydream. Crossing Harrison, it occurs to me that students will be reading essays about their fathers today. I would have had a hard time with this assignment myself. I'm not sure I remember my father.

Ed Finke came home sick from work on my third birthday: December 23, 1961. Two weeks later he died of a heart attack.

Congress Parkway. This is our hardest street to cross. Four lanes, traffic going both ways, rushing in and out from the suburbs. Lots of pedestrians cross here, though, so the traffic is forced to stop. Hanni and I go with the flow, allowing me to think more about my dad. The heart attack. The ambulance arriving. My mom, Flo, being told to wait in the kitchen. We kids were asleep, so a neighbor came to sit with her. The paramedics went into the bedroom, then returned. Your husband has expired, they told Flo. "I didn't understand what they were saying," she told me decades later. "I didn't know what that word meant, 'expired.'"

Van Buren Street. One-way traffic, going west. Not as well-traveled as some other Chicago streets; an easy cross.

Ed Finke's death transformed his 45-year old widow from a housewife to a working mom. I went with Flo to work, held her hand as we walked to her job at a neighborhood bakery, played by myself in the back while she waited on customers.

Flo and I shared a bedroom, too. I can't remember which room I slept in before I moved in with my mom. And why did she want me in her room, anyway? Was she lonely?

West Jackson Boulevard. "Be careful at that corner," my friend Bonita, a longtime Chicago resident, has told me. "People get hit by buses there all the time." Hanni stops at the curb at Jackson. I feel pedestrians rushing past us. They're crossing, but the traffic on Michigan hasn't started yet.

My face betrays my confusion. That, or the guy next to me is a psychic. "It's red, but there's no traffic," the mind reader says. "We can go. You want my arm?"

I tell him thanks, but I'm waiting for them – I point to the traffic on Michigan – to go before I cross.

"Okay," he says. But it's one of those okays like "Okay, I tried to help you, but if you're crazy enough to stand here all day, be my guest."

When I hear the Michigan Avenue traffic start up, I say "Hanni, forward!" We're off. "Good girl!"

I was seven when my mom switched from the bakery to an office job. Peeking out from the covers of our double bed each morning, I'd watch her squeeze into a girdle, methodically unwind and garter her support hose, and lean into a bra. Flo was not a complainer, but she did groan about that girdle. I didn't blame her. All that yanking and tugging and strapping in – the process looked painful. When she slipped a dress over it all, though, it was like magic. She looked beautiful. I was proud to watch her walk out the door, start the car, and take off for work each morning. My sisters Marilee and Bev were left to shepherd me out the door in time to walk to school with neighborhood friends.

My voyeurism stopped when I started peeing in the bed at night. Embarrassed about waking up wet, I'd throw off the covers and race to the bathroom to change into dry pajamas. Flo would shove an old book, a stick, sometimes a wooden spoon, under the wet spot to keep the sheet away from the mattress pad. It looked like a circus tent for Barbies. You wouldn't want to pull Barbie's Malibu sports car up to that campsite, though, P-U!

The bedroom door was kept closed. I loved Flo for this, helping me keep my accidents a secret from my older sisters. The Barbie tent would air out during the day, then be laundered after Flo returned home from her office job.

Friends assured Flo I'd grow out of it. My bedwetting was a reaction to her new job, they told her. They said the change in routine must be affecting my behavior. We didn't know then that frequent urination and bedwetting are signs of undiagnosed type 1, or juvenile diabetes. Months went by before I was diagnosed. And it wasn't until some 20 years later, in 1985, that we'd find out that diabetes is the leading cause of blindness in working-age adults.

West Adams. The Art Institute is right across the street, so lots of kids. "Look at the dog!" "What's that thing on his back?" "Can I pet him?" A cop comes over and introduces herself. "Wanna hand crossing?" I say yes and grab her elbow.

We're almost there. My mind flashes back to the present, today's class, what they'll be reading. And what I've been writing.

National Public Radio had contacted me that week. Christopher Reeve died. "Is this something you have any special interest in?" they asked. I did.

So while my seniors were working on essays about their fathers, I was working on one about Christopher Reeve, the promise of stem cell research, and my hope that someday a cure would be found for chronic diseases like type 1 diabetes.

We turn left on Randolph. The homeless man selling *StreetWise* there calls out a hello. I use my free hand to wave towards the sound of his voice. Hanni guides me up the stairs, lifts her nose to the door handle, and we enter the Chicago Cultural Center. She darts right, left, then right again. No need for me to know what obstacles she's avoiding, I just hold on tight and trust her as she leads me into the classroom.

Follow the Writing

I KNOW WE'RE in the right place when I hear one student explode from her seat, "I heard you on the radio!"

"You were great!"

"Encore, encore!"

"My daughter called me, she heard it to!"

"Three cheers for Beth!"

Heat rises to my cheeks. I am blushing! I rub Hanni's head, look toward her face, and stage whisper to her, "We must be in the right room!" They all laugh. I laugh, too.

The success of the Christopher Reeve essay I'd recorded for NPR's Morning Edition gives me the resolve to announce a new rule in class: no more than 500 words per essay.

"And look! I've brought a timer for backup." They seem to approve the old-fashioned kitchen timer I discovered at our neighborhood hardware store. Mike had helped me squeeze a dot of rubber cement onto its five-minute mark.

"500 words. That's how long my NPR essays are. They say

6

24

short essays help listeners to, you know, stay tuned."

They groan at the bad joke, but seem perfectly fine with keeping their essays short. Especially Lita, who hadn't been able to read hers after we'd run out of time the week before. This week, she had arrived early to claim the spot right next to mine. With nine empty chairs to choose from, Alice took the one right next to Lita. My head was pretty big after my NPR appearance that week. I figured they'd come early to nab a seat next to the teacher.

I was wrong.

Without giving it much thought, I'd been having the writer on my left read first every week, followed by the writer next to them. I might have been born at night, but it wasn't last night. Students are starting to come early to get a good place in line.

Time to try something new. Ripping a sheet of paper into squares, I write a number on each little piece, fold the shreds, place them in the small clean bowl I carry to give Hanni a drink in a pinch, and pass it around. Each student picks a number.

Eyebrows up in exaggerated anticipation, I ask, "Who has number one? That'll decide who reads first." Two students answer. Eyebrows down. My handwriting suffered after I lost my sight. My sixes look like zeros. My nines look like zeros. And I guess my sevens look like ones.

So back to the old method. The students go around the table, introducing themselves aloud before they read so I'd know who – and where – they are. Sylvia isn't there. No one there to object to the 500-word rule. I'm relieved, yet sorry my outburst has driven her away.

The seniors who hadn't been able to read their travel essays the week before go first. After that we hear about fathers.

Hannelore grew up in Germany and learned English in her 20s when she landed in America. In her eighties now, she still has a strong accent. The lyrical story she reads about her father mentions a private bathroom. They were the first family in their neighborhood in Mannheim, Germany, to have one, and strangers would come to their house to admire it. The other students are intrigued. "You should write more about that," one of them suggests. "Tell us more about that bathroom." The idea had never occurred to Hannelore before.

Pretending surprise, I ask, "What? You never thought we'd want to hear more about the bathroom in the house you grew up in?"

"The house in which I grew up, Beth," she corrects me, feigning authority, then breaking into joyful laughter. Hannelore's knowledge of English grammar is far superior to that of her teacher. Or most of the other writers in class, for that matter.

Hannelore makes her opinions known, but she does so in such a lighthearted way that it makes us laugh. Delighted with our questions about shiny porcelain and hot, hot bath water, she can't wait to get home and start writing.

Minerva's story mirrors mine. She was the baby of her family, and her father died when she was young. His death wasn't from natural causes, though. He died in an accident, hit by a streetcar on his way home from work.

Olga's father, a tailor, had emigrated from Poland.

Ida's father was strict. He never let his daughters out of the house at night. Not even on Halloween. "He always made sure we had the party at our house that night," she laughs. "That way we wouldn't beg him to let us out!"

These stories about fathers help explain how we ended up where we are now. With Sylvia gone, we have time to discuss each piece. Not to talk about the writing, of course. To talk about the experience.

"What street car did your father take to work, Minerva?"

"Oh, yeah, my dad took the #7."

"Olga, did your father sew at home?"

"Oh, you're right! Milwaukee Avenue. All the tailors had shops there."

"Ida, you mean you really couldn't go out at night? Ever? You're not kidding. He really was a strict father."

There's even time left at the end of class to discuss next week's assignment. Memories of Flo sticking that wooden spoon under the wet bedsheet so it'd lift off the mattress pad and my questions of why I was still sharing a bed with my mother when I was seven years old had been rattling around in my head. I want my students to write about the first time they can remember having to change beds.

"You mean the first time I changed my own sheets?" Hannelore cackles.

"No, no, no!" I say, laughing along with her. "I want you to think back to the very first time you had to switch which bed you slept in. I'm guessing this happened when a younger brother or sister was born, or a grandma died, or you had to move," I say. "Not the first time you went away to visit some-one and slept in a different bed for a short while, or the first vacation you remember taking. I mean the very first time you made a change that would last, and you started sleeping in an entirely different bed. How did you feel about the move? Excited? Angry? Scared? What made you feel that way?"

I also ask them to describe the event that had forced the change. "Give us the date of that event. If you can't remember the specific date, give us the year," I say. "Besides what was going on in your family or personal life right then, what was going on in the outside world? Mention that, too – it helps place your readers in time."

Above all, I want my writers to be honest about their feelings. If a move to a new town required the switch in sleeping quarters, and that move made them angry, excited, anxious, I want them to explain why. "Say it in your own words, as if you were sitting at a table with a friend and telling him or her about it."

I ask them to let their readers know how things worked out in the end. "Were you right to be angry, excited, scared? Or did the move work out much differently than you expected?"

Hannelore won't be following my "switching beds" assignment. She makes that clear right away. "I'll write about a cradle instead," she announces.

I am getting used to this. When I told students to write about getting to school in the cold, Lita came back with a song. The week I assigned "vacation fiascos," Ida wrote about the Chinese classes she took after she retired. I do not object. These students are 75, 88 and 90+ years old. They don't have to take orders from anyone anymore. Besides, we are learning that part of the joy of writing is finding out where it leads you.

7

First Time in a New Bed

SYLVIA RETURNS THE next week.

"Sorry I had to miss class, but we were on vacation, visiting my daughter and our grandchildren. And just seeing them, especially my one granddaughter, she just reminds me so much of my daughter as a child, I wrote up a little something about her, and I can't wait to read it for everybody."

I give her a cheerful, "Welcome back!" And I really mean it.

I start class by letting them know I've come up with a new ritual to solve the which-writer-goes-first problem. Each writer will close their eyes, fiddle through a zippered, woven cloth pouch the size of an iPhone, choose a Braille Scrabble® tile, then ceremoniously pass the pouch to their neighbor. Whoever picks "A" reads their work aloud first, then "B," and so on. Letters on the tiles appear in print as well as Braille. "If you learn to read Braille," I tease, "you could cheat and pick the tile you want."

Fascination with the Braille on the tiles keeps the writers from getting miffed about who has chosen "A" and who got "X." We don't announce who will be the next one to read; the element of surprise keeps us all listening.

"I'm F!" Sylvia calls out after "E" finishes reading. I hear her shuffle her papers. Many papers.

Buoyed from the positive reaction to the Scrabble tiles, I stick my neck out and tell her about the Christopher Reeve radio essay she'd missed, and how, after the positive response that short radio essay had received, I'd decided to limit our word count to 500 words. "That's five minutes of reading," I say.

I'm ready for her objections – I've researched this. Experts recommend people speak between 140 and 180 words a minute if they want to be understood clearly. Five minutes gives each reader plenty of time.

No comment from Sylvia. She just starts reading.

Our kitchen timer dings when five minutes are up. "Okay, you'll have to end there."

"But I'm not done yet!"

"Remember our new rule?" My eyebrows are up. The other writers catch on.

"I'm G!" Minerva calls out. I love that woman. We all turn our attention to her, and Sylvia gives in.

After Minerva, Alice reads her essay about the day her family's house burned. She was five years old. Her father was away at work, but her mother was home and carried her out to safety. Assured her daughter was safe, Alice's mother went back in the house to save Alice's baby brother. She never came back.

Alice ended up being raised by her father as an only child. She doesn't shed a tear while reading her piece to us. "That was the first time I ever remember switching which bed I slept in," she says. "Otherwise I probably would have never written about that."

8

1968

MY RESPECT FOR the writers in my class grows. They are, after all, older and wiser than I am, and they like having plenty of room to interpret subjects in their own way.

Knowing that many of the writers were young adults in Chicago back then, I assign the topic "1968." Few of them choose to write about the Democratic convention that year. "We had jobs," one of them scoffs. "We couldn't take off work to go downtown and bother with that mess." Their essays definitely speak of the times, though.

From Tom's essay we learn that he grew up on Chicago's South Side, where he and his wife were raising their three boys in 1968. Their oldest son would be starting high school that year, and as Tom delicately puts it, the neighborhood was "changing." Tuition was so high at the Catholic high school that he and his wife opted to move their family to the suburbs.

Gwen reads next. She and her husband had also decided to move their family to a new house in 1968.

"On the day of the closing we took our sons out to see their new home," she reads, explaining it was located in the Rosemoor neighborhood on Chicago's far South Side. "Our boys were excited to have a larger home, although they didn't want to leave their friends. My husband and I were happy that the house had been vacated by the former owners and we had immediate possession."

But Gwen's husband called her at work the next day with disturbing news. Someone had tossed a chemical into their house – the chemical simmered throughout the night, eventually burning through the floor. A worker from People's Gas Company who had been sent out to take a final meter reading the next morning noticed the windows were all black from the smoke. He called the fire department.

"The fireman, who knew how to enter a burning house, told us that if we had opened a door, the house would have exploded and been completely destroyed," Gwen writes. "We were completely unaware that we were the first Black family to move into that block. Had we known, we would have skipped that area. I did not want to put my children in danger."

Their three-year-old was afraid to enter the house, so the family moved into Gwen's brother's attic for a few weeks until her husband decided it was time to clean up the house and move in. He checked on it every evening during the process, hoping the culprits would return.

"But of course they didn't," Gwen reads. "And I was glad. I didn't want a confrontation."

After about a year, the family finally moved in. But Gwen tells us it took a long, long time before they could relax in the house. "It seemed that every time we started feeling comfortable there, the weather would turn humid and the smoke smell would seep down from the attic." They lived there for 20 years, and after the kids were grown they moved to the south suburbs.

Gwen can barely speak for sobbing, but as she nears the end of her essay, she straightens herself, catches her breath, and finishes without a hint of anger or bitterness: "We cannot allow the actions of a few to poison our minds and cause us to react in a manner that would be completely contradictory to what Martin Luther King and other Black leaders have preached and marched against."

When Gwen is finished reading, Tom says he thought that kind of thing had ended long before then. He had no idea people were still burning houses down like that in 1968. A quiet chorus of "uh huhs" rises from the other South-Siders in class. Gwen says she'd buried this whole ordeal deep inside until I gave the assignment to write about 1968. "It all came back to me then," she says.

Change of pace: Louise reads next. By now I know to expect that she didn't follow my assignment. She always writes on the same subject: her son. Each time it's her turn to read, she shifts in her chair and ceremoniously gathers her papers as if she's about to give a presidential address. Instead of the State of the Union, though, we hear about the state of her clever son. Each piece is more dramatic than the last, and now that her tooth is fixed, she can read with flourish.

It didn't take a psychic to read the other students' thoughts. Oh no, they were thinking. Here we go again, another essay about that son of hers, and Beth's too chicken to tell her to stick to the topic. Chairs would creak. Ida would harrumph. "Him again," Alice would mutter.

This week is no different. Louise's story gets off to a slow start, and in an effort to speed things along, Lita picks up her papers and arranges them over and over. And over. And over. Finally satisfied, she uses the tabletop to level the stack. It isn't easy to hear Louise above the din, but when her tone suddenly changes we all fall silent and listen.

On what would be her last day in class, Louise reads a different kind of story about her son. A son who suffered from alcoholism. A son who, in his 30s, surrendered the battle and returned home to live with his mama. A son who died at home, under her care, less than a year ago.

The pack of Kleenex Louise had used weeks ago to cover her missing tooth comes in handy once again. As she concludes her essay, she begins to weep.

In talks I give about memoir writing at conferences and writers workshops, I evangelize about the power of writing, how it can be therapeutic, how writing can help bring order and clarity to messy and chaotic lives. But the messy and chaotic experiences in my own life can't compare with the ones I am hearing about in class. I haven't buried a son. My mother did not die after rescuing me from a fire and returning for my baby brother.

The class is very still. Silence makes me nervous – I feel a compulsion to break it. Searching desperately for a line from my "Writing as Therapy" speeches, I ask the writers who shared stories of personal tragedy if getting those stories down on paper helped at all.

Louise doesn't answer my question. She simply shoves the papers my way and says, "I want you to get this one published." I thank her, grab the sheets of paper, and stuff them in my bag.

I turn to another spot at the table. "How about you, Alice?" It has been weeks since we'd learned that a house fire had killed her mother and baby brother. I ask her if writing about that had been cathartic at all. When she doesn't answer, I bite my tongue, resisting the temptation to break the silence. "Yeah," she finally says. And then, "I guess so,"

Hardly convincing. "I guess it's good to have it in writing?" I ask. She concedes.

Viewing her indifference as a sign she doesn't want to dig deeper, I turn to face the other students and remind them I can't see Alice. "Can you tell from looking at her that she was in a fire?"

A chorus of no's rings out. One woman says, "She's beautiful."

Alice seems pleased to hear that. She starts rolling up one of her blouse sleeves. "I still have scars," she says, showing them to the class.

Taking this as my cue to assign a lighter topic, I think quickly. Something about love, maybe. "How I Met Your Dad." No, some of the women in the class never married. Some don't have children. And what would Tom write? I need something more generic.

"Okay, everybody ready?" I ask. "For next week, I need you to fill in the blank. The assignment is: "How ___ and I Became Friends."

"You can fill in the blank with a thing if you want. 'How Chocolate and I Became Friends.' 'How Chicago and I Became Friends.' Or try writing about a person: 'How My Daughter-in-Law and I Became Friends.' Fill in the blank."

To write this one, I suggest they find a place to get comfortable. "Close your eyes and relax before writing anything down," I say, encouraging my writers to replace the noises of the outside world with the sounds they might have been hearing when this friendship began. I want them to think of songs from that time, what the weather was like when the friendship blossomed, how it felt to think they'd made a new friend.

"Then, and only then, open your eyes," I say. "You'll be ready to write."

9

Change

JUST FOR FUN, I decide to switch things up a bit.

As writers gather and search for seats, I fumble through my backpack, distinguishing items by their texture: flimsy doggie pick-up bags, hairbrush prongs, smooth leather wallet, strips of gum, cold metal house keys, skinny tube of lipstick, sandpaper nail files, wrappers twisted around the hard candy I carry around in case of low blood sugar. At long last, a Ziploc® bag full of loose change.

"Pick a coin," I instruct. My plan is to explain next week's assignment while the bag is going around the table. Silly me. I should have anticipated how averse older adults can be to, well, change.

One writer chooses a coin, passes the bag.

"What's this?" the next writer says. "Where are the tiles?" She gives in, chooses a coin, passes the bag.

"What's this?" the next writer asks. "Why are we picking pennies? What happened to the tiles?" He passes the bag.

"What am I supposed to do with this?" the next writer asks. "Do I add a penny? I'm not sure I have a penny."

When the Ziploc bag comes back around, I pull out our kitchen timer and turn the knob. The bell always gets their attention.

"Read the date on the coin you chose," I say. More bedlam.

"I can't find the date!"

"The print is too small!"

Alice to the rescue. "Wait!" she calls out, digging in her bag. "I have a magnifying glass!"

Once we're all settled, the student with the earliest date reads first.

At the end of class, we are calm enough for me to give next week's assignment: write about something that went on in your life the year that's on your coin.

"I got 1978," one of them whines. "I can't remember anything that went on in 1978!"

I suggest that if they got a year that doesn't ring a bell, they can do some research, find out what happened in the news that year to jog their memories.

"Keep in mind, though, I want you to write a memoir, not a report."

"If your coin says 2006, I don't want you coming back with something like: 'The year 2006 was the year a coal mine disaster trapped 13 miners. Some newspapers got it wrong and announced early that all the miners had been rescued when, really, they hadn't.'

"That is all very interesting stuff," I tell them. "But it's a report, not a memoir. I want a memoir. If you pick a coin with the year 2006 on it, and researching the coal mining disaster jogs your memory, reminds you how sad you were about that tragedy, how it made you think of your grandfather who was a coal miner, or how much the news inspired you to live more fully, then go ahead and mention the coal-mine disaster in your essay," I expound.

"My people weren't coal miners," one writer says. "What if you don't have any coal miners?" I tell her to see me after class.

A gaggle of other students joins her with more questions. One still can't determine if her coin says 1966 or 1968. "How about if I write about 1967?" she asks.

Fine.

10

Minerva

MINERVA WASN'T BORN with that beautiful name. "My birth certificate says Minnie," she admitted one week. "I changed it to something a little more dignified."

The name suits her. She is the essence of dignity. The whole class treats her with special respect, and not just because, at 86, she's our oldest member. From her essays, we've learned that she graduated *cum laude* at age 63, then received a master's degree in English at age 70. So when it's her turn to read, we settle in our chairs and shove papers aside. We want to focus on her words.

Poised and proud, Minerva's diction is exquisite. Her essays are short, to the point, read with confidence. And like everyone else in class, she's led a life worth writing about.

Still, I never feel competition in the air. She listens while others read, waits politely for her turn, and appreciates the class's compliments on her pieces. "Thank you," she always says, never adding false humility or mentioning weaknesses in her work. It isn't arrogance, it's confidence. I can tell she has done this many times before.

She hinted at her experience once, when she confessed to reading an essay she'd written years before. "I only needed to revamp it a little bit to make it fit with the assignment," she'd said, apologizing for cheating. Her husband of 65 years had been in the hospital that week.

"Pneumonia. I brought a pad and pencil with me when I was visiting Walter, but I just couldn't make myself write." I forgave her.

I'm sure Minerva would benefit from more difficult writing assignments, challenges about narrative, point of view, plot. I wish she would speak up, let me know how I might help with her writing. But outside of reading her essays, she rarely speaks at all. I would be glad to talk to her after class, but she always rushes off for her long bus ride back to Chicago's South Side. She's in a hurry to get back to Walter.

This week she shows up early, and I decide to put those few minutes alone with her to good use.

"Minerva," I ask, "How long have you been taking these kinds of classes?"

"Ever since I retired," she laughs, patting my hand. It feels nice. "And that was 20 years ago!"

We chat about her poetry classes, her journal-writing classes, the screenwriting class she'd tried. I ask her opinion about a suggestion I've received from one of her classmates. "She wishes we'd spend more time critiquing our writing," I say. "She wants me to go around the table after each person reads, ask everyone to give a comment on what they heard."

"Oh, please don't do that," she begs. She sees no sense in talking if you don't have anything to say. "Another teacher made us do that. It made me so uncomfortable that I finally quit the class."

What a relief. With the Minerva Seal of Approval, I'll keep doing what I've been doing: make a positive comment after each essay, ask if anyone else has a comment or question, let them chime in if they want to.

Then Minerva speaks admiringly of Debra, another student in our class, for managing to publish her own book. I want to tell Minerva how plodding and dull Debra's writing is, how her "book," an homage to herself for taking care of her father while he had Alzheimer's, was actually a pile of her unedited essays stapled together. But to Minerva, Debra is a published author.

"Minerva! I know you have written enough essays to make a book," I tell her.

"Oh, you don't know: I'm a bad housekeeper," she says. "I've got piles of writing all over the house. I'd be dead before I'd get them all arranged."

It is one of those moments when I wish I could see. I'd love to visit Minerva's house, go through her piles of writing, help her arrange them into book form.

"Have you thought about just getting a few of them published?" I ask. "Like in a magazine or something?"

"I wouldn't know how to get started," she says.

Other students begin trickling in. Minerva lowers her voice. "How'd you do it, Beth? How'd you get your first article published?"

My first published essay appeared in a local weekly

newspaper. It was about a job I took in the late 1990s, modeling nude for art students. I'm not sure I want to tell Minerva about that. She is a church-going woman. I am a woman who has taken her clothes off for money.

One of the new arrivals interrupts us. "It's 1:30!"

Minerva finds her place at the table. In that split-second, her unanswered question has given me an idea. Next week, I'll bring magazines to class.

11

Magazines

OVER THE YEARS I've collected names of magazines that welcome essays submitted by readers. *Newsweek*'s "My Turn" is very popular. But lots of other magazines – *Southern Living, Education Week, Spirituality and Health,* to name just a few – regularly feature essays sent in by readers.

The first essay I ever got published in a real-live glossy national magazine appeared in *Dog Fancy. Dog Fancy* had a special "Perspectives" page each month featuring a 1000-word reader essay. My first Seeing Eye dog, a beautiful Black Lab named Dora, was slowing down, and *Dog Fancy*'s agreement to publish an essay about her looming retirement meant revisions would be emailed back and forth to editors. Voila! I had a connection with an editor, a name and email address to submit future story ideas. A half-dozen or so of my articles were published in *Dog Fancy* every year, and eventually I was named a contributing editor.

Most of those glossy magazines are online now, making it much easier to look over the titles to see if any spark an essay idea.

I often encourage new writers to check out the table of contents of publications they like and look for words like "Readers Write," "Your Say," "Memoirs," "Perspectives," and strongly encourage them to read and follow the submission guidelines exactly. Most publications receive far more essay submissions than they have room to print, so bending or ignoring a rule just provides the editor with a good reason to disqualify you.

I decide to bring my magazine list to the Borders Bookstore.

The poor guy at the information desk! He looks up oodles of never-heard-of magazines – *Irish American*, *In-Fisherman*, and so on – and finds what he can on the shelves. I ask him to check the table of contents for me, to make sure each magazine has the "Readers Write" feature I am looking for.

Satisfied, I feel through my wallet for a twenty-dollar bill, folded in half, of course. Paying close attention when the cashier gives me my change, I fold the new bills into their appropriate shapes, stick them back in my wallet, and shove the magazines into my backpack.

At the end of our next class, I surprise everyone with my idea.

"Now, I know some of you are writing your memoirs down for your children and grandchildren," I say. "And some of you write to jog your memory, or to get things off your chest." I sense their heads nodding, the students placing themselves in one category or another.

"Well, I've been listening to your essays all these weeks, and you know what?" Only Hannelore answers. Unaware of the appropriate American call and response, she doesn't say "What?" She says, "Yes!" as if to say yes, she already does know what.

I smile her way and continue. "You all should submit your work to magazines!" With that I fling the magazines willy-nilly over the tabletop, instructing my students to each choose one they want to write for.

"Take the magazine home, look through it to see what sorts of articles they publish. Then go to the section where they publish essays from readers and see what you have to do to submit one of your own."

Some of the students catch on right away. Doris, a 70-year-old who'd ridden on the back of a motorcycle in her 20s, snatches up *Rider*. "That was the only time I was ever on a motorcycle," she says. "I still remember it." Alice and her husband never had children, but they love dogs. She grabs *Dog Fancy*.

"I don't get it," Lita says. All that's left is a copy of *Canoe and Kayak*. "You want me to write an opinion piece about canoes? I don't really have an opinion about canoes."

"The essays you write for this class are not op-ed pieces," I explain. "They're personal essays." That is exactly what I want Lita to write for *Canoe and Kayak*. "Write a personal story, a memoir that has a canoe or kayak in it. The story will be all yours, Lita. You're the only person who could write a first-person narrative like that."

Lita falls silent. Is she miffed about being stuck with

47

Canoe and Kayak? Or is she thinking through her life history, searching for something, anything, that includes a canoe? In the end, like a petulant schoolgirl, she accepts the teacher's Stupid Assignment.

Other students are more interested in flipping through their magazines than worrying about Lita's plight. I move on, pointing out the blank cassette tape on the table. "That's for anyone who wants to write an essay for National Public Radio," I say, using myself as living proof that they take essays, too.

I'd taped a list to the cassette: "How to Get an Essay on Chicago Public Radio." It was something I'd put together on the fly, tips like: send completed essays, not just essay ideas; keep it short, no more than 600 words; use short sentences; write as if you are talking (remember, it's radio!). Most important: mention something about Chicago – a place, an event, an organization, a person, anything – because then they'll be more likely to accept it.

Zip. Unzip. Zip. Zip. I know that sound. Class is drawing to a close. Writers are making room for magazines in their handbags.

My search for a weightless backpack and the sleeping dog under the table is interrupted by a delicate tap on my shoulder. "Beth, it's Minerva." She's selected Chicago Public Radio for her assignment. "Do you want me to put my essay on tape?"

I tell her she doesn't have to. "But it's a good idea, just to hear how it might sound on the radio. That can be a lot different from the way it looks on paper."

Minerva is eager to get home and give this a try. Before

darting out the door, she confides that she'd always wanted to be on the radio. "Way back, when I graduated from high school, I wanted to be a radio announcer." But her mother sent her to secretarial school instead. "She thought the radio idea was ridiculous."

12

Minerva Records

ONCE HOME, I get right to work on my own radio essay. My editor at Chicago Public Radio had called a few days earlier to ask if I could come into the studio on Monday to record.

I told her I can't record on Mondays – it's the day I teach.

"You're a teacher?" she asked.

Am I? I am still having trouble thinking of myself that way. "Well, I suppose it'd be more accurate to call me a facilitator," I conceded. "I just give assignments. They go home and write, then bring their essays to class and read them aloud." The class meets right downtown, I explained, "So it's easy to get there with public trans. The students come from all over the city."

"You should write us an essay about your class," she suggested. What a good idea! I accepted the assignment.

"The writing class had been promoted for beginners," I start. "Flyers with exaggerated punctuation marks – 'So you think you can't write?? Think Again!!' – were plastered on walls at the Chicago Cultural Center..." and I was off.

I write by ear, and I copyedit by listening to the robotic voice on my talking computer or hearing Mike or generous volunteers read my finished work aloud. So radio essays come fairly easy to me. It takes just a few days before I email the rough draft to my editor at WBEZ. She returns it with edits and suggestions.

Once we both agree on the finished product, I drop the bomb. "I'm ready to record it," I say. "But only if you follow it up with one of my students reading something they wrote, too."

I know Minerva has that tape at home. I know I will love whatever she puts on it.

Chicago Public Radio likes my idea.

Minerva likes my idea, too. She decides to adapt an essay she wrote for an assignment I gave to have the class work on dialog. "Bring a pen and notepad to some public place," I told the writers. "When you hear people talking, write down what they say." I knew they'd discover that people rarely complete their sentences. When they do, their statements are surprisingly short.

Minerva brought her pad and paper to Grand Crossing, a post office on the South Side of Chicago. It was her own idea to write about herself in the third person.

Grand Crossing
By Minerva Mills Bell

The short, slightly stooped, elderly woman stood quietly awaiting her turn in the long line at the Grand Crossing Postal Station.

The clerk at Window 1 called out, "May I please serve the next in line?"

A small bird-like man at the end of the line darted forward. Clerk No. 1 chided (as if speaking to a naughty child), "Now, you know you are not the next in line!"

"Well, I am a senior citizen!"

"Bully for you. Then you're not in a hurry. You don't have anything to do but stand there and wait for your turn."

The other patrons in line raised eyebrows and chuckled.

The clerk at Window 4 was a striking woman. She sat there, queenly, surveying the customers. As if they were serfs, eagerly awaiting her largess. She called out "Next!"

The little old lady came forward, laid some money on the counter and said, "Good morning. I would like two books of self-adhesive stamps. If possible, I would prefer stamps that do not say 'LOVE.'"

The queenly clerk was very erect. Her makeup was impeccable, and her hair was beautifully coiffed. Disdainfully, she turned her face and spoke loudly, so that everyone could hear: "All I have is 'LOVE' adhesive stamps. Anyway, what difference do it make?"

"I don't like putting 'LOVE' on envelopes when I'm paying bills."

"That's stoopid! Dumbest thing I ever heard. You ought to be glad you can pay your bills. Whole lotta people can't even buy the stamps, much less pay their bills!"

They glared at each other over the counter. Clerk No. 4 slapped down two books of "LOVE" stamps and some change.

The customer said, "Thank you very much."

Clerk No. 4 did not answer. She looked past her, right over her head and called out, "Next!"

Chicago Public Radio doesn't think an 88-year-old "short, slightly stooped, elderly woman" should have to make her way from the South Side of Chicago to their studios to record a story. So Matt Cunningham, the sound engineer who'd worked on all the WBEZ essays I'd recorded up to then, offers to come to our class and record Minerva at the Cultural Center instead.

Matt is mature and confident about his work, but his voice and energy level betray his youth. When I introduce him to Minerva, it is love at first sight. "I want her to be my grandma!" he tells me.

Matt escorts Minerva to a quiet room nearby to record her essay. They aren't gone long. "We only needed to do a couple takes," he says, sounding surprised.

Class has already started, so Matt politely escorts his would-be grandma to her seat at the table. "Okay if I stay and record some of the class, too?"

I turn to my writers and ask. The chorus of sures, of courses, and yeses I get in response is music to my ears. They are proud of their work, confident enough about their writing to let the nice young man from the radio station stay and listen.

Matt fiddles with his recording equipment, chairs squeak as writers shift in their seats to get ready. I don't have to be able to see to know they are patting their hair and refreshing their lipstick. It's radio, ladies. Not TV. I don't say it, I just smile and take it all in.

Matt finishes recording, thanks the class, and heads back to the WBEZ studio to share the audio clips with his editor.

THE EDITOR MUST have liked what she heard. She suggests only one change. "You repeat the word 'seniors' too much," she says to me. She asks me to come up with a "gentler" word. When I can't think of one, she says, "How about golden agers?"

When we finally hear the finished product, Matt has interspersed clips of seniors reading throughout my introduction. If we listen very closely, we can hear me choke every time I call the writers "golden agers." And I sure wish I'd followed my own rules: the intro is longer than 500 words – too long. WBEZ listeners are rewarded for their patience, though. They get to hear Minerva's steady and confident reading at the end.

13

Gus

MINERVA SAILED THROUGH her NPR recording like a pro. My first attempts were much less natural.

The best way to do a piece on radio is, of course, to read it. I've studied Braille, but I'm no Helen Keller. It can take me nearly an hour to read a single page. Instead, I memorize my essays so I can recite them on-air. When I was in the studio in late 2002 to record an NPR essay about our son, Gus, they had to call in an expert to coach me.

Gus was born with physical and developmental disabilities, and my essay was about his move to a residential facility in Wisconsin when he turned 16.

When the moment to start recording came, the engineer pointed me toward the mic and I began: *"Our teenage son wears diapers."*

It's a line I know will grab listeners' attention, but I sound stilted. "Cut!"

I try it over and over, and over and over again, until

producer/coach Ari Shapiro comes up with a brilliant solution. His voice comes into my headphones: "Start out saying, 'Okay, here's how it is,'" he suggests. "Then say the first line."

It works. Ari stops me countless more times throughout the recording, asking me to redo certain phrases, assuring me that NPR sound editors will edit my stammers and splice it all into one coherent piece. "You'll sound like you sat down and read it all at once."

And sure enough, I do.

Group Home
By Beth Finke
As Aired on NPR's Morning Edition

Our teenage son wears diapers. He can't talk or walk. If his food isn't cut into bite-sized pieces, we have to feed him. Gus's genetic condition doesn't have a name, like Downs or Asperger's. It's known by its clinical description: Trisomy 12p.

Mike loved his son from the day Gus was born. It took me a lot longer. Truth is, I was angry at Gus. He wasn't the baby I expected. A baby was supposed to bring us joy. The way I saw it, Gus brought nothing but trouble.

I did therapeutic exercises with Gus. I cuddled him, played the piano for him. But none of it was heartfelt.

Until one night, when I was singing Gus to sleep. Suddenly understanding washed over me: none of this was Gus's fault.

"You didn't want it to be like this," I said, starting to cry now. "It's not your fault, is it?" Over and over I repeated it. "It's not your fault, Gus." I kissed and hugged him, finally able to love him and to tell him so.

Sixteen years later, Gus communicates by crawling to whatever it is he needs. When he wants to hear music, for example, he scoots to the piano. Gus laughs and sings with the tunes and claps with delight whenever he hears live music. He loves to hold hands, especially while swinging on a porch swing.

But as Gus has grown bigger, Mike and I have grown older. Shortly after Gus's sixteenth birthday, we realized it was time for him to move away. Mike and I placed him on waiting lists all over the country. A facility four hours away contacted us last summer. They had an opening.

Gus cried his entire first weekend away. So did we. "It'll take some time for us to all get used to each other," the social worker assured us over the phone. On our first visit, we found Gus happy and smiling, yet not quite sure what to make of these visitors on his new turf. I sang to him. He felt my face. Suddenly he burst out in laughter, realizing it really was me. When I stood him up to transfer him from the wheelchair to the car so he could join us for lunch, I realized how much he'd grown. He was up to my chin!

As I leaned down to kiss Gus goodbye, he took off. Couldn't wait to wheel himself back to his friends in the activity center. Now, when we visit Gus, it's all fun. No hoisting him onto the toilet, no muscling him into the shower, no changing his diapers. No drudgery.

He seems relieved, too, finally allowed to do things independently of his parents. Hmmm...maybe Gus has more in common with other teenagers than I thought.

14

Class Over

EIGHT WEEKS HAVE passed, and the "Me, Myself, and I" class has run its course. Hanni guides me into the classroom for the last time.

Olga is already in her spot, arranging papers at the table. "When do we meet again?" she asks.

Another voice rings out from behind me. "Yeah, will there be a summer class, Beth?" It is Ida, lumbering to her seat. I don't know her as well as some of the other writers, but I sure like her so far. Her laugh is good-natured and joyful; I am certain she has one of those smiles that goes ear to ear.

"I called to sign up for the next session," she says. This news surprises me. She had missed many of our classes, and I assumed her absences had been due to lack of interest. "They said it wasn't listed."

Chicago's Department on Aging had contacted me days earlier with bad news: there was not enough money in the budget to continue our class. Funny, even without being able to see, I can't face Olga and Ida to give them the disappointing news. "I really don't know," I say instead, leaning down to distract Hanni from leftover nibbles under the table.

But I can't hide down there with Hanni all day. I finally come up and explain. "I asked my supervisor if we could extend the class, but she told me there isn't enough money in the budget." The students pay $1 for every writing class they attend. The Department on Aging subsidizes my pay.

Olga groans in disgust. "We were just getting started!" Ida says she will call the center to complain.

"To be honest, I'd teach the class for free," I offer.

Ida nearly jumps out of her chair – not easy for her to do. I judge fitness by the size of a person's upper arm. Ida once offered her elbow to guide Hanni and me out of the building after class. That's when I found out: she is a sturdy woman.

"Don't you dare!" Ida chides. "Beth, you should never, ever offer your skills for free. You'll lose your credibility."

Ida's first essay revealed her to be a college graduate with a long career at IBM. Quite an accomplishment for any woman who finished high school in the 1950s. A second essay told me more: Ida is African-American.

One might think I'd have figured this out earlier from Ida's speech pattern. Sometimes I can tell a person's background or race by the way they talk, but it's unreliable. Harry Connick, Jr.: jazz piano player, from New Orleans, accent, good sense of rhythm, and he can swing. Must be Black. And it was such a breath of fresh air for me to hear the entertaining voice of James Carville, a sexy African-American man, during those Clinton campaigns. Wrong on both counts. And when I first heard

Colin Powell speak? I was sure he was White. When it came to Ida, prejudice seeped through, even without my being able to see. IBM. World travel. Corporate job. Must be a White woman.

But through Ida's writing I learned that all her public schooling had been in segregated schools on Chicago's South Side. She stayed on the South Side for college, too, and graduated from the University of Chicago.

So I take Ida seriously. I promise I won't offer my skills free of charge.

Other students arrive, most of them not quite as disappointed as Olga and Ida to learn the class is ending. Georgia, who'd offered to be the bad cop for me, will enroll in higher-level writing classes. Anita, who had perfect attendance without ever writing an essay of her own, says she had enjoyed hearing everyone else's stories but writing just isn't for her. Louise hasn't shown up again after handing me the essay about her son.

And Sylvia, of course, will be traveling anyway, it is so fun to get out on the road, such a wonderful wide country, and then to get out of the country and see different parts of the world, it's so fascinating, so amazing to see different cultures and the different ways people go about their daily lives....

Ding! Ding! Ding! My hand twitches back and forth on the timer, ringing it repeatedly to call our final class to order. I am sorry the class is ending. I tell them so. "But you all have your memoirs started," I say. "All you have to do now is arrange the essays you've written and fill in the gaps."

I suggest they each invest in a hole-puncher. "I think they still make them," I say with a laugh. "Get three-ring binders,"

I add. "Arrange the essays into some sort of order. The stories don't have to be in chronological order. You don't have to start with what happened first in your life. You can group them into themes if you want."

The class is silent. I have them in the palm of my hand. Marching on, I explain how their "Father" essays might fit with "Vacation Fiasco" essays, if a father happened to be along for the fiasco. A "Getting to School in the Cold" essay might be grouped with other essays written about school or about school friends. "This way you can write about what you want to write about when the moment strikes. You know, rather than forcing yourself to write in chronological order," I say. "The good thing about using a three-ring binder is that you can mix and match, move your essays around."

They keep listening. I keep talking. After putting their essays in order, they'll have to figure out which pieces from their lives are missing. "Tom, your 'Getting to School' essay mentioned an Uncle P.J.," I say. "We don't know who Uncle P.J. is. Write about him."

The murmur I am starting to hear sounds positive, not rebellious. They are already talking out loud about which essay might go where in their binders. I feel victorious.

Realizing the Scrabble tiles have already been passed around, I interrupt their revelry. How'd it go with your "Good Advice" essays?

Lita goes off-topic with an essay about a painting on her bedroom wall, Sylvia writes about Hawaii, and Hannelore brings us a story about the Blaupunkt radio she and her husband bought when they settled in Chicago. The rest of them are

61

stories about advice these writers have heard over the years, and we enjoy them all.

Alice tells me she has three essays ready to submit to *Dog Fancy* and asks me, "Can you take a look at all three of these, Beth? I need to know which one I should send in."

The essays are all in longhand. Alice doesn't own a type-writer, much less a computer. Someone will have to read all three essays out loud on a cassette for me, then I'll transcribe them onto my talking computer to edit them.

Here's a dirty little secret: it takes me longer than my sighted peers to get my work done. I'm not supposed to admit this. Thing is, seventy-five percent of people who are blind like me are unemployed. And most of us would like to work. So we're supposed to say we're just like everyone else. You know, so employers won't be afraid to hire us.

But we're not like everyone else. Braille takes longer to read than print. Searching a website by ear with a talking computer takes up more time than scanning the screen. Cutting and pasting is slower with a talking computer, too. Transcribing taped interviews takes much longer than just jotting down notes the way sighted reporters do.

So I get up early. I work extra hours to get my work in on time. We blind folks get our work done, we just work longer and harder to get there. Time is precious to us, and we don't like to waste it.

But transcribing Alice's essays will not be a waste of time. It will be an honor. A victory, even. She sees me not as someone who needs help, but as someone who can help her. A teacher.

As long as I'll be asking someone to read Alice's stories onto a cassette for me, I figure I may as well add to the reading pile. Scrounging around for a clean sheet of paper, I pass it to Lita on my left and ask everyone to write down their names, addresses and phone numbers. "I'll get in touch with you if the class ever starts up again," I promise.

As the list goes around, students scratch the contact information down on their own scraps of paper. We all want to contact each other outside of class. Immigrants and native Chicagoans, Blacks and Whites, wealthy and middle-class, Cub fans and Sox fans, Catholics and Jews, Baptists and Atheists, sighted and non-sighted. We have one thing in common: we are all writers.

15

Chicago Sides

WBEZ IS A very popular public radio station. After our essays about my memoir classes air, Chicago organizations start inviting me to talk about memoir writing at their events. I invite a writer from class to come along and read an essay aloud at each gig. Minerva is always my first choice, but when she can't make it, others volunteer.

So when a Barnes & Noble bookstore schedules a book signing and reading of *Long Time, No See*, I call Minerva. Would she like to come with me? She sounds very eager.

"Where's it at?" she asks. I give her the address. The phone goes silent. I can barely hear her when she finally speaks up. "Oh, Beth, I don't think so," she says. "I'm afraid of the North Side."

Chicago is one of the most racially-diverse cities in the country. Mike tells me that if you look at the people milling around in the Loop on an average workday, you see all sorts of racial differences. My Monday memoir class meets downtown, and it's so easy to reach via public transportation that seniors come in from the city's predominantly-Black South Side, White North Side, and Asian neighborhood pockets. Some meet for coffee afterwards, but once class is over, we all return to our segregated neighborhoods.

Mike and I are White, and I regularly say we live on Chicago's South Side. If Mike is within listening distance, he regularly adds, "Not really."

Chicago's address numbering system uses a grid that claims Madison as its East-West axis, and we live six blocks south of Madison Street. Printers Row, our neighborhood, is a part of a larger section of Chicago called the South Loop. We are fans of the White Sox, Chicago's South Side baseball team. Chance the Rapper attended our neighborhood high school. I stick to my story.

Mike knows that claiming the South Side as home leaves some people worrying about our safety, but the South Side of Chicago is far more than gangs and guns and street violence. And I'm so used to hearing White people say "I'm afraid of the South Side" that hearing Minerva say the same about the North Side is oddly refreshing.

And I can't say I blame her, really.

Minerva was born in 1920, not long after the Chicago race riot of 1919. That riot started after a group of White men pelted stones at a 17-year-old African-American boy who crossed an unofficial barrier between the city's White and Black beaches. The teenager died, and police officers who arrived at the scene refused to arrest anyone. Fighting continued for days, and no doubt Minerva grew up hearing about the shootings, beatings, and arson attacks that left 15 Whites and 23 Blacks dead.

So okay, Mike is probably right. He and I don't live within those barriers. We are so close to the Loop downtown that Printers Row may not really count as South Side. That said, until now all the events I've been doing with Minerva took place south of Madison. And essays she and other South Siders are sharing in class are helping me understand and respect her fear.

I don't pressure her, I just tell her how much I enjoy having her with me. "Your writing boosts my confidence," I say.

In the end, Minerva does join me – her daughter drives her. The audience loves her. And me? I sign lots of books. "You need to come out with yours now," I tell Minerva.

16

My Turn

AS THE CLASS facilitator, I consider it my job to keep the class moving. I encourage others to comment on the essays they hear, and I do my best to keep my own stories to myself.

But now it's my turn.

I am one of seven children, and as Mike likes to say, we are not a family, we're a nation. So we have lots of stories.

I'll start with my father.

I don't remember much about Ed Finke, but from stories I've heard I know he grew up in small-town southern Illinois. In exchange for a scholarship to a teacher's college near Chicago, he was required to teach at a Lutheran elementary school after graduation. He taught one year, quit, and never looked back.

Why did my dad quit teaching? What happened that first year to change his mind? Maybe Eddie Finke never intended on a career in education. Did he accept the scholarship to escape rural life? Or his overbearing mother? Or to leave grief behind after his 7-year-old sister Wilma died of diphtheria?

I never got to ask him.

One of my dad's college friends told me that Eddie was a good writer. If he had put some of his own life stories on paper, I might know him better.

Before she met my dad, Flo waitressed at the Dew Drop Diner. Sometimes she didn't get off work until 11 p.m. "I used to walk home by myself," she told us. "We didn't think anything of it." One night in 1935, her cousin Evelyn talked her into making a visit to the Concordia Teachers College. Claiming they were cousins to one of the guys in the men's dorm, they got in. And guess who lived in that dorm? Ed Finke. Our dad.

Florence told Eddie about a street dance coming up in Elmhurst. Smitten by her blue-eyed beauty, he said he'd come. Flo lit up every time she repeated this story. "There was going to be a chivaree for Edna Felbinger that night, too!" Another fella also offered to meet Flo at the street dance. "I figured I'd just go with whomever showed up first."

To our great fortune, it was Eddie. A year and a half later Eddie chose a very romantic setting – our Grandma Moos' kitchen – to sit Flo down at the table and ask her to marry him.

Florence Moos and Edgar Finke were married at Immanuel Lutheran Church in Elmhurst on November 27, 1937. "Evelyn was my maid of honor," Flo said. "I couldn't choose between all the cousins, it could have been Rose, Toots, so many. But Evelyn introduced your dad and me, so I chose her." It was a beautiful day, especially for November. "We didn't need coats or anything." The bride wore a blue velvet gown – "It was depression times, you couldn't get silk."

Eddie and Flo Finke

Our dad didn't own a car, so Flo's new in-laws drove the newlyweds to their "honeymoon" in Springfield, Illinois. "Your dad was teaching there," Flo explained. "They dropped us off on their way back to Litchfield."

Eddie fulfilled his one-year teaching obligation for a monthly paycheck of $40. Monthly rent was $20. First Bobbie was born, then Doug, then Ron, then Cheryl. By that time they were raising four children in my Grandma Moos' upstairs apartment. They all shared one bathroom. "You just do what you have to," Flo always said.

After three more children, in 1960, the Finkes moved to a newer, bigger house, next door to one of Flo's childhood friends, Marion Denny, and her family. Uncle Ray helped our dad finish the basement, including a bedroom for Doug and Ron plus, get this, a second bathroom. They built a two-car garage, too. Things were looking good.

And then, in December, 1961, on my third birthday, our dad came home sick from work. Flo believed most people were her superiors, and she did what her superiors told her. So when doctors said he had a minor heart condition, she knew if we followed doctor's orders everything would be fine.

Finke siblings portrait taken November 27, 1961,
as a 24th anniversary gift for their parents

The four older kids were out and we three younger ones were in bed a few weeks later when my dad got up and leaned on the closet door, clutching his chest in pain. My sister Marilee was eight years old then, and she and I slept through it. Six-year-old Bev woke up and saw it all.

It was January, 1962, and 9-1-1 wouldn't become the national emergency number until 1968. After walking our dad back to bed, Flo rushed to the kitchen, lifted the receiver off the phone on the wall, put her pointer finger in the "O," dialed clockwise, listened to ten clicks register, waited for the operator to answer and then finally, finally got to ask for an ambulance.

We three little ones stayed in our beds while Flo went alone to the front door to greet the emergency team. Confident Eddie would be all right, she stayed in the kitchen as ordered while the ambulance staff "worked on" him. But it didn't work.

My oldest sister was the first one called. Married for two years by then, Bobbie left their baby son with her husband and rushed to our house. She arrived just in time to see the workers take our dad down the front steps in a body bag.

Nineteen-year-old Doug, a trombone player, was doing a two-week stint with the Smokey Stover Firehouse Band in Detroit. Flo reached him after midnight, once his gig was over. "She got to it right away," Doug said. "She said she had bad news...." Heavy snow made the trip home by Greyhound Bus challenging. "It was a long ride, with no one to talk to. I'd take cat naps, but I kept waking up and wondering if this was really happening."

Eighteen-year-old Ron had been out drinking nearby with his buddies. "But he sobered up the minute he walked into the kitchen," Flo recalled years later.

By the time my fifteen-year-old sister Cheryl got home from a dance at the park district's Teen Club, Bobbie had already come and gone.

Marilee remembers waking up the next morning and seeing our mom and dad's bed made like usual. "No one told me anything," she said.

Bev was a teenager before she told any of us she'd woken up that night and seen our father standing and grasping his chest.

I only remember it all through everyone else's stories.

My dad didn't have a life insurance policy. Flo received Social Security after he died, but it wasn't much. So she found a job at a local bakery that let her bring me with her to work on weekdays. Marilee and Bev came along on Saturdays, too. Cheryl's nights at The Teen Club were over – she spent them waitressing at a nearby diner instead. Ron worked nights for a moving company, and he and Cheryl started paying Flo rent to live at home. Doug went back on the road with his jazz band.

Saturday afternoons we'd go to the cemetery. When the peonies in our backyard were in bloom, Flo would rinse out an empty juice bottle, cut a bunch of flowers, and bring them along. I learned to walk around the graves, not across them, to get to the life-size depiction of the Lord's Supper on the long cement wall near Daddy's grave. I could identify Jesus in the etching – he was the one in the middle – but never did figure out which of the disciples was Daddy.

Life wasn't all work and no play, though. Flo took us to

hear Doug any Saturday or Sunday night he was performing nearby. When he drew a low number in the draft lottery, he enlisted. We all breathed a sigh of relief when he got into the 3rd Marine Air Wing Band in El Toro, California. Playing for national parades and ceremonies in the United States kept him out of Vietnam.

Before he left home, Doug bought us a piano. Flo scrimped and saved and insisted that Marilee, Bev, and I take lessons.

When I started kindergarten, a part-time worker named Nina walked me to school from the bakery, holding my hand the whole way. My elementary school recognized our family situation and moved me up to first grade during the Christmas break. Now Flo could take classes and find a higher-paying job.

My siblings had taught me to read, and Flo instructed me to write my father's full name as "Edgar W. Finke" to fill out school forms on my own. She taught me to spell d-e-c-e-a-s-e-d. "That's what you write on the line where they ask for your father's occupation."

Flo studied typing at night and eventually took a full-time job as an office clerk at Reliable Electric Company. We three youngest girls were now latchkey kids.

Thirteen-year-old Marilee was in charge, keeping the house clean and fixing dinner in between peeking at *Dark Shadows* on TV. The hardest part of her job was corralling Bev and me inside, seeing to it that we were seated around the Formica kitchen table for supper the minute Flo walked in from her long day at the office.

Money was still short, but Flo kept that to herself. Instead, she'd scold, "You're wasting electricity!" if we forgot to turn the lights off. Or, "Those calls cost money!" if we talked on the phone too long. But she never complained about money, not even when I made things worse.

When I turned 15 and got my driver's permit, Flo was hesitant to let me practice using our car. She didn't point out that she needed the car to get to work. She didn't whine that we didn't have gas money. She just said no. I thought she was mean.

My friend Terri had her own car, an orange Chevy Nova. She helped me practice and drove me to my driver's test. But even with a license, Flo hardly ever let me drive.

Except for one memorable Sunday in 1976. York High School's percussion ensemble was practicing that afternoon and I had to be there to play my piano parts. Since church ran long that morning, it was too late to call friends for a ride or take my bike.

Flo handed over the keys, making it clear she wasn't happy about it. Well, neither was I. Why was this always such a battle? It wasn't like I was heading off to the forest preserve to do bongs – I was heading to the high school band room!

Keys in hand, I slammed the back door and stomped across the cement slab into the garage behind our house. I slipped into the driver's seat, turned the car key, revved the engine and backed out of the garage – right into the back corner of the house.

Why stop? I pulled forward, jammed the car into reverse, missed the house on the second try, sped down the gravel driveway, and took off.

Rehearsal didn't go well. Hard to play piano when your hands are shaking.

Flo was wiping off the kitchen counters when I got home. Her back to me, she didn't turn around as I walked in the door. She wordlessly opened her hand, accepted the car keys, and placed them on the key hook. I never drove that car again.

Flo worked at Reliable Electric for 20 years, burned the mortgage on our house, and retired at age 70. Which was the same year I lost my sight.

During one of my visits to schools on Long Island, a precocious fifth grader asked me one of the most difficult questions I've been asked since losing my sight. "If you could see for one day, and then at the end of the day you wouldn't be able to see again, what would you do that day?" My answer?

1. I'd spend the morning with Mike reading the newspaper and sipping cappuccino at our local coffee shop
2. I'd look over my photo albums, try to memorize what everyone looks like
3. I'd drive over to Flo's, help her with errands, then sit on the couch with her and listen to traditional jazz on the console hi-fi. Her face would light up, her blue eyes would sparkle, and she'd cock her head and say, "That's my kind of music."

17

Minerva Takes Printers Row

MIKE AND I live in Printers Row, a revitalized neighborhood two blocks south of Chicago's loop. It's the perfect location for someone like me who can't drive. We're near every mode of public transportation Chicago offers: trains, subways, buses. We can even walk to Lake Michigan and take a boat to Navy Pier if we're feeling adventurous.

Printers Row used to be the city's bookmaking hub. Now it's the home of the Printers Row Book Fair, the largest free outdoor literary event in the Midwest. Nearly 100,000 bookworms come every June for two days of author readings and panel discussions. Tables line up along five city blocks so that booksellers, publishers, and literary and cultural organizations can sell and promote books and merchandise. Eleven stages with huge tents block the streets. Book lovers line up after events to get their favorite authors' autographs.

At the 2004 fair last summer, I did a presentation and signed copies of *Long Time, No See*. Mike and I threw a party for dozens of friends at our apartment right before my event, then shooed everyone out so they'd be at my tent on time. Good strategy! My tent was packed. The Book Fair organizers noticed. Will I please come back this year?

Sure, I say, but how about I do a presentation on memoir writing. "And I'd like to have one senior citizen from my writing class read at the presentation, too. Will that be alright?"

Minerva explodes in joy when I ask her over the phone. "That would be wonderful!" Her voice sparkles. I know I can count on her to wow the audience.

Since my sisters live all over the country, we get together once a year for Sisters Weekend. This year we decide to meet in Chicago for the Printers Row Book Fair. Flo has heard so much about Minerva that she wants to come, too.

Our presentation is slated for 1 p.m., too early for us to bribe friends with another pre-event party. Instead, we invite all the seniors from my now-defunct class to come to a celebration party afterward, hoping the thought of food and drink to follow will entice them to come hear Minerva first.

The Book Fair's tony hospitality suite is replete with fancy sandwiches and drinks. They ask us to check in there an hour before we appear so they know where we are when it's our turn to speak. When Minerva and I arrive, volunteers ceremoniously place ribbons over our heads à la *The Wizard of Oz*. A badge at the end of the ribbon proclaims each of us "Author."

Minerva brings in friends. I bring my sisters, Flo, and Mike. All are given badges saying "Author Relations." Other authors check in without stopping for food. Us? We all gush at the spread. "Cloth napkins, too, girl!" Minerva titters, patting my knee under the table. We snarf.

When it's time, a volunteer escorts Minerva and me to our presentation room. We enter to chaos. It's Standing Room Only! People line the hallway – organizers are turning a lot of them away. When my sister Marilee notices a friend of Minerva's is about to be bounced, she grabs her elbow and yanks her inside.

One of my students pushes her way to the front to whisper that she's going to leave. She hopes I don't mind. "It's too crowded in here!" she says. "And besides, I know what you teach in class."

I'm getting nervous. Without being able to see, I can't judge exactly what sort of crowd it is. Distract yourself, Beth. Think about something else. How about that iced tea brewing at home? Won't that taste good when we finish here? Assuming the student is still standing in front of me, I tell her I hope she'll come to the party afterwards.

"You bet!"

Next thing I know, I'm being introduced. Hanni leads me to the podium and takes her time getting comfortable at my feet. The audience laughs. I do, too. It feels good.

My talk is short, a brief overview of the merits of getting memories down on paper. Start out by giving yourself short assignments, I tell the audience. Pick a theme and limit yourself to 500 words. "Small pieces are easier to take on because you might actually finish them."

Then I show them how writing can be used as a form of therapy. That's what *Long Time, No See* was for me. Social workers over the years had urged me to talk about my feelings, vent my frustrations at not being able to see, at having a child born with disabilities. I don't like to dwell on those subjects. And let's be honest: people aren't always ready to hear our feelings once we do decide to let loose. So writing is much easier. I can do it when I feel like it, when I can devote the energy. I can take time to search for the perfect word or phrase.

I share an example from my own life: back in 1985, when the retinal specialist told me the surgery to restore my sight hadn't worked and I would never see again, how did I feel? Scared? Angry? Bitter? Serene? Relieved the surgeries were over? Thinking so hard to find the perfect word put me right back in the situation, forcing me to work through my feelings.

I want to read them a passage from *Long Time, No See*. I tell the audience that Braille would be the easiest way to do that, but I'm still learning it. "So to read at presentations like this, I put in an earpiece and listen to my book on tape," I say, showing them my cassette recorder and the earpiece. "It's like the ones we used with transistor radios, remember?"

As they chuckle and share transistor-radio memories with their neighbors, I double-check to confirm I'm at the right spot on the tape. Once the crowd noise dies down, I start listening to the words, simultaneously repeating what I hear:

I was struck by a sudden feeling of freedom and relief. No more lasers, no more operations, no more weekly visits to Chicago, no more worrying whether or not this all was going to work. We'd been at this for nearly a year; now it was finally over.

I swiveled my head as if to look around. I saw nothing.

Mike talked to the doctor, asking sensible questions, I suppose. Turning toward their voices, I asked if this was really it, if we'd really exhausted the possibilities.

"I'm a religious man," the doctor answered, "and in the religion I follow we believe in miracles. I believe God has cured all sorts of ailments. This could happen with you, but there's nothing else I can do for you medically."

We stood up to leave. I reached out for the doctor's hand. He clasped mine with both of his, and I thanked him for all he'd done. He was shaking. I felt sorry for him; I would've liked to tell him we were going to be alright.

I pause, then explain that once I'd written all that down, I was able to set it aside. It's there if I ever need it, but I no longer have to be burdened by the memory.

"And all those social workers who accuse me of denying my feelings can read it, too," I say with a laugh. "We could put a lot of therapists out of business!" I hear the audience laughing with me and feel them nodding in agreement.

I point out how writing can help your brain. "So many older folks are worried they don't remember things the way they used to," I say. "Writing, and thinking of the right word to use in an essay, helps your brain. It's like doing a crossword puzzle, but better. If you can't come up with the right word, it's okay to look it up."

But enough about me. Finally, the moment comes – I introduce Minerva. "Some of you might recognize our next reader's voice," I say. "Minerva Mills Bell recorded a short piece on Chicago Public Radio."

Minerva glides to the podium and greets the crowd like a preacher giving a Sunday sermon. "Good afternoon, everybody!"

she calls. The audience responds with a lively, "Good afternoon!" She thanks everyone for coming, introduces friends and family members who are in the audience, and takes off reading.

But really, Minerva isn't reading at all. She must have memorized half the funny story she reads about her son Marvin. Instead of looking down at her paper, she surveys the crowd. I can hear it in the way her voice projects. It is mesmerizing.

My sisters are the only ones young enough to spring to their feet when she finishes. The rest of the audience roars with applause instead. Minerva takes it all in. We are a hit.

After the presentation, Minerva's friend Wanda Bridgeforth introduces herself to me at the front table. "Minerva and I have been friends since high school," she boasts. "DuSable, Class of '39. I'd love to take your writing class."

Minerva joins us and surprises me with a hug. "Thanks for keeping me alert, Beth. And interested!" I am nearly thrown off my feet. Not by her strength, but by her words. Minerva is a wisp of a woman; I have to be careful not to break her when I hug her back.

18

Afterparty

THE PARTY BACK at our place is even better than the presentation. At home Hanni doesn't wear her harness – I know my way around and don't need her to lead me. Finally off duty, she spends half her time that afternoon on her back enjoying belly rubs from dog lovers who had obediently resisted the temptation during all those weeks of class.

Ida is among the last to arrive. Right behind her is Queen Minerva and her entourage, who enter to much applause.

Turns out they'd returned to the hospitality suite after our presentation. Minerva's friend Lynn says they'd almost been turned away. "But Minerva just pointed to her badge, said *'author,'* and paraded us all in!"

Mike and I have asked a few friends from outside of class to come to our party, too. My sisters mingle. Flo chats with Minerva. I sit at the piano, playing and staying out of Mike's way while he puts out appetizers.

When our friend Lydia arrives, she comes right to the piano and introduces me to her friend Brian. When he asks a few questions about my piano and the chord changes I was using, the light bulb over my head goes off. This is Lydia's friend who plays piano with Second City. "You wanna play?" I ask.

His answer is so resounding that I know he'd been dying for me to ask.

The party really takes off after that. Brian knows all the old songs. One writer knows the words to one tune; another knows the words to the next. Slowly they all drift towards the piano.

The one tune every single one of them knows the chorus to: "Don't Get around Much Anymore." "Isn't that fitting?" Ida laughs.

By 4:00 in the afternoon, all the guests are gone. Gotta get home before the traffic, you know. Best. Party. Ever.

Later that week I write the Commissioner of Mayor Daley's Department on Aging to thank her again for giving me the opportunity to teach these fabulous students. I tell her about the SRO crowd at Printers Row and our wonderful party afterwards. What a shame it is that the class cannot continue.

Two days later I get a call from the Chicago Cultural Center. "When can you start teaching again?"

19

Friends

MINERVA AND WANDA have been friends since DuSable High School opened in 1935.

"Minerva told me she was going to be in the book fair with her teacher, and I should come and meet Beth Finke," Wanda says. Minerva hadn't mentioned that I was blind, and Wanda was sitting so far back that she didn't see Hanni at my feet until she walked up to say hello. "I said 'Holy Toledo! A blind lady teaching a writing class? This I gotta see!'" I invited her to sit in on a class, and she signed right up.

Minerva and Wanda bring a slice of Chicago history with them. Tens of thousands of Southern blacks flooded into Chicago during the Great Migration of the early 20th century. The friends' essays describe Bronzeville, the segregated neighborhood they grew up in, as a "city within a city." Overcrowding, joblessness, and poverty was a fact of life, but so was literature, jazz, blues, and gospel music.

DuSable High School, the first Chicago high school built exclusively for African-American students, opened in the Bronzeville neighborhood in 1935. Minerva transferred in as a sophomore, and Wanda was a freshman. "I was in the birthday class," Wanda reminds us.

DuSable was built on Chicago's South Side 15 years before the Brown v. Board of Education decision. Wanda says it was built to keep schools segregated. "We were blocked in," she writes. "We knew not to cross Cottage Grove, 51st Street or the train tracks." Everyone inside those boundaries was Black. "That was our neighborhood, and DuSable was our neighborhood high school."

When DuSable first opened, some neighborhood parents applied for permits to get their children into nearby White high schools. "Their parents didn't think a Black school could be any good," Wanda writes, adding that she felt sorry for those kids. True, DuSable classes could be very crowded; she remembers 50 or so students squeezing into classrooms. "But at those other schools, if you were Black and you wanted to be in a play, you had to be a maid or a butler," she writes. "At DuSable, we did everything, we were in all the plays, we wrote the school newspaper. We were having such a good time at DuSable."

Between the two of them, Minerva and Wanda were at the high school between 1935 and 1939. During those years they walked the hallways with some pretty impressive classmates, including Nat King Cole; John H. Johnson, publisher of Ebony and Jet magazines; Harold Washington, first African-American mayor of Chicago; Redd Foxx; and Dinah Washington.

"Nat Cole added King to his name later," Wanda tells me with a laugh. "You know, like Old King Cole!"

They remember Dinah Washington when she was Ruth Jones, and they knew Redd Foxx as Jon Sanford. "His brother was Fred, that's who *Sanford and Son* is named for," Wanda tells us. "They changed their names once they were stars."

DuSable's initial fame was in its music program, and Wanda and Minerva both sang during "Hi-Jinks" student talent shows there. "We were in the background, but we put on shows that were better than what was going on in Chicago professional theatres," Wanda writes. "With musicians like Ruthie Jones and Nat Cole and all of those guys, we couldn't miss!"

20

Hannelore

YOU MIGHT NOT think that listening to a person read aloud for five minutes once a week would give you much insight into their life. You would be wrong.

Hannelore has macular degeneration. She found us through the volunteers at Blind Service Association, who read her mail out loud to her every week. "They are the ones who told me about this blind lady who teaches a writing class," she says. "I just had to come and find out how she does it."

From Hannelore's essays, we have learned that she grew up in a German industrial city called Mannheim, that her family was Jewish, that they owned a substantial home and butcher shop, that she was only 19 when she escaped Germany, that others of her family didn't make it out in time. She and her future husband, Eugene Bratman, met on the MS *Saturnia* on their way to America. When they arrived here, no one could pronounce her name, so she changed it to Hanna.

When I assign "First Grade," Hannelore takes us

back to 1920s Europe with her as she reads out loud in her German accent.

First Grade, Mannheim, 1926
By Hannelore Bratman

I had graduated from the Froebel seminar which was just around two corners from our house in E.5.3. I knew the school at K.5 was just five blocks from our house.

The city of Mannheim was founded by the Romans who had explored the country around the rivers Rhine and Neckar. The old city was laid out in blocks, and instead of names it had the alphabet and numbers. It was easy even for young children to figure out where you had to go.

Our Laden Fraulein Rosa accompanied me to my new school. I will find my own way home, I assure her. When we are at the school I bid Rosa goodbye. I carried a big cone of candy and goodies, and wore a new dress and apron. My teacher, Fraulein Ackerman, handed out slates, chalk, and little sponges. She told us our homework is to tie the sponges to the slate with some string and to wet the sponge at home before coming the next day. I put it all in my new backpack. It is my first backpack, a brown leather bag. It is big and heavy.

The next day a little wet sponge to wipe the slate dangles out on a string as we walked to the Volksschule, the school at K5. Six blocks straight down towards the Ring by the Neckar. I cannot get lost. I have practiced walking this stretch several times under the watchful eye of our Kinderfraulein. All the school supplies have been secured at Jesselsohn's, an office supply store, the store next to our butcher shop.

The slate had a little wood frame. It was black, with white lines for writing on one side. On the backside, there was half a grid for numbers and math. The other half was blank. We used white chalk mostly. For new homework, you just washed off whatever was on the slate. It was important to have a clean slate because the teacher made you do your homework over if you didn't. Sloppiness was not tolerated, and punishment followed promptly.

I also had a brand new abacus with its many colored beads. I knew how to use it, had played on my brother's abacus many times, and I loved counting and adding.

Fraulein Ackermann was a skinny, tall woman, who carried a long bamboo stick. She had a loud voice. She used the stick and sometimes just slammed it down on your desk. I was scared of the stick. She also slapped it on your hand if you were naughty, but I did well.

We had homework, had to learn how to recite poems, write stories, and then read them out loud to the class. When I started to have problems after my father's and little brother's deaths, she put up with my antics. I was promoted with honors to second grade and a different teacher. All I remember about the second grade was that we were supposed to learn how to read and recreate maps.

Fraulein Ackermann entered my life again in 3rd grade. I loved her then. Her long bamboo stick was no longer part of her attire. I am very grateful she was so strict. She gave my education a good foundation.

21

Out of the Mouths of Babes

I LEARN A lot about the writers in class by the way they sound. Some days the spectrum of wisdom, comfort, humor, flirtation, anger, even crankiness that transmits through 60, 70, 80, and 90-year old pipes is disarming.

On most days? It's charming.

When Hanni and I enter elementary school hallways, we are surrounded by the happy-chatterbox din of kids heading to their classrooms. That makes the awestruck silence when my Seeing Eye dog leads me into their room all the more astonishing. Their honesty and thoughtfulness shines through when they start asking questions.

Hanni and I love taking Amtrak, so that's how we get to Horace Mann Elementary School in West Allis, Wisconsin, on this particular school visit.

After getting settled in a classroom, I talk to the children circled around Hanni and me about my daily routine, about Hanni, about what it's like to be blind. I tell them that, even when my eyes are open, all I see is the color black.

At school visits I recruit a teacher or staff member to call on students who have questions. A second-grader's hand shoots right up. Okay, I can't see her hand shoot up, but it comes through loud and clear when I hear the excited "Oh! Oh!" in her voice before she is chosen.

The little girl's question? "Is it the kind of black you see when you're sleeping, or the kind of black you see when you wake up and open your eyes?" The questions go on from there:

How do you drive?

If you can't see red or green, how do you know when it's time to cross the street?

Do you see different kinds of black, like light black and medium black and dark black?

How do you know which dog is your favorite if you can't see them?

How do you tie your shoes when you can't see your feet?

You mean you really can't see any colors? I feel so sad for you if you can't see colors.

I thank the thoughtful boy who feels sad for me, and try to assure him that even though I can't see, my life is still pretty colorful. "I just have to use my other senses to do things you do with your eyes," I say. I describe how I read and write books, swim laps, bake bread, play piano, go to plays, meet with friends. "And if I wasn't blind, I probably would never have known what it's like to love a dog."

From there I explain how Seeing Eye dogs are trained and what rules the kids should follow if they encounter someone with a guide dog. I list the commands that Hanni knows and show them how responsive she is.

The thoughtful boy who had felt sad for me must have been really pondering his feelings as I talked. Before we leave to catch our train home, he raises his hand to tell me he doesn't feel that sad for me anymore.

"Really, you're lucky," he says. I'm expecting him to add something about how I get to take Hanni with me wherever I go. But he surprises me with a new twist on the lemonade-out-of-lemons notion.

"You don't have to worry about ever getting blind," he reasons. "You already are."

22

All Aboard with Wanda

MY AMTRAK RIDE that week inspires the next writing prompt: "All Aboard!" "Write about being a passenger on a train, an airplane, a ship," I say.

Wanda's story takes us back to when she was seven years old, making her first solo train ride from Chicago to visit her grandparents in Mississippi. When Mama and Wanda's beloved Uncle Hallie B. take her to the station, Hallie B. runs ahead to help get her on board. The Pullman porters don't mind – most of them already know Hallie B.

Reasoning that newly-freed slaves and their sons and grandsons would make excellent servicemen and work for long hours at little pay, Pullman only hired Blacks as porters. Pullman was the largest employer of blacks in the country back then, and the greatest concentration of Pullman porters lived on Chicago's South Side.

From the 1920s through the 1940s, porters helped Blacks from Mississippi migrate north by bringing back information on available jobs and housing in Chicago, most notably by distributing copies of *The Defender*, Chicago's Black weekly newspaper.

Aware that porters were willing to deliver goods for friends and family north and south of the Mason-Dixon line, Wanda's Grandma Lula Johnson would regularly bake birthday cakes for her offspring in Chicago and send them north with a porter. Hallie B. would head to Chicago's 12th Street Station on every birthday to collect the cake. "The porters all knew my Grandma Lula," Wanda says with delight and pride.

Wanda tells us later that at seven years old she had no idea she was riding in the "colored only" car, purposely located next to the engine where noise, smoke, and soot were at their worst. Every single Black person who boarded a train had to cram into that first car, along with the conductor, the porter, and other "colored" train personnel, even when cars in the White section remained empty.

All Aboard
By Wanda Bridgeforth

Standing near the door leading to the platforms, we listened to hear "All Aboard for Columbus Mississippi, Track Five." Mama grabbed my hand and clutched it to her chest as we ran down the wooden platform past the Pullman sleeper, the club car, the dining car to the first coach behind the engine. My Uncle Hallie B. passed us and was on the steps of the train car waiting to help us board. I was traveling alone to visit Grandma and Grandpa Johnson. I felt all grown-up in my Sunday dress, coat, hat, patent leather Mary Jane slippers, and purse. Pinned to my coat was a slip of paper with my name,

Grandma and Grandpa Johnson's name, and their address in Columbus, Mississippi.

As I stared open-mouthed at the huge black locomotive engine the engineer leaned out of the window and yelled, "Howdy, little lady, are you riding with us today?"

"Yes sir, I'm going to Columbus, Mississippi, to visit my Grandma and Grandpa Johnson."

"Well, what a coincidence. I'm from Columbus. Is Mac Johnson your grandpa?"

"Yes sir!!!"

"Well, I'm honored to have you on board."

The porter and waiter assured Mama and Hallie B. they would keep an eye out and deliver me safely.

"Board!" More passengers began to fill the car behind the engine. Hallie B. put my suitcase in the rack over my seat. Mama settled me into the first seat by the window and set my lunch of biscuits and fried chicken wrapped in a tea cloth tucked inside a shoe box beside me.

The coach wasn't full so I had the whole seat to stretch out and sleep. I was almost seven and felt so grown up I could hardly contain myself. The conductor shouted the final "Board." The engine began to chug, steam belched from the pipe on top of the huge black engine, Mama and Hallie B. hugged me, got off the train and stood on the platform waving, I'm sure until the train was out of sight.

The porter brought me a blanket and pillow and the waiter brought me a Coca-Cola and some water.

Every time I heard "Board" I looked out of the window to watch the passengers getting on and off the train. The thrill of *my first solo trip is one of my happiest memories. I know the conductor was supposed to say All Aboard but I only remember hearing "Board!"*

23

Hanni and Beth: Safe & Sound

NO MATTER WHERE I'm presenting, or what the occasion, when it comes to the Q&A, nearly every question is about one thing: my Seeing Eye dog.

"How old is she?"

"How does she know where to take you?"

"How do you know when she has to go out and, you know, pee?

It took me three years to write *Long Time, No See*, then ten years to find a publisher. Children's picture books are only 24 pages long. It's a no-brainer. My second book will be a children's book about dogs.

So in between memoir-writing sessions, I write a story about Wags, a Seeing Eye dog who doesn't always like his job. Other dogs get to play Frisbee in the park, but day after day, Wags has to follow commands and lead a blind woman around. The woman doesn't always go where Wags wants to go, and speaking of going...other dogs get to lift their legs on any tree they want. Wags has to wait until his human companion takes his harness off and gives him permission. I call my new book *Long Time, No Pee* – a sort of canine sequel to *Long Time, No See*.

I send my proposal to a long list of publishers. The rejections come quickly, most via postcards I can't read myself. Poor Mike has to be the messenger.

Then it's back to teaching.

Just like I can't read those postcards, I can't read or edit handwritten essays. Eyebrows up! Little by little the writers learn to use email. I devise a simple editing system: I write my comments in ALL CAPS, and put {brackets} around words I suggest they delete. They can take or reject my ideas before they read their essays at the next class. It's the perfect feedback loop.

Magazines and newspapers are starting to accept my stories via email, too. When my talking computer isn't chirping away helping me write edits to senior writers, it is busy parroting the words I type for magazine and newspaper assignments. It's a busy time.

So I've nearly forgotten about *Long Time, No Pee* when, *ding!* A note from Blue Marlin Publications pops up in my inbox. Publisher Francine Rich likes my writing. "But the story needs to be about you and Hanni, not some made-up Seeing Eye dog," her message says. "The kids will be meeting you and Hanni during school visits, so the book has to be about you."

She insists the title needs to be changed as well. Books with the word "pee" in the title are not welcome on school library shelves.

I am disappointed, but I understand. No *Long time, No Pee*. I'll change the title, and rewrite the manuscript, too.

Not in first person, though. After all that work writing and publishing a memoir, I am sick of myself. "How about I write it from Hanni's point of view?"

Francine loves the idea. Rough drafts go back and forth for months. My sister Marilee, an elementary school teacher, coaches me. Finally, a manuscript we all like. I sign the contract and cash my advance check.

Now to find an illustrator.

Francine Rich likes to involve authors when it comes to choosing an illustrator. "But you can't see. Is there a way we can involve you?"

Over the years, Mike has become an expert in describing visuals. So I tell Francine not to worry. Her potential illustrators can send their sample drawings our way and Mike will describe them to me.

Francine submits my manuscript to a handful of illustrators and asks them to paint or draw a sample illustration for any part of my story. After looking over the samples, Francine mails them to Mike.

My husband is a creative guy. After first letting me know which part of the story is being illustrated – Hanni guiding me down the sidewalk, watching me bake bread, sitting at the ballpark – he entertains me with descriptions of the samples. One he likes is "kind of like a circus poster." Another is "a bad rendition of a Beetle Bailey comic strip." Mike hates comic strips. We reject that artist.

An artist from Japan chooses the first page of the book, where Hanni says, "Look at me!" He paints her off-center in front of a fireplace with her paw pointing to the mantel. "She's pointing to a photo up there," Mike says. "It's of her, wearing her harness." Clever!

Next comes an oil painting from Anthony Alex Letourneau. "It springs off the page," Mike tells me. Tony has illustrated other Blue Marlin books, and Francine sounds eager to work with him again. Mike, Francine, and I all agree. Tony is our man.

Tony lives with his wife and three kids on a hobby farm two hours outside Minneapolis. We introduce ourselves over the phone and Mike agrees to mail photos of Hanni and me so Tony can get to work. "I'll send some sample drawings to Mike from time to time," he tells me. "Mike can check to see if I'm on the right track."

The first sketches Mike gets in the mail are just a teeny bit off. One of them shows Hanni using her body to block me from a hole in the sidewalk. But Seeing Eye dogs always, always stay on the side of the person they are guiding, a little ahead, facing forward.

It's clear that Tony will get a better "picture" of how Hanni and I work together if he sees us in person. There's no time to lose – he has to finish a painting every two weeks to complete the project within a year. So off Hanni and I go on a Megabus trip to Minnesota.

Ten hours and several feature-length comedies later, Hanni and I emerge in Minneapolis. My niece Caren is waiting at the bus stop, ready to deliver us to a coffee shop where Tony and his family are waiting.

Tony has his sketchpad and pencils all set up, and he wastes no time before asking Hanni and me to pose. When Hanni needs a break outside, he follows us and takes notes on how she and I work together. After taking photographs of us back in the coffee shop, he laughs. "People think we're from Hollywood!"

The illustrations are a success. People who look at the book tell me they've never seen anything like it. "The artwork is beautiful!" they say, admiring each oil painting. "The drawings look just like Hanni...and like you, too!"

It doesn't bother me to hear people react to illustrations I'll never see myself – it makes me smile. Just more evidence of how important it was for Tony to see Hanni and me in person. "I gotta believe that's how he was able to get our coloring right and see how we move through space," I say. "Otherwise we spent 20 hours on a Megabus for nothing!"

And really, our friend Steven's comment to Mike after flipping through the pages was all the confirmation I needed. "Beth looks hot in these pictures!" The illustrations really do look exactly like me.

24

Easterseals

"HELLO, BETH FINKE?"

It's a woman named Shirley. She works for a national non-profit called Easterseals that helps people with disabilities. "I heard one of your essays on the radio," she says. "Would you be interested in an internship?"

I thought internships were for college kids. I am in my 40s. I don't tell Shirley that, though. I just let her go on.

Easterseals is headquartered in Chicago, and they've just received a Technology Opportunities Project grant from the U.S. Department of Commerce. "We're working with a software developer to find out if blind people can create and manage web content," she says.

I have no idea what web content management is. I don't tell her that either. I tell her I'll come in for an interview.

No one at the interview seems surprised or bothered by my age and inexperience. Or if they are, they don't mention it. We like each other and I accept their offer. The paid part-time internship will end by the time *Hanni and Beth: Safe & Sound* is in bookstores, leaving me time to promote the new book.

Easterseals supplies me with a talking computer and gives me classes to learn how to use assistive technology with online calendars and office software. There's a permanent spot for Hanni's bowl under the sink in the women's bathroom. I have my own cubicle and learn the joys of conference calls and business meetings.

On Friday afternoons Shirley and I meet for a "weekly download" to go over my progress. One Friday, we find out the office will close early, so we decide to do something special. We'll have our meeting at Jake's Pub, Shirley's favorite bar in Chicago.

Before I leave the office, I search for Hanni's bowl. It's gone. Cleaning staff take it by mistake? Oh, well. It's 3 o'clock, and Hanni has to eat. So I spill her Ziploc bag of dog food right onto the floor in the bathroom stall. "C'mon, Hanni! C'mon, hurry up!" I want her to finish before someone comes in and catches her licking the bathroom floor. "Hurry up, Hanni!"

After finally, finally finishing her food, Hanni leads me downstairs where we pile into a cab with Shirley and head to Jake's. What a thoroughly modern working woman I am, joining my boss for cocktails at happy hour!

One drink leads to another. I start getting hungry. Jake's doesn't sell food – not even beer nuts. But I'm prepared. I reach down into my bag, feel for my pouch of almonds, set them on the bar and start to munch.

Ugh! Yuck! I fumble frantically on the bar for a napkin and spit. Dog food! No wonder it had taken Hanni so long to eat her dinner in the bathroom stall – I'd given her my almonds!

I should be horrified, but I have to laugh. My boss laughs, too. She's seen a lot at Jake's, she says, but until now she's never seen anyone belly up to the bar for dog food.

25

Near Miss

HANNI'S NOT LIKE Lassie. I don't just say, "Memoir Class, Girl! Let's go to the Cultural Center!" and expect her to guide me there. I study routes, memorize which intersections have stop signs or stoplights, and which do not.

Hanni's job is to get me to the end of each street safely, stop, and wait for my command. I listen for traffic. When it sounds safe to go, I tell her to either go "forward," "left," or "right." She looks both ways, confirms it's safe to proceed, and pulls me where we need to go.

Some days Hanni's job is harder than others.

On our way home from a presentation at the Union League Club, a swanky private club on a busy downtown street, Hanni stops at a side street. The sound of traffic rushing by at our parallel tells me it is safe to head straight.

"Forward, Hanni!" She looks both ways, judges it's safe, steps into the street, and in the blink of a blind eye, she jumps back.

I follow her lead. A car rushes by inches in front of us, precisely where we'd just been walking. My heart stops, then it races.

I know what to do. We practiced this very thing during training at The Seeing Eye school. Walk backwards. Get on the sidewalk before praising her.

I am back on the sidewalk hugging Hanni when I feel someone run behind us, shouting down the street. Seconds later, a man is bending down to pat me on the shoulder.

"You alright, Miss?" He is out of breath, panting. "I work at the Union League Club. I saw the whole thing." It was a cab that had sped around the corner, he explains. The driver hadn't even slowed down to make the turn.

"Was that you shouting?"

"Yeah, I was trying to catch him," the doorman says. "Sure you're alright?"

Hanni's tail is wagging, we'd escaped a near miss, and a doorman in shining armor had galloped down the street to seek vengeance on our wrongdoer. All right? "I'm fantastic!" I say, giddy with appreciation. And relief.

26

Launch

"THE PICTURES LOOK just like you!"

"Look at Hanni! There she is!"

"It's so beautiful!"

Hanni and Beth: Safe & Sound has finally arrived. "Hey, guess what!" I say, pulling the hardcover children's book out of my backpack and holding it up, hoping it's not upside-down.

My writers have been along for the whole ride, from writing the story, pitching the story, finding a publisher, rewriting the story, finding an illustrator, all the way through to today. A few of them hope to publish children's stories, others have grandchildren, so everyone's excited.

Someone takes the book from my hand and starts passing it around. When it reaches Minerva, the more mobile writers move to look over her shoulder as she turns the pages. Wanda comes close to hear Minerva read.

They start chattering about all the kids they know who they need to buy copies for – grandchildren, neighbors, cousins, nieces. Finally someone asks me, "Where can we get it?"

I tell them it's available at Sandmeyer's, the independent bookstore near our home in Printers Row. "But here's an idea," I say. "Go to your favorite bookstore, put your hands on your hips, and say, 'I can't believe you don't have Beth Finke's book on your shelves!' They'll order it for you, and maybe some extras, too." They like that idea and arm themselves for battle.

Even better, our friend Carol has volunteered her posh apartment for a book launch party, and everyone is invited.

On the day of the party, our friend Ellen Sandmeyer loads 60 copies of *Hanni and Beth: Safe & Sound* into a red wagon and walks the four blocks from her bookstore to Carol's apartment. Writers, friends, neighbors, and family – my sister Cheryl surprises me by bringing Flo – we all mingle in luxury, enjoying the view of Grant Park and the crowds walking their way to Soldier Field on this beautiful October day. I sit at a table with Ellen, signing, Brailling, and rubber-stamping Hanni's paw print into books for anyone who wants to buy one. And lots of people want to buy one. Or two. Or three! One of our writers buys seven: the first member of the Safe & Sound Frequent Flyer Club.

Ellen notices the pile of books getting shorter and shorter. My sister Cheryl volunteers to sit with me and supervise the signing so Ellen can dash back to Sandmeyer's and grab extra copies.

Back at Sandmeyer's Bookstore, sales have already started. "There's not another book like it," Ellen's husband Ulrich Sandmeyer says, marveling at the illustrations. "I knew it was going to sell." After helping Ellen grab copies off endcap displays inside the store, he yanks the copy from the front display window for her to sell, too.

Ellen returns to the party laughing – and panting. "I've never, ever sold out of books at an event before!" she apologizes. "We could have sold more!"

No apology necessary.

That night, Mike and I take my own copy across the street to Hackney's, our local tavern. Jim – one of the owners – grabs it and shows it off to everyone at the bar. I'm so busy answering questions about the illustrator – "He lives in a farmhouse two hours north of Minneapolis. No, I didn't know him before. The publisher chose him. Hanni and I took a bus up there from Chicago, he watched us working together and sent sample drawings to Mike. Oil. Each page is a painting." – that I don't hear Jim slip away downstairs.

He re-emerges with a couple of big bottles in hand. "Champagne!" Mike exclaims with a hug. Real champagne glasses, too. Ooh la la! Toasts, celebrations – and let the touring begin.

27

Hanni and Beth Hit the Road

HANNI AND I have made lots of free visits to schools and libraries. But now I've learned a wonderful secret.

Published children's book writers can get *paid* to give those sorts of presentations.

Conferences and conventions started offering air fares, per diems, speaking fees, and hotel rooms after *Long Time, No See* was published. And now with a children's book out, schools and libraries are starting to offer honoraria, too. All the hoopla has taught me yet one more thing I didn't realize before I lost my sight: I love staying in hotel rooms. Especially when someone else pays for them.

Solo trips to O'Hare are surprisingly easy from Printers Row. Airport shuttles pick Hanni and me up at our front door and drop us off at curbside check-in.

I always check my bag – Hanni has a hard enough time threading me through a crowded airport as it is. We'd have to fly a bright orange "wide load" flag if I towed a bulky bag along, too.

"My bag is green, right? With a red ribbon attached?" After I double-check that with the curbside workers, they print my boarding pass and tell me where to wait for a skycap.

Skycaps almost always roll up with a wheelchair and guide me to sit in it. I'll have plenty of time to sit on the plane. So I plunk my carry-on backpack in the wheelchair, grab the sky-cap's elbow with my right hand and Hanni's leash with my left, and we're off. Escalators aren't safe for Hanni, so I rely on the skycaps to know where all the elevators are. They know how to cut to the front of the security line, too.

Hanni lives for the moment when her harness rings the alarm in security. Any other time she's wearing her harness, she's working and no one should touch or pet her. But when security folks ask to wand her, I relent. She squirms joyously and wags her tail like she knows she's getting away with something. My quip to the TSA worker that "she's the only creature I know who loves going through airport security" almost always gets a laugh.

Once through security, I hand my boarding pass to the skycap, plunk my carry-on back in the wheelchair, and we're off to my gate.

I love talking to the man or woman beyond the elbow. So many stories! I've learned about Pakistan's health system, Nigerian economics, and stray dogs in Somalia. Every once in a while, though, I get a skycap who doesn't talk. Tired? Shy? Not particularly proficient in English? That's okay. I can rely on my own tricks to tell me where I am and whether we're close to the gate.

I've memorized the gate number, so once Hanni and I clear security, I listen – and feel – for clues that we're getting close.

Hallways are usually tiled, gate areas are carpeted. Counting the TV sounds in each waiting area helps me know how much farther we have to go. Restaurants have cash register sounds and fried-food smells, and restrooms are usually located near the food areas. The sound of flushing toilets is another cue, and I give my skycap a break so Hanni can lead me inside for a quick stop. Shoe sounds confirm I'm at the right bathroom entrance: women's heels click on tile floors.

At our gate, I check in before asking the skycap to guide us to an empty seat as near to the jetway as possible. If I miss the pre-boarding announcement, I'll hear employees talking and figure out it's time.

Once seated, I file through my wallet where I find twenties folded in half, tens folded lengthwise, fives in triangles, singles unfolded. I pull out some bills and thank my skycap. Hanni gets comfortable under my feet while I fumble with headphones, listen to audio books, and check my cell phone periodically until pre-boarding is announced.

The walk down the jetway is the easiest one Hanni and I take all day. It's impossible to make a wrong turn – just straight down the hallway and onto the plane. A flight attendant tells me which row I'm in, and Hanni pulls me forward. I try to count seatbacks, but the flight attendant usually cries out, "Right there! To your right!" to alert us which row to sit in. I command Hanni to sit, then shove her bottom under the seat in front of me. She's remarkably comfortable there, and the feel of a loveable Lab head between my feet is better than Xanax.

Once we land, Hanni is happy to guide me off the plane and up the jetway. I arrange ahead of time to have a skycap meet us there, lead us to the baggage claim, and help us find a shuttle or taxi. I tip well.

At the end of the rainbow: my own hotel room. I ask the desk clerk to snip a corner off my key card so I know which side to slide into the door lock. A hotel staff member guides us to my room, and the questions begin. "How do I dial downstairs? What's the number for room service? How does the thermostat work?" Rummaging through my bag for a rubber band, I ask which bottle is shampoo. I put a rubber band on our hotel door knob, too, so I'll know for sure we're at the right place when we go out. One last question. "Is the radio alarm on?" While he checks, I feel through my wallet again. A tip and he's gone.

Now comes my favorite part. Hotel rooms are predictable, simple, easy to get around. The furniture is rugged, sometimes even bolted to the floor. Nothing fragile on the dressers or countertops. I can't break anything.

Sometimes I eat out, but I usually order in and charge it to my room. Maybe add a glass of red wine. I'm alone in a hotel room. Independent. I like the feeling.

OUR FIRST MAJOR *Safe & Sound* tour takes us to Long Island, to visit elementary schools in the vicinity of Blue Marlin Publications.

Poor Hanni! She starts every school presentation with a whine and a moan. She isn't scared of the kids. She wants to play with them.

Who can blame her? Hearing them ask questions in their adorable Long Island accents makes me want to gather them all up and play with them, too. Some examples:

What happens when you have to go down stairs?

How do you eat ice cream?

How can you write books if you can't see?

How can you use the remote to watch TV if you can't see?

But what if the ice cream is in a cone?

How come you are so pretty?

Dr. Who started in 1963 and you could still see, did you ever watch it?

Can your dog have babies? Why not?

I liked the Fourth Dr. from the planet Gallifrey and he had a robot dog named K-9 and I liked it when Nyssa was on, too, so which one was your favorite Dr. Who?

How do you feel if you're blind?

What if you had a glass and you were walking to the couch and you went to sit down and your dog was there and you got to the couch and you dropped the glass and it broke and got all over the place?

Whew! We spend three days in a row with students, and trust me, Hanni and I both sleep well afterwards. No wonder teachers get the summer off. They need it!

28

Protest

EVERY TIME MINERVA reads, we learn something new.

She sang in the West Point Baptist Church choir with Albertina "Queen of Gospel" Walker.

She memorized "We Real Cool" when she discovered Gwendolyn Brooks in a weekly poetry column in *The Chicago Defender*. "Gwendolyn Brooks lived in our neighborhood, which I considered quite a wonder."

She ran against Ebony publisher John Johnson for DuSable High School senior class president. "He became a millionaire. I was an also ran." Hardly.

But not all of Minerva's memories are fond ones. We shake our heads when we hear these sentences from the essay she wrote when I asked the class to write about something that happened in their teen years that changed their lives:

"Way back, when I graduated from high school, I wanted to be a radio announcer." She even attended broadcasting school. Only for one day, though.

"I arrived for that first day of class, and I was told to leave. No coloreds allowed." So that's why her mother sent her to secretarial school instead.

Some of Minerva's essays are poetic. In "My Grandfather's Job" she packs a lot into just a few lines:

> *Grandpa's Grandpa must have been captured in Africa,*
> *Far across the sea,*
> *Chosen due to his stature and girth,*
> *Fulfilling a role, far from the land of his birth.*
> *There's no written record of Grandpa,*
> *No word of his work or his deeds.*
> *We just know that he worked as a farmer,*
> *And we know that he planted seeds.*
> *Most likely he did not choose his name.*
> *He had to learn new speech.*
> *He must have been a survivor,*
> *Much must have been out of his reach.*
> *No, I can't tell you much about my Grandpa,*
> *Or what the Master's plan might be.*
> *All I know is, I am here in America,*
> *Where so many other people long to be!*

We share in Minerva's grief when we learn of her husband Walter's death. "He died in peace," she tells me. "And he never had to go live in a nursing home."

She may be closing in on 90, but Minerva still has ideals to uphold. Barack Obama's candidacy and the possibility that we may soon have an African-American President is exciting to her. She writes:

I am happy that I lived to see this year 2008 when I may cast a vote in an election I never expected to see.

Furthermore, I am very glad that Barack Obama's grand-mamma did not raise him up on a diet of humble pie like I was.

Ideals aside, Minerva is pure determination when her efforts to get to class collide with a May 1st immigration rally downtown. When I assign the writing prompt "Protest," Minerva stands and delivers the most feisty essay of the day:

Protest

By Minerva Mills Bell

That immigration protest in downtown Chicago had nothing to do with me. I have no quarrels with the immigrants, legal or not. I don't bother them; I don't expect them to bother me. I am just an 88-and-a-quarter-year-old lady who wanted to go downtown and meet with my Monday afternoon memoir-writing class at the Chicago Cultural Center.

All I had to do was to take the #3 King Drive bus, cross the street and enter the building. Class over at 3 pm, walk outside, board that #3 bus and return to 85th and King Drive. Was it too much to ask the CTA to give this old lady as much consideration as it did making accommodations for all the other Chicagoans, whether legal or illegal? Apparently so.

I, and all the other folks who favored me, stood waiting patiently as bus after bus after bus after bus after bus after bus drove past us, discharging many passengers who ALSO did not favor us. And taking on lots of others who did not favor us. One young lady finally piped up. "I've been standing here

45 minutes and have not seen one #4 or #3 pass this stop."

She voiced this again to a driver of one of the buses that paused there as he made his duly appointed rounds. He responded, "Don't you people know? Neither the #3 bus or the #4 is going to come here today. Your buses are being turned around at Roosevelt Road. You've gotta get there and get a southbound bus." He added, "Someone was supposed to come here and instruct you."

This little old lady said, "How can I get there? I can't walk all the way to Roosevelt Road."

"Then you've gotta walk over to Wabash and get – he named some color transit line of which I was completely unfamiliar – get off at Roosevelt Road and transfer to a #3"

So this old lady, who almost never walks a whole block, set out and walked over to Wabash. She could not find a bus stop and asked a meter maid who responded that she did not know where there was a bus stop. She only knew when she had to ticket those overdue parkers.

As I stood there wondering what to do, a uniformed CTA man said, "Lady, all you have to do is climb up those stairs and take the train to Roosevelt Road."

I said, " I can't climb up all those stairs!"

He said, "Well you asked me how to get there, and I told you. The only other thing you can do is walk over to State Street and take – then he added some other colored line, of which I was unfamiliar."

So then I struck out and walked over to State Street.

At State Street another uniformed CTA man told me I would have to descend the stairs, take the train and get off at Harrison.

I did what he told me to do, but when I did, after walking the long way down, taking the noisy subway, the escalator at the Harrison stop was out of order. I had to ascend what felt like three long flights of steps to reach street level.

I was gasping for breath by that time, and another CTA person attempted some humor by saying to me, "Now all you have to do is go back DOWN those stairs and...."

He could see that I did not respond with like humor. So he took me by the arm, escorted me across the street and placed me at the proper place for the next bus, for by this time I was completely disoriented and could not tell left from right or north from south.

He repeated several times, "Now, when you get on this bus, tell the driver you must get off at Roosevelt Road."

In my prayers at night I ask the Lord to bless him.

In the meantime someone else had to tell me, "Walk two blocks over to Michigan. THIS way! Cross over to the southeast corner and catch a #3."

After about 15 minutes a #3 bus came and I boarded. Later I heard the driver saying, "I'm only going to 79th Street. I'm not going to 95th."

When I asked, "Do you mean you'll give me a transfer?" she replied, "I kept telling you I was not going all the way."

Bristling, I retorted. "That's not what you said when I got on at Roosevelt Road."

By this time I was quite ready to do battle rather than pay for a 15-cent transfer.

The driver at 79th Street said, "Ah, go on and get on this bus, lady."

Which I did.

When I walked into my house it was three hours since I left the Cultural Center.

I protest.

29

ASPCA Seal of Approval

SOUND THE TRUMPETS! *Hanni and Beth: Safe & Sound* just won the Henry Bergh Children's Book Award. A press release from the American Society for the Prevention of Cruelty to Animals (ASPCA) says it best: "Named in honor of ASPCA founder Henry Bergh, the annual awards recognize books based on their exemplary handling of subject matter pertaining to animals and the environment."

Hanni and I will be traveling to a special ceremony at the 2008 American Library Association's Annual Conference in Anaheim to accept the award.

I want my award-winning dog to get her nails painted for the big event. Hanni guides me to Doggie Bath House, a new business right down the street, but the owner stops us in our tracks.

"We don't *do* nails, we don't paint nails," he tells me. "We only do nails, as in *nail trims*."

For a short moment I consider going elsewhere. But when

the owner introduces us to Atlas, we have to stay. How can I deny Hanni the chance to be bathed by a pro wrestler?

Atlas tells me he grew up with dogs, and dog grooming is the perfect way to supplement his pro-wrestling income. "You can make good money wrestling, but I have a daughter now."

Does the responsibility of fatherhood make a pro wrestler more careful in the ring, less interesting to the audience? Does the thought of a daughter at home distract him from crushing his opponent? Does he get paid less if he loses?

Atlas never explains, but it's easy to imagine fatherhood forcing Atlas to cut down on travel to faraway cities. Chicago has 12 venues for pro-wrestling, he says. "But the work is only there on weekends."

And so, during the week, Atlas grooms dogs.

Hanni does her best to be stoic in the pro wrestler's presence, but truth is, she hates getting soaked. She hardly ever gets bathed, really. Guide dogs are almost always attached to their owners, so unless I go playing in mud puddles, or get caught up with skunks, or tangle the two of us in brambles, Hanni stays pretty clean. Trainers at The Seeing Eye teach us how to brush and comb our dogs, and if we do that every day, baths are unnecessary.

Hanni sparkles on our special day in Anaheim. Sure, her nails are still their same old black color, but thanks to Atlas, when she guides me across the stage to accept our award, her fur coat absolutely shines.

30

Cheating the Lottery

MY PRESENTATIONS ABOUT memoir writing continue, and attendees like what they hear. Many of them sign up for my class.

Too many, it turns out.

I'm willing to teach twice a week, but Chicago's Department on Aging can only afford to subsidize one class at a time. So they develop a lottery to make things fair. Everyone's name goes in a hat, and the first 18 chosen get a spot.

I start getting phone calls from writers whose names weren't picked. "Those decisions are out of my hands," I tell them. I try to sound disappointed, but truth is, my hands are full leading that class. I really don't want to be responsible for scheduling it, too.

Until Minerva doesn't get chosen in the lottery. I tell her to come anyway. Word gets out, and others who hadn't been chosen start showing up, too.

By now I've gotten used to officials letting me get by with things because I can't see. Mike claims that even before I was blind, I had a tendency to ignore certain rules. "I suppose so," I shrug. "But it's a lot easier to get away with when you can't see."

At Easterseals HQ, my co-workers have to fill out seven-page reports for permission to work from home. But when the Chicago weather gets particularly harsh one winter, I simply announce I'll be working remotely from now on, and no one asks me for paperwork. Amtrak riders can't place luggage on the seat next to them, but I always do, and conductors never complain. Rule-bending seems to come with the territory.

But my supervisor tells me I'm screwing up the system. They make budgetary decisions based on the number of students in class, and besides, sneaking my favorites in is not fair to new students who want to try my class.

She doesn't fire me for breaking the rules. Instead, she lets the punishment fit the crime: no lottery for the next eight-week session. Anyone who signs up is allowed to attend. I end up with 24 writers.

They're an eager bunch. Lots of them email pieces for me to edit, and when I suggest we have 12 writers read one week and the other 12 the next, they say no. They all want to read every week.

I trim our word limit from 500 to 400, and set our timer to four minutes per reading. No time for questions, no time to talk about what we like about each other's writing, no time for fun.

Eight weeks later? I beg my supervisor to bring back the lottery. She does, and I haven't broken the rules since.

31

Myrna's Opening Line

WRITING ABOUT OURSELVES in the third person can give us objectivity and perspective. It's a good self-awareness exercise. So I decide to ask writers to pen their own short biography.

Myrna, one of the pillars of our class, writes this about herself:

> *Myrna Knepler has spent nearly all her life in Chicago, a city she loves dearly. For the past seventeen years she has been living just a block away from the building she lived in as a child. She retired from teaching at Northeastern Illinois University seven years ago and enjoys reading, painting, writing, and walking along the Chicago waterfront.*

Having a smart woman like Myrna as a student could be intimidating, but she is so patient, encouraging, and downright sweet that we just can't be nervous around her. Plus she has a terrific laugh.

The little bio Myrna wrote about herself is a good introduction, but the essays she reads in class tell us there's more of Myrna to know.

After reading a story in the *New York Times* about people who, like her, have birthdays on September 11, she shows up in class with an essay on the subject.

"I am one of those people whose routine compliance to a request for identification at the bank, the airport, and the doctor's office elicits comment, and sometimes commiseration," she writes. "Unlike other days marking tragic events like Pearl Harbor, this event, like the festive 4th of July, is known by the date it occurred. Most people can't help commenting."

Myrna has learned to say that her birthday is "the eleventh of September" in hopes of avoiding those comments. Some people with her birthday limit their celebrations. Myrna tries to ignore it as only a coincidence. Still, there is always a sense of tragedy on her birthday morning. When she turns on the radio or opens the newspaper, there it is.

On the day of the tragedy, Myrna was supposed to celebrate her birthday at dinner with two of her daughters. Instead, they spent the evening of 9/11/01 at the Red Cross blood bank. "There were lots of people there, and strangers talked easily to one another. The Red Cross was overwhelmed with people wanting to give blood, and gave us an appointment for another day," she writes. "We grabbed a bite to eat and went home."

Sharing a birthday with a national tragedy does give Myrna perspective, however. When we speak about it at her 80th birthday party, she says, "After what happened that day? Well, aging just seems like a minor worry."

Since our memoir class has been meeting for several years now, the writers decide to put an anthology together – sort of a greatest hits. One essay per writer, 18 in all, they name it *Been There, Done That.* Myrna volunteers to collect and format the pieces. I'm given the job of writing an Editor's Note before each essay.

Myrna's story in the anthology is a window into how an Eastern European Jewish family came to settle in Chicago in the 1930s. My Editor's introduction: "Myrna is the patient soul who collected and formatted these essays for us – Thanks, Myrna! In class we all agreed that her opening line to this essay was the best we heard all session long. I think you'll agree."

How I Came to Chicago
By Myrna Knepler

I came to Chicago in utero, attending the 1934 World's Fair in that state. I stayed to be born in Grant Hospital. But my parents' home was seventy miles away.

My mother, father, and maternal grandmother had settled in my father's hometown, Walworth, population 800, not too many miles across the Wisconsin border. My mother had been raised in Chicago among many siblings and half siblings. In addition to the advantage of being close to her own family, the added security of giving birth to their first child in a major city hospital led her to spend the last month or so of her pregnancy in the home of an older sister in Hyde Park.

My father stayed behind. His family ran a small department store in Walworth, and he and most of his brothers and sisters worked in it. My paternal grandfather, Meyer Cohn, had come to the Midwest in the late nineteenth century, and like many Eastern European immigrant Jews started out as a peddler. After some time he was able to open a small general store, then a somewhat larger store. Finally he built a two story, solid brick building that sold furniture, clothing, and other items to a town that was growing in prosperity because of wealthy second homes in nearby Lake Geneva. They were the only Jewish family in town and, from all accounts, well liked and respected by the townspeople, though the Klan, active in the 1920s throughout the upper Midwest, at one point burned a cross in the central square in front of the store.

The family returned to Walworth after my birth. My parents had set up housekeeping in a comfortable house on the outskirts of town. Walworth seemed to them to be an ideal place to raise a child. Since my paternal grandfather had died suddenly less than a year before my birth, my parents expected that my father and his brothers would inherit the store and run it.

This was not the way things turned out. One of my father's younger brothers was given sole control of the store. Two other brothers apparently had other plans, but my father clearly expected to remain. Why he was not chosen, I will never know for sure. There must have been some monetary settlement, but clearly my parents had to leave and my father find work elsewhere. My mother blamed it all on the wife of the inheriting brother, the only person in her husband's family she could never get along with. They would never speak again. Though generally inclined to see the good in people, throughout my childhood she would describe her sister-in-law in terms that reminded me of the witches in the fairy tales she read to me.

I think my parents tried to move to St. Charles, another small town, just across the Illinois border to establish a business there,

128

but were discouraged by other members of the family who lived there. A year after my birth they settled in a busy neighborhood on the north side of Chicago and opened a small dress shop and named it after me, Myrna Mae Frocks.

I often think about the ways my life would have been different if I had grown up in a town of less than a thousand rather than in the midst of a big city.

32

On the Air with Hannelore and Wanda

ALL THE NEWS stories describing our financial crisis as the "worst recession since the Great Depression" leave me wondering. My life now, in 2008. Is it anything like life during the Great Depression?

When it comes to questions like this, who needs Google? I go directly to the experts. Next week's assignment: "The Great Depression."

"Those of you who lived through it – tell us how it was," I say. "If you remember hearing stories from family members, write those down."

Writers who weren't around in the 1930s have the option to write about how they or their loved ones deal with mental illness or depression. "Or use the prompt as an opportunity to call or visit relatives who were alive back then," I suggest, knowing from experience that people take questions more seriously when told the information is needed for a class.

To get them started, I tell one of my own family stories. My Grandma Moos, Flo's mother, was 33 years old when the stock market crashed. Flo's father drank so much that when Flo and my Uncle Ray started high school, Grandma made a courageous and quite unconventional move: she got a divorce.

Left to raise two teenagers by herself, Grandma cleaned houses, did laundry, babysat, ironed clothes, stretched curtains – anything to bring in income and pay the mortgage. She walked to all her jobs. Grandma never owned a car; never even got a driver's license. Her carbon footprint was far smaller than her real one, the one she left all over my hometown of Elmhurst, Illinois, with those practical black leather shoes of hers.

The Great Depression taught my grandma to recycle way before the word "green" came to mean "environmentally friendly." She kept up her green ways when I was growing up, cutting frayed worn-out wool coats into long ribbons, sewing those strips into tubes and weaving them into throw rugs. Burnt-out light bulbs were never thrown away – Grandma Moos shoved them into socks so she could darn holes. She saved old nylons to stuff her hand-sewn pillows.

But back to class. The next week, many writers return with essays about their parents' view of the Great Depression. Wanda and Hannelore are the only ones in class old enough to have lived through it. Wanda is 87 years old now, and Hannelore, the oldest writer in class, is 88. "I'll tell you this, Beth," Hannelore repeats to me just about every week in class. "I've always been very, very lucky."

The stories the two of them read aloud are so moving

that after class I contact my "connections" at Chicago Public Radio and ask if they'd be interested in recording Hannelore and Wanda's stories. WBEZ answers yes. They'll do a three-or-four-minute bit.

I meet Wanda and Hannelore at WBEZ, and the producer welcomes me to join them in the studio and cheer them on. Once the two ladies start telling their stories, the producer cancels his next interview. He has Wanda and Hannelore stay for an entire hour.

After the interview, I come home to find this email message in my inbox:

> "Because both stories were so compelling, we just can't cut them too short. So, we're going to air them in two separate parts, on two separate days, as a short 'series.' So, Wanda's will air tomorrow, and we'll then try to run Hannelore's within a week. I'll let you know about that one when we have an air date for that.

> So, I hope that's cool with you and them. They would have been powerful together, but I think they're just as powerful on their own."

And so they were.

Money
By Hannelore Bratman

This is what my mother told me, this is what I remember. Before the Great Depression, 1926, the inflation in Germany. I was 6 years old when the highlight of the day or for a treat I was allowed to count the 10 Pfennig (cents) coins on the dining room table after dinner. My mother and Rosa, our Ladenfraulein (saleslady) counted the bills and recorded the proceeds for the day's sales. Suddenly coins were no longer valid currency; there was only paper money. Large bills filled the whole big table that accommodated 10 comfortably. The money was put in different bushel baskets, one hundred, one thousand, five thousand, ten thousand. Next day that money bought less than the day before and the government printed more bills, million Mark bills, they were beautiful to look at but had little or no value. I remember on my birthday my mother took such a bushel basket to the store to buy me a doll buggy. I was scared.

I was hoping I was just dreaming all this. I called my friend, ten years older than I. She was then about 16. I asked how her family managed. She reported that her father, who was in the manufacturing business, would put money nightly into a shoe box for her mother to buy food for the day. Shopping was done daily, and often her mother came home with too little food for the day. She remembered that all they often had was bread for a meal. I feel better, at least I am not hallucinating. I also remember. A friend of the family and my mother owned a 4 story apartment house in C.3.4. When he no longer could pay his debts and support his family, he jumped out of a window.

My mother was able to hang on to our butcher shop. Eventually things stabilized, new currency was introduced, even coins again. Everybody lost. There was a huge unemployment problem. Those now worthless beautiful million Mark bills were used to wallpaper rooms.

This instability gave rise to a lot of different political parties, and the National Socialist was one of them. All the different political parties fought each other and in 1932 the National

Socialist party won the upper hand. Hitler promised jobs. He was going to build a big network of roads, the Autobahn. Everybody was going to be able to buy a Volkswagen. Everybody was taxed and given savings credits on their Volkswagen investment.

Memories of the Great Depression
By Wanda Bridgeforth

Chicago was especially hard-hit by the Great Depression. Men couldn't find jobs, especially Black men. Here was my father, with a degree in chemistry, and he could not get a job. He was humiliated. And really, that's when he started to fall apart, and that's when Mama started working "in family." She told me that this was the way it had to be. We either survive doing it this way, or we don't do it and we don't survive. So I went to live at Uncle Larry and Aunt Gert's house. My neighborhood was known as the Black Metropolis. Louis Armstrong had lived there, and Ida B. Wells.

Uncle Larry was actually a cousin, but we called him uncle as a term of respect because he was the head of the household. Uncle Larry was a big black man that had been injured in WWI, where he fell in love with a White German woman named Gert. He married her and brought her home to the Black Metropolis. Aunt Gert was a very heavy woman but had very small feet, I think she wore a size three-and-a-half shoe. All her shoes were too big on her, so we could always hear her clomping down the hall.

I had to learn to share. 19 of us lived in Uncle Larry's six-room apartment. The grownups had the bedrooms. Where we slept, in the daytime it was a dining room. We each had a roll-away bed, really a cot on rollers with a cover. At night we took the leaves out of the dining room table and took down our roll-away beds. That was our all-purpose room. We ate in that room, did homework at the table, played cards there and slept there.

Some of the people in the apartment were on relief. Everybody but Aunt Gert would go out every day to try and find work somewhere. Aunt Gert ruled the household. She did the cooking and sent us out.

Every Saturday, some people living there would get ration cards. We would take baby buggies to a warehouse and use the ration cards to get our vegetables, fruits, and dairy goods. Auntie Gert baked a pound cake every Saturday and whipped the batter with her hands. We just loved it when we heard her slapping that bowl. We knew we were in for a treat.

She formed committees, and I was on the committee to churn the ice cream. We would always fight over who would get the dasher.

Aunt Gert would bake the cake, but we didn't get it right after dinner. After dinner the boys were sent to the kitchen to clean the linoleum floor. Once they were done cleaning the floor, she would sit in the corner and play the guitar. That's when the rest of us would know to take our shoes off and come in our stocking feet to spread the wax and wax the floor. She'd say "Clarence, get over to that corner, it needs more wax!"

We would make so much noise that others in the building knew it was time to join us. Nobody reported us for being too noisy because they were all involved.

In the summertime Aunt Gert would play her guitar on the porch and we'd dance in the yard.

We were kids, and we didn't know we were poor. And actually, we weren't poor, we were po'.

33

Tough Guys

MY EASTERSEALS SUPERVISOR must have kept my bar food preferences under wraps. When my internship there ends, they not only hire me part-time, but they dispatch me to New Orleans for their national convention.

On my flight to The Big Easy, I sit between two guys returning home from Africa. "Were you there with a church group?" I ask.

They both laugh. "We're not missionaries," Chris, the guy on my right, says. "We're mercenaries!"

They are mechanics. Caterpillar had sent them to Nairobi for a month to build boat engines. "We built ten engines in four weeks," Timmy, the guy on my left, says. "That's a lot – they're big engines."

They describe how hard it was to be away from their families and how cramped the living conditions had been. But it sure beat working on oil rigs at home, they say. That's what they'd been doing before they got the job with Caterpillar.

Chris had escaped the oil rig life relatively unscathed. Timmy hadn't been as lucky: two back surgeries, three knee surgeries, and one operation on his elbow. Pain management classes and martial arts helped him survive, he says. He'd agreed to go to Africa after Caterpillar offered him a supervisor position there – the work wouldn't be as physically demanding. "Plus it paid $500 a day," he says, sounding embarrassed by that huge amount. "I have two sons. I need to make as much money as I can. You know, while I'm still able to work."

Timmy takes care of Hanni when I leave to go to the bathroom. Chris jumps up to take my backpack from the overhead bin any time I need it. They chorus lyrical tales of duck hunting in Louisiana, families back home, surviving hurricanes. I lean back, enjoying the music of their voices.

Our flight to New Orleans, well, it flies by.

When we land, Chris reaches up to get my backpack for me. "You go ahead," he says. "It's been a long flight for Hanni."

A long flight for Hanni? They'd left Nairobi 36 hours ago and still have a three-hour drive ahead of them. I urge them to go first. They won't hear of it. So Hanni and I say our goodbyes, and as she tries to lead me through first class, a passenger pulls me aside and asks if I am okay.

"Yeah," I say, shrugging my shoulders. "Is something wrong?"

"Well, those men they sat you with," he says, lowering his voice to a whisper. "They look very rough."

I'd look rough, too, if I'd just flown from Nairobi to London, London to Chicago, and Chicago to New Orleans. I was so taken by their stories that I hadn't thought much about what Timmy and Chris looked like. "Did they have tattoos?" I ask First Class man.

"Oh, yes," he shudders. "All over. You sure you're okay."

"I'm sure," I assure First Class Man. After thanking him for his concern, I give Hanni's right ear a scratch, lift her harness, and feel a huge smile spreading across my face. "Hanni, forward!"

34

Something Missing

"I AM LOSING my friends, and my car keys, and my car in the parking lot. Not only that, I am losing my hair."

Minerva's "Something Missing" essay betrays her weariness with growing old. In it, she travels back to a nostalgic 1960s reverie. "I wish I had let my hair go natural like Pulitzer Prize Poet Gwendolyn Brooks in the 60s," she writes. "Remember the 60s? That was a wonderful period in our growth: Dr. Martin Luther King, Jr. gave us a dream. Stokely Carmichael taught us that 'Black is beautiful,' that we should resent being called 'colored,' that freedom isn't free, and we learned how to sing 'We Shall Overcome.'"

She ends her 500-word piece on aging with a poem:

I love my new bifocals,
My dentures fit just fine,
My hearing aid serves me very well,
But I sure do miss my mind!

"Minerva always closes her eyes when she recites poems," Wanda whispers from her seat next to me. "She did that in high school, too." Good idea. I lean back and do the same.

Soon after the 2008 election, Minerva tells me she will be taking a few months away from class to compile her writings into book form. "Those piles of papers are taking over the house!" she laughs.

I don't.

Minerva's dignity and poise in class are contagious. How will the other writers behave without her around? Her confidence rubs off on me, too. How will I fare without her?

I phone during her absence. Minerva always sounds happy to hear from me, but she is embarrassed to admit the lack of progress on her book. So I stop asking about it.

On her birthday, she calls with some very good news. "I got the most marvelous present!" she gushes. Her family has secretly gathered her essays, arranged them into book form, and presented the compilation as a birthday gift.

It isn't long after that birthday that the call comes. I recognize Minerva's daughter's voice on the line. "I just want you to know my mother passed at home last night."

Class is on break, so I call Wanda a few days later to find out about the funeral. Hanni and I attend, along with Sylvia and Alice. And of course, Wanda.

"Queen Albertina Walker is up there with the choir," Wanda tells me from the West Point Baptist Church narthex before Hanni leads me into the sanctuary. "She's on oxygen now, but I won't be surprised if she takes that mask off to belt out a song for Minerva."

Sure enough, she does.

During the service, Minerva's great-grandson Jabril shares memories of his grandma. How they would play Scrabble, and she would always win. He reads excerpts from her memoir, and I close my eyes to listen.

Her words are poetry to my ears.

35

Wait Until Dark

THE STAGE MANAGER at Chicago's Court Theatre notices me on a TV interview and gives me a call. An audition? No. Equally as good, though.

"We're staging a production of *Wait Until Dark*," she says. "The actress playing the Audrey Hepburn role isn't blind in real life." They need someone to 'show them the ropes.' "Would you be willing to come to a rehearsal?"

As a kid, I remember finding the movie absolutely terrifying. One of the many complications of type 1 diabetes is blindness, and the Audrey Hepburn character was too close to home: a cool-as-ice psychopath smooth talks his way into the home of an unsuspecting blind woman who has no idea she has valuables hidden in her apartment.

I'm pretty sure we don't have valuables hidden in our apartment (unless you count my Seeing Eye dog), and I feel fortunate to have no expertise in anything psychopathic. I do, however, know what it's like to be newly blind and married to a man who can see. And that's what the cast wants to know about.

How can I say no?

During the first rehearsal we just sit in a circle and talk. One actor – he might have been the guy playing the psychopath – asks, "If someone was standing in your apartment, not moving, and not saying a word, is there some way you would just sense they were there?"

Nope.

"If a person you'd met before came your way again, but this time disguised his voice, would you know it was him?"

Absolutely not.

I'm horrible with voices. On our street here in Printers Row, passers-by often call out a friendly "Hello, Beth!" I'm not that famous. If they know my first name, I've met them before. If they were standing behind the counter at the bank, or in the coffee shop I frequent, or sitting at the bar in Hackney's, I might recognize their voice. But out on the sidewalk? I have no context. If they disguised their voices? I'd be totally clueless.

"But that's just me," I remind them. "I don't speak for all blind people. We all have different skills we use to make our way." The cast seems to understand.

"How do you think the friends you've made since you were blind are different from the friends you made when you could see?" This question comes from Emjoy, the actress playing the lead.

After thinking it over a bit, I say, "I think the friends I've met since I lost my sight are surprised to find out they actually like me." Does that make sense? I don't think so. "It's kind of like if I were the first Black kid to go to an all-White high school.

144

People want to meet me so they can think they're cool, they're open-minded, you know, they can tell other people that they have a friend who has a disability."

One of the guys around the circle laughs. "You're telling our story!" he says.

Unsure of what he means, I just continue. "And then if they take the time to get to know me, they're surprised to find out they like me."

Another cast member phrases it better. "They're surprised to find out there's more to you than being blind." I nod.

We sit in that circle for almost two hours. They ask questions, I answer, we get off subject, then back on track again. "This is probably a dumb question…" they start off, then ask some of the most interesting questions I've heard since losing my sight.

Time up, they have to get back to work and rehearse. As I button my coat to head out with Hanni, I think about that guy who said I was "telling their story" and realize I have a dumb question of my own.

"Is the whole cast Black?" I ask.

Emjoy says no. "I'm Filipina," she explains. "But my husband in the play is Black."

Another cast member chimes in. "One cop is White," he says. "The other is Black. Gloria, the little girl who comes down and visits from the apartment upstairs, is Hispanic."

"Did you cast it this way on purpose?" I ask. "Or was it just by coincidence, those are the people who tried out?" I didn't realize the director has left the room, but the actors seem more than happy to call him back in to answer my question.

Ron OJ Parson is known as one of Chicago's best directors of realism, and he's nationally known for his work directing the plays of August Wilson. *Wait Until Dark* is traditionally done with an all-White cast, he tells me. "But it's a new era," he says. "We've got a Black President now." He was the one who decided to cast Emjoy Gavino, a Filipina, in Audrey Hepburn's role of Susy. "We didn't have to change a single line in the play to make this work," Ron said. "Just think about it. This play is set in Greenwich Village in the 60s. These are the sorts of people you would see there."

36

The Turn of the Key

A WEEK OR so later Hanni and I take an Amtrak train to give a presentation in Milwaukee. I'm sound asleep in my hotel room when I hear a key card go into the slot on our door. Then out. In, then out again.

Someone is trying to get in. Did the key work? Is he in our room? What's that sound? Someone breathing?

Finally I get up, go to the door. There is Hanni, wagging her tail, hoping someone might come in to play. She wouldn't be acting like that if a stranger really were in the room. Or would she?

I crouch down, give her a big hug, and feel my way along the doorframe on my way up. When I get to the security lock, I flip it shut and turn around. "Anybody in here?"

No answer.

I find my way back to the bed, crawl under the covers, and spend most of the rest of the night awake. Listening.

ONCE HANNI AND I are back home safe and sound in Chicago I get another call from Ron, the Court Theatre director. He barely gets a word out before I interrupt with a curse and a laugh.

"That damn play of yours, it's got me scared!" I say, describing the scene in my Milwaukee hotel room. "If someone had used the wrong key for my hotel room before I met you guys, I would have figured some drunk just made a mistake and gone right back to sleep."

"That's what we're after," Ron says. I hear him smiling over the phone line. "We want the audience to be as afraid as that blind woman on stage."

The scenery will be up on stage soon, and Ron is calling to see if I can come to another rehearsal. "We want to watch how you find your way around the set," he says.

I usually don't like people observing how I get around, but this is different. It is art. I am happy to oblige. I'll be feeling my way around a strange environment, but I won't hurt myself or fall. One thing I know for sure: the stage will be more neat and organized than my own apartment is.

A lot of people who can't see keep immaculate houses. I'm not one of those people. I never liked cleaning house when I could see, and my cleaning skills didn't improve after I lost my sight. If I were to write an essay on how this blind person does housecleaning, it would be too short to publish: Mike. Does. It.

Most of the action in *Wait Until Dark* takes place in the kitchen and dining room of an urban apartment. Emjoy asks if she can come to our place. "I'd like to watch you get around in a space you're familiar with," she says. Seeing me in action might help her portray a blind woman at home more accurately.

Spend an afternoon alone with a real actress? Of course I say yes.

Mike isn't home the day Emjoy visits, and rather than make a vain attempt to straighten things up before she gets here, I just leave the place a mess. She can be there to watch me tidying up on my own.

When she arrives, Emjoy is glad I need to wash some dishes by hand. "I want to watch," she says. "Susy does the dishes in the play." She watches me empty the dishwasher, put dishes away in the cupboards, wipe the counters, wash out the sink. She follows as I pad down the corridor to the garbage chute, one hand carrying the sack, the other trailing the wall.

Back in the apartment, I find my way to the couch and sit down. Emjoy has lots of questions. "Do you have the furniture close together like this for a reason?" Yes. I like right angles. "When you rush to answer the phone, do you have to feel around for it? Or can you tell where it is by the sound?" I don't know. Susy uses a white cane in one quick scene, so I show Emjoy how I'd learned to use mine.

When we sit down again, Emjoy gets quiet for a bit. She seems hesitant to ask the next question. "That night in the hotel," she finally says, acknowledging that Ron the director had told the cast about the stranger trying to get into my room with the wrong key card. "Did you jump up out of bed right away?" she asks. "Did you hurry to figure out what was happening?"

"Oh, no," I tell her. "No way. I had to listen first. I had to sit still and stay quiet to figure out what was going on." I remind her I'd heard the key card go in the slot, then out. In the slot, then out. "If I'd jumped up and started moving around,

I wouldn't have been able to focus on what I was hearing."

After I thought I knew what was happening, I'd shouted towards the door. "You've got the wrong room!" The key went in again. Or was it out? Then silence. I stayed there in bed, listening, for a long while. I called Hanni. She didn't come. I finally got up then to figure out where she was. That's when I found her wagging her tail at the door.

"That's good," she says, thinking to herself as she talks. "That's good. That's what I thought."

In one scene of the play, when things are getting scary, Emjoy has been told that maybe she should move around to try to figure things out. "But I thought maybe I should stand still, just listen. And from what you just said, I think I might be right about that."

Emjoy's visit to our apartment confirms a lot of things she has already thought through, and she thanks me profusely for letting her come over. As she starts putting her boots back on to leave, the phone rings. "Perfect!" I exclaim, rushing over to answer it. The verdict? I don't have to feel for the phone. I can tell where it is by the sound.

37

Hiding in Plain Sight

THE NEXT WEEK stage management contacts me again. The stage is set up for previews. Could I come check it out? Of course I say yes.

Enjoy introduces me to the set when I arrive. She and Ron ask me lots of questions during the tour to confirm they are doing the blind stuff right – not just waving a hand wildly over a tabletop, for example, but coming at it from the bottom first, then gently, gently brushing over the top to find what you're looking for.

They'd had a few preview nights before my little stage tour, and audience members had been invited to stay after for a question and answer session. A question from one audience member is really bothering Ron. In a scene where the thugs are in the apartment, standing still, not breathing, the blind woman is on the phone, nearly two feet away from one of the actors. She doesn't notice he is there.

The audience member told Ron that the cast lost him right

there. He said there was no way the blind woman wouldn't know the thug was there – he was just two feet away. The guy in the audience didn't believe anything in the play after that.

I start worrying that these theater types are not going to be able to pull this play off. So many people have preconceived notions about "the blind." We have super powers. We can hear things others don't perceive. And if someone is near us? We can just feel their presence.

"I told that guy in the audience that Beth Finke told us she wouldn't know!" Ron tells me. I laugh. Beth Finke, expert in all things blind.

Ron asks me back to one last rehearsal for an experiment. "I want to have the actors stand still at different parts of the stage," he says. "Would you mind coming up, walking around, let us know when you can tell where they are?" I don't mind. I mean, it is a weird idea – kind of like playing "Marco Polo" on dry ground. But, hey – I am the technical consultant. I am there to help.

So I get on stage. After getting my bearings, I start walking around, just a few steps at a time. Emjoy has taken such care to describe the set that I feel somewhat familiar with my surroundings, and I've come to know the cast so well that I trust someone will stop me if I get too near the edge.

By the time our game is over, I've only discovered one actor. He was standing near the coat rack, and when I reached out to touch the coats, I felt a human arm instead. Scary.

Truth is, if I hadn't been told to try to hear the actors, I wouldn't have known anyone was there at all. Even knowing I was supposed to find them, I'd lost that hide-and-seek round.

Once the actors start breathing and moving around again like normal, I have a better sense of where they are. An actor who'd been standing in a closet said the experiment unnerved him. "That was freaky. You were looking right at me. You looked me right in the eyes." He says his heart raced when I was so close to him. "I can't believe you didn't hear my heart beating."

A few more questions from different cast members, a few more experiments with sounds – can you hear the blinds? Do you notice different footsteps? – and it's break time. Time for me to go home.

As I stand waiting for someone to lead me out of the theater, I start preparing myself mentally for the hangover I am sure to have once I get home. It happened each time – after the first rehearsal where we sat around the circle, after the visit with Emjoy, and then again later after Emjoy accompanied me to a lecture about how people with disabilities are portrayed in film. I'm just not used to thinking about disability and blindness so much.

And so, as exciting as it is to be the center of attention at the theater for a while, to have very smart people ask me all sorts of questions about the things I do, and to realize I can show these very smart people something they couldn't figure out for themselves even if they put blindfolds on, well...those guys can get off the stage, quit acting once the play is over every night. I can't.

I am lost in those thoughts when the actor I'd "looked" right in the eye interrupts me. "It must be sort of Zen, being blind," he says. I'd never thought of it that way, but the notion brings me back to the benefits of being blind. Emjoy's visit to our apartment had pointed out one I hadn't recognized before: I'd always been a lazy housekeeper, but blindness provides me with an alibi for being messy. And now this actor just brought up another benefit I hadn't thought of before. People who can see are distracted. Too much in their way. Big-screen TVs. Magazines at grocery checkout lanes. Billboards. YouTube. iPhones. I tell the actor he is right. It is Zen-like. "I'm relieved of vision," I say. "I have more time to think."

Ron invites Hanni and me to sit on stage with the cast for the Q&A on the final night of previews. The very first comment comes from an audience member who says her husband is visually impaired. "That actress was fabulous," the woman says. "I was so glad she didn't play it like we see in TV, where the blind person spends the whole time looking up to the sky." That same woman said she was startled when Emjoy came out at the end for her curtain call. "She walked down the steps like someone who could see."

DAYS LATER MIKE and I are given tickets for opening night of *Wait Until Dark*. We are invited to stay for the "opening night toast" afterward, too. I feel like a star, celebrating with cast members. But just like after the rehearsals, I find the experience somewhat bittersweet. This is a more standard type of letdown, though. Nothing to do with my blindness, really. Just an "empty nest" sort of thing. Emjoy and the cast don't need me anymore. They are doing fine on their own now. A review in the *Chicago Sun-Times* confirms my assessment:

> "[Emjoy] Gavino, a most skilled and charming slip of
> a girl, deftly manages to shift from Susy's initially blithe

self-confidence into shrewd counter-insurgency mode as she refuses to become the classic female victim. She also makes you begin thinking as Susy does, with a heightened awareness of sounds and smells and space and the little strategies required for living blind."

Emjoy is surrounded by well-wishers at the opening night toast, but she does manage to make her way towards Mike and me before we leave. After uncoiling from our congratulatory hugs, she says she would have brought a thank-you note along for me but knew I wouldn't be able to read it by myself.

"So I have something I want to tell you," she says. "When I'm playing a role, I like to put songs on my iPod that the character would listen to. It helps me get into the part."

She reasoned Susy would be a jazz fan, Greenwich Village in the 60s and all. "I've been listening to Miles Davis, other jazz. Joan Baez. Bob Dylan," she says. "And I copied all those songs from my iPod onto this CD for you."

She reaches for my hand and presses the disc into my palm. "Its music Susy would have listened to."

38

Mustang Beth

THIS IS SHAPING up to be my year for doing gutsy things. A few weeks after being on stage, I get invited to drive a car. What?

I wasn't a good driver when I could see. Our family only had one car, which I famously backed into the house. I miss riding my bike far more than I miss driving. But for other blind people, especially those who don't live near public trans like I do, driving is #1 on their "Things I Miss" list. So I feel a certain responsibility to take one for the team.

The story starts with an email from a public relations company. It sounds spammy: on May 7, a blind man is going to live out his dream in a 2010 Mustang. It's part of Ford's campaign to give 10 people the chance to test-drive the new Mustang before its official release date. "Please join us to witness Roger's experience and listen to him describe the drive in his own words. You will even have the opportunity to put yourself in his shoes and take the 2010 Mustang for a spin."

I ask Mike to have a look at the email. He says it looks legit. "The new 2010 Mustang is kind of a big deal, Beth," he says, sounding impressed.

And a little jealous.

He asks, "You remember what the Mustang looked like back in the 60s?" I do. My sister Cheryl bought a Mustang in 1967. Marilee was 14, Bev was 12, and I was 9. We were all awestruck by Cheryl's new sports car.

Apparently the new Mustang looks a lot like the old one, only better. He says I should go for it.

Bev, Beth, and Marilee in front of Cheryl's
1967 Mustang

I have misgivings. I don't want it to be a freak show. And how on earth will I be able to drive without seeing where I'm going?

On the other hand, I've lost plenty of opportunities because of being blind. On the rare occasion that blindness actually gives me an opportunity I wouldn't have had otherwise, say, driving a Mustang before its release date, I should take advantage, right? If I'm honest, I have to admit things like this can help take the sting away from losing my sight.

So I call the number listed on the email message and come clean: I don't know much about cars, and getting behind the wheel again is not on my "bucket list."

No problem. They've done their research and they're ready for me. They know I'm blind. They know I write for magazines. And they know I do commentaries for NPR. "We just want you to come out to Phoenix and enjoy the experience along with Roger," they say, apologizing for the late notice. "If you can get out here this week, we'll be happy to make flight arrangements." Other journalists will be there covering the story, too.

The trip is on them? That clinches it. I'm in.

I'm in Arizona sharing lunch with a bunch of sports car-enthusiasts and journalists. Roger Keeney, the blind man mentioned in the email, has already driven the Mustang that morning, and journalists on hand will be driving the new Mustang after lunch. One caveat, though: in the spirit of the occasion, the journalists have to agree to drive blindfolded. Except for me, of course. No blindfold necessary.

A man named Tommy introduces himself from across the picnic table, and conversation drifts to where we're all from.

Tommy has lived in Southern California his entire life. "Well," he adds, "all but two years." After everyone chimes in on the beauties of Santa Monica, Marina del Rey, etc., etc., I finally butt in. "I'm curious – where'd you live the two years you weren't in California?"

For one year he lived in Las Vegas. The other year, Indianapolis. Indianapolis?

"I was in a crash," Tommy explains. A mechanical failure in his race car. "I broke both feet, both ankles, both knees, both legs." The crash happened at Watkins Glen, NewYork, but the surgeon who mended him was in Indianapolis. "I wanted to be near the surgeon while I was going through physical therapy," he says. The PT took a year. "People thought I'd quit racing after that, but I got right back in."

Tommy excuses himself to talk to a friend who'd just shown up, and I'm rewarded for eavesdropping: Tommy casually mentions a recent conversation with Paul Newman.

I tap the journalist next to me and ask for Tommy's last name. It's Kendall. Tommy Kendall.

Lunch over, Tommy Kendall says, "Whenever you're ready, we can go."

He walks me to the passenger seat and gets behind the wheel. Here I am, Beth Finke, in a sports car with Paul Newman's buddy Tom. I'd been nervous about driving all morning. The temperature in Arizona is 103 degrees, but suddenly I feel very, very cool.

Tommy drives me out to the asphalt flat. It's 1500 feet long, 700 feet wide. "I just want you to get a feel for how the Mustang rides," he says. We switch sides, and once I'm belted behind the wheel, he asks what I'd like to do. Do I want to start slow, to get a feel for it? Go straight out, hard and fast? Do I want to try doing donuts?

I toss out a laugh and say, "Absolutely not!" He laughs, too. I'm smitten.

I want to go straight out, I say.

We journalists had been put through a safety drill earlier, and now Tommy goes through it again. If he calls out "left," I should turn the wheel just a few degrees in that direction. If he says "left" again, I should turn it just a few more degrees left. "Like that?" I ask, turning the wheel 3 or 4 degrees. "Exactly," he says. "Same with right – just a few degrees at a time."

He assures me nothing will go wrong. "Race car drivers have big egos, you know," he says. "We're all about self-preservation. I wouldn't be doing this if I didn't think it was safe."

He reminds me that in the very rare case something does go wrong, he'll shout out the word, "abort!" At that point I should pull my hands off the wheel and bring my knees to my body. "That way your feet will come completely off the pedals."

Tommy didn't have any controls on his side. We were in a regular 2010 Mustang convertible. It wasn't fixed up especially so that blind drivers could give it a spin. "But I can reach the parking brake," he explains. "I'll make the car stop if anything goes wrong. But trust me, it won't."

My foot's on the brake. "Put your right hand on the column," instructor Tommy says, addressing me as if this is the most normal thing in the entire world, a blind woman sitting next to him, about to take him for a ride in a 2010 Ford Mustang. "Pull back on the column until you hear four clicks," he says. "That'll mean you're in Drive."

Click. Click. Click. Click.

"Okay, Beth – whenever you're ready!" I can hear Tommy smiling.

I lift the ball of my foot off the brake. The car inches forward. I turn my head to the right one last time, just to make sure Tommy is serious. "Press the pedal all the way down?"

"All the way!" Tommy exclaims, that smile still in his voice.

I floor it.

Seconds later, we are flying across the pavement.

"You're going 40," Tommy says. I start to smile. "You're going 60!" he shouts, making sure I hear him over the engine noise beneath us. I start to laugh. "You're going 80, Beth!" Tommy exclaims. My cheeks get hot – blood is rushing to my face. It is absolutely thrilling.

"Okay," Tommy yells. "Brake!" I slam on the brakes. Tires shriek. Rubber burns. The antilock braking system kicks in – I feel the brake pedal pulse in my foot. The steering wheel shakes in my hands.

And then, as quickly as it started, it's over. All is quiet. The car is still. So am I. Speechless. Thrilled.

"You did it, Beth!" Tommy exclaims. "You were going 80 mph!" I put my palm up, expecting a high five. Instead, Tommy Kendall grabs my hand and holds on. A triumphant hand-to-hand embrace.

39

Bea's Short Story

SOMETIMES 500 WORDS are just too many.

Bea Schwartz's essays are always, always short. And so is she! Under five feet tall, Bea never married. After her parents died, she became the caregiver for her developmentally disabled sister.

When Bea first joins our class, she is very subdued. Her sister has just died, and she really misses her. In spite of her sadness, she packs a lot of life into her short essays. So much so that I often use Bea as an example of how an essay can be "short and sweet." She is a great addition to our group.

Which is why, when she misses a few weeks in a row, we all notice. Especially Wanda.

Wanda has an uncanny way of knowing when something is about to happen, or if something isn't quite right. When I ask how she knows, she always comes up with the same answer. "I'm physic!" she laughs, fully aware of the mispronunciation.

Wanda has seen a lot of life, and understanding that her

fellow writer is essentially alone in the world, she tries phoning multiple times on different days.

No answer.

Familiar with the City of Chicago's protocol for situations like this, Wanda goes through channels until she connects with the proper agency. What is Wanda's relationship to the missing person? Does she know of any other relatives? Wanda says no. "There's no one else that we know of."

The city official dials Wanda's phone so she can act as witness to their check on Bea. With cell phone in hand, the official goes door-to-door through Bea's building while Wanda, Bea's only connection, sits at her kitchen table at home, phone pressed to her ear.

Wanda hears the knock, knock, knock on every door. To any neighbor who answers, the city official asks: "Have you seen Bea coming or going recently? Have you seen Bea Schwartz?" No one has.

The only option left is to open Bea's front door. Wanda's fellow writer is taken to the hospital. The official calls Wanda again later to let her know. Bea was pronounced dead on arrival.

Wanda brings us the sad news in class the next Monday. We are not completely surprised, and we are very quiet. I can't see the expressions on everyone's faces; I let the silence speak for itself. We wish there was something we could do. There is no service to attend, nowhere to send sympathy cards. This is especially unsettling for Wanda. "I don't know what they did with her body," she worries, eventually finding a spiritual resting place for Bea in "Mount Eternity," alongside Wanda's relatives who have passed on before.

So we speak of Bea to each other and keep her memory alive in our small way. Any time a new writer wonders how they can possibly tell an entire story using no more than 500 words, someone inevitably recites the quintessential essay Bea wrote when I assigned "Driving Lessons" as a writing prompt.

Our Car
By Bea Schwartz

> *My father took one driving lesson.*
> *He drove into a bunch of garbage cans.*
> *End of driving lesson.*
> *We made do with buses and streetcars. Or cabs. Or bicycles.*
> *The End*

40

Birthdays with Flo

WHEN YOUR MOM is in her 90s, every birthday is a gift. So we make sure each one has its own story.

Last year, Flo celebrated her 92nd birthday dancing with a stranger. My brother Doug's jazz band was performing in Louisville that day, and a young man brushed right by me and my four sisters to ask Flo if she'd like to swing. "Sure!" she said, and off they went.

Later that year she flew with us to Orlando and danced at our niece Jennifer's wedding. The dancing was exhilarating for her, but struggling through an airport was not. After Orlando, Flo announced that was her last flight. From here on out, birthdays would be spent closer to home.

So for Flo's 93rd birthday this year, Bobbie, Cheryl, Marilee, Bev, and I take her to a beautiful restored old inn in Geneva, Illinois. It is only an hour away from her condo, but to hear Flo talk about it, you'd think we brought her to Switzerland. Trying out her poster bed, enjoying her first ever massage, peeking over the balcony at the series of brides being photographed in the courtyard...Flo is enthralled.

We walk around town some, but spend most of our time in our adjoining suites reminiscing, laughing, and toasting to Flo's good health.

Bev has her laptop with her, so she Skypes her son Brian, who is teaching English in South Korea. Flo can hardly believe her eyes – she is talking to her grandson on the computer screen from all those thousands of miles away. "I just can't keep up!" she says. "I'm not in this world!"

That phrase becomes the theme for the weekend. She even uses it on her first trip to our hotel bathroom. It isn't the bidet that throws her off – it's the phone. "It's right by the toilet!" she giggles. She's never seen – or imagined – such a thing, and she can hardly get over it.

With us egging her on, she goes back in the bathroom, picks up the phone and gives my husband a call. She practices her lines out loud as his phone rings. When he answers, she's ready for him.

"Mike?" she asks, somehow managing to stifle a laugh. "You know where I am?"

"Well, you're probably all sitting at a round table, each with a glass of wine, right?" It's a pretty good guess. Flo is delighted to tell him he is wrong.

"No," she says, taking another big breath to avoid laughing. "I'm sitting on the pot!"

Mike is stunned to silence. Flo repeats, "I'm on the pot!" and bursts into giddy schoolgirl laughter.

As the weekend draws to a close, we ask Flo what it is like, living into her nineties. She says she doesn't really think about her age much. "One thing, though," she says. "Every year, something new happens. And it's always something I would have never, ever have thought of myself."

41

Printers Row Pen Pals

FLO LIGHTS UP whenever I share stories about Wanda. "And she's on the radio, too!" she marvels. "I want to meet her."

Marilee flies in from Florida, Bev trains it from Michigan, and Mike drives Flo in from the suburbs, all to see Wanda on stage with me at this summer's Printers Row Book Fair.

Our favorite bartender, Billy Balducci, will be tending bar at Hackney's that day. "Flo's coming here afterwards, right?" He doesn't mean it as a question. It's a command. "I'll save her a seat."

That's crazy. Printers Row Book Fair is second only to St. Patrick's Day when it comes to crowds at Hackney's. "I'll reserve a seat for Flo all day until she gets here," he insists. "I'm all about Flo."

I've written a promo piece for Wanda's appearance at our "Getting Your Memoir Off the Ground" presentation:

"Wanda Bridgeforth, a student from the memoir-writing

class Beth Finke teaches for senior citizens, will read one of her stories during the presentation. The two will offer tips on how to get started on a memoir, and then what to do to keep yourself going from there."

Wanda is the perfect living example of how this works – since starting my class she's written enough stories to fill the first volume of her own memoir. With Wanda Jr.'s help, Wanda self-published *On the Move* last fall – just in time to give the book to family and friends for Christmas. Flo owns a copy, of course, and Wanda brings extras to show off at our workshop today.

The promo piece seems to have done its job. The room is full when my 88-year-old co-presenter steps up and reads in that plucky and playful Wanda way of hers.

My Favorite Toy
By Wanda Bridgeforth

I must have been a really good girl in 1927 because Santa left an ironing board, electric iron, sewing machine and the "Eff & Bee" Rosemary doll all of my friends and I asked for. Her curls and eyelashes were natural hair. Every time I sat her up or laid her down she opened and closed her eyes and said MA-MA! That was enough to melt a little girl's heart. Without hesitating I named her Geneva after my Mama.

In late spring 1928, Dad's company closed their chemistry lab and he was laid off. Mama and I moved into a bedroom with Aunt Gert and Uncle Larry on 51st Street and Dad went to live with Uncle A.S. and his wife at 42nd and Vincennes.

Mama showed me how to wash and iron Geneva's dress, panties and bonnet.

Mid-summer Mama went to work "in private family." I abandoned all of my toys except Geneva. She became my confidant and bedfellow. I guess you could say she was my security blanket. I took her everywhere. The kids began to tease me and called me a "Big Baby," so, when I left home I hid her under the pillow on my bed.

Every Tuesday after school I washed her clothes so she would be nice and clean when Mama came home on Wednesday, her day off. The three of us would sit at the kitchen table and exchange the events of the week. Geneva's clothes were almost faded white.

Christmas 1931, "Cousin Sugar," the lady I was staying with, made Geneva a new outfit. Mama and Cousin Sugar assured me the new clothes did not need weekly washing.

Some of my friends boasted about their dolls made of rubber that could drink milk or water from a tiny bottle with a tiny nipple on it. I looked at Geneva. Her mouth was open and she had a space between her lips. I bought a tiny bottle with a tiny nipple on it from Woolworth's 5 & 10 Cents Store and fed Geneva.

After a while Geneva developed a horrible odor and her body became damp. Cousin Sugar and Mama cut a slit in her body. The straw stuffing had mildew and mold and her plaster body had melted. Only her head was intact. I didn't realize her straw insides absorbed the liquid instead of passing it through like the rubber dolls did. I was inconsolable Geneva was DEAD!

I decided she must have a funeral. Mr. Brunow, the janitor, dug a grave in the far corner of the back yard. Dressed in our parents' black clothes, my friends and I marched behind the Radio Flyer Wagon lined with black crepe paper.

We sang a hymn and sent Geneva, My Favorite Toy, dressed in her Christmas outfit to live with the Angels.

After her reading, the star is surrounded by family and friends. Wanda only has a few seconds to chat with Flo, and really, that's all they need. The two of them agree to become pen pals on the spot, and our crew – Flo and her walker, me and Hanni, and all – thread our way through thousands of book lovers to the entry to Hackney's.

There it is. A seat. A veritable throne, which Billy has guarded for Flo.

Eventually seats open next to Queen Mom, and we all get to hunker down around her. Predictably, Billy charms Flo, who transforms rather easily from shy and matronly great-grandmother to giggly schoolgirl. Billy is good on his word.

42

Of Course It Was Illegal

I DIDN'T USE a white cane or a guide dog when I first started losing my sight. I quit driving, but I could still see well enough to walk to my university job counseling students on study abroad options.

As my eyesight worsened, I started making mistakes in the office. I ran into tabletops. I spilled grounds when I tried to make coffee. I sat unusually close to the computer screen to see the words. At one point my boss took me aside and told me I wouldn't be going to the annual conference with my colleagues that year. "You'll embarrass the office," she said. The next month, she terminated my contract.

That all happened in 1985. The Americans with Disabilities Act was passed in 1990. Today, a decade later, an employer would never dream of firing someone simply because they couldn't see well.

Or would they?

Just this year the *Chicago Daily Law Bulletin* reported that a job recruiter named Jocelyn Snower had been fired after her boss realized she was blind.

What? He didn't notice when he hired her? Something tells me this will make a good article. I find Jocelyn's number and give her a call.

The lilt of her voice over the phone tells me she smiles a lot. The words she says tell me she thinks a lot, too. It is easy to understand why the owner of Balance Staffing would want to hire her, and difficult to understand why he let her go.

"I have enough usable vision to ride my bike," she says, explaining that's how she got to that job interview. "I don't use a white cane, and I don't have a guide dog."

Her employer was at her initial interview, but after that, he only communicated with her by phone. He had no complaints about her work until she used a copy of her official State of Illinois ID instead of a driver's license on an internal HR document. He learned Jocelyn couldn't see well enough to drive, and he fired her.

Jocelyn took her case to the Equal Employment Opportunity Commission, and a consent decree required Balance Staffing to pay her $100,000. The judge's decision was good news, Jocelyn said. "But really, I felt like I'd already won when the EEOC decided to take on my case. It meant they believed me. They knew I could work. They knew I'd done a good job."

The Americans with Disabilities Act works for those of us with disabilities who want to keep our jobs, but if you ask me, it fails when we're looking for a new job. Employers are so leery of lawsuits down the line that they craft job descriptions with ways to avoid hiring us at all. Many of us resort to working for ourselves. Jocelyn runs her own successful job recruiting business now, specializing in finding nannies. I own my own writing business. And the story I write about Jocelyn appears in the *Chicago Tribune* in 2010, the 20th anniversary of the Americans with Disabilities Act.

43

94 And Counting

FLO READS THE newspaper every morning. She passes her driver's test yet again, and starts the car every other day. "You know, just to make sure it's still running."

Her hearing is fading, but she doesn't grouse about it. When she can't hear us, she just cocks her head and says, "Hmm?" in an adorable Cindy Lou Who voice that always makes me smile.

For her 94th birthday this April, we sisters decide to take her to a musical. During the car ride to dinner afterward, Cheryl asks Flo how she liked the play. "It was good," she says. "I just wish I could have heard what they were saying."

"I know what you mean," I call out from the back seat. "I wish I could have seen what they were doing, too!" Flo laughs. We all do.

From then on, I start spending the night with Flo more often. Slumber parties at Flo's are like staying at a spa. She keeps the thermostat in her condo at sauna-high temperatures, and doesn't have a computer or Wi-Fi. Instead, her living room boasts a console hi-fi. She knows how to create a calm setting – stack traditional jazz music on the record changer, sit back in a favorite comfy chair, and enjoy. She encourages all guests at Spa Flo to do the same. When day turns to night, the slow, deliberate movements she makes to get ready for bed allow Spa Flo guests plenty of quiet time to sit on the couch and meditate.

A few months after her birthday, Flo has outpatient surgery and a skin graft for a malignant melanoma. Cheryl's wonderful daughter Janet takes Flo to all her doctor visits, but with four kids, Janet can't stay with Flo at home during recovery.

The teenager in me boldly offers to do night duty. This, even though I have no idea how I'll check Flo's wounds to make sure they are okay. Not to mention what I'll do if Flo can't get out of bed by herself. Or if she needs help in the bathroom. Or if she can't feed herself.

Under normal circumstances, Flo can take care of herself just fine. But this is not a normal circumstance.

Janet drives Flo to the hospital the morning of her surgery. My cousin Darrell and his sweet girlfriend Carolyn meet Hanni and me at the Elmhurst train station and drive us to Flo's apartment. Janet and Flo are already there when we arrive. Flo is fast asleep in her own bed. Janet leads me to the kitchen, places my hand in the bowl where the pain pills are, gives me directions on what to do when Flo wakes up, and takes off to relieve her husband at home.

I sit on Flo's couch and try listening to a book. I can't concentrate. What have I gotten myself into? All that time I'd been saying "No problem, I'll take the overnight shifts, I'll stay with Flo?" Secretly I'd been hoping someone would step in, remind me that hey, Beth, you're blind, you can't take on that responsibility. But no one did.

On one hand, I am tremendously flattered. They actually think I can handle this. The baby sister has achieved her goal – in the eyes of my older siblings, I look like a grown up. On the other hand, I'm feeling pretty uneasy. But I'm here.

Two hours later Flo wakes up, finds her walker, and makes it to the living room. I jump up from the couch.

"You okay, Mom?" She is fine, she says, in a way that sounds like I can't believe you are asking me if I'm okay, of course I am fine.

"You hungry?" she asks me.

And so it goes, Flo mostly taking care of herself, me just reminding her to keep the wound dry, not touch it, sit down, rest.

Flo is stubborn about taking medication and only comes to the kitchen once for painkillers. When she gets to the bowl in the kitchen to find them, she shakes the vial in a panic.

"These are all whole pills. I thought Janet was going to cut them in half for me!" She only wants to take one-half of the pill. I join Flo in the kitchen, fish through the bowl and pull out a Ziploc bag.

"Janet only cut a couple of them in half," I remind Flo, pressing her fingers to the Ziploc so she can feel them herself. "You're supposed to take one-and-a-half for pain, remember?"

She pulls one entire pill from the vial, and I hear her swallow it with a drink of water. I hand her a half-pill from the Ziploc bag as a chaser.

We make a good team. Flo can see, I have a good memory for details, and Janet is just a phone call away. I have my laptop with me, but I can't get a good internet connection. That is a blessing. I slow down. Hear Flo's stories. Tell her mine. Join her outside on the glider. Welcome visitors. Brush Hanni. Listen to the radio. Talk about the workers paving the parking lot across the street. Ask Flo how she'd ever learned to drive. Find out her teenage boyfriend, Huntz, taught her. "He was good looking," she smiles. We keep the glider rocking.

The only time we fight is when she wants to make my coffee, or go to the other room to get something for me. "I'm supposed to be helping you, Flo!"

She laughs and insists she doesn't need any help. "I'm fine," she says. "You sit down. I'll get it."

44

Hanni Earns a Rest

HANNI IS TEN years old now and starting to slow down. No surprise, and no problem, either. I can walk slower, too.

Good idea...in theory. But when we step off the curb downtown with a crowd of pedestrians one afternoon, we get halfway across and horns start blasting. When a car speeds by right behind us, I know. The other pedestrians are already on the next sidewalk. Our light has turned red. Hanni and I are still in the middle of the street.

"Stay THERE!" a woman calls out. "C'mon! Keep Coming!" a man yells. Shouts ring out from all directions.

"Don't move!"

"Watch out!"

None of the commands jibe with each other. Embarrassment outweighs my fear. I want to correct our mistake, I just don't know how.

A Good Samaritan finally braves the traffic and pulls us across. Hanni's tail wags a thank you all the way to the curb. She is still enthusiastic about her work, she just can't keep up.

She has to retire.

We'd been living in small-town Urbana, Illinois, when I first brought that two-year-old ball of fluff home from The Seeing Eye. Hanni took Chicago by storm when we moved here in 2003. Her confidence was contagious. In her seven years with me in the big city, she's helped me get to and from my Easter-seals job in Chicago's tallest building, guided me to our memoir classes, and flown all over the country with me to promote our children's book. She's worked hard and kept us, well, safe and sound. She deserves a long, happy retirement.

But the mere thought of Hanni's aging does me in. "It's all because I'm blind," I sob into Mike's shoulder. "If I could see, I wouldn't need a dog."

Mike sounds uneasy. "But I thought you liked dogs?"

"That's the problem," I say, using his shirtsleeve for a tissue. I didn't know much about dogs before I trained with my first Seeing Eye dog, Dora, and I got along fine, but I'd really fallen for Hanni.

"If I could still see, I would never have had a dog," I reason out loud. "And then I'd never have fallen in love with a dog and had to go through all this goodbye stuff."

I have three options. First, I can bring Hanni back to The Seeing Eye school, and they'll find someone to adopt her. Second, I can find a friend to adopt her. Third, I can keep her as a pet, so when I return from training with a new Seeing Eye dog, we'll have two dogs.

I can't bear the thought of training with a new dog while Hanni's stuck in a kennel waiting for a new owner, so option one is out. I know I won't be able to devote myself to a new guide dog if Hanni stays with us, so that eliminates option three.

Our friends Nancy and Steven in Urbana offer to adopt Hanni. Eyebrows up! This could work. I can always visit her at their place. Mike and I stay with them whenever we visit our old stomping grounds at the University of Illinois, so Hanni feels comfortable at their house, and with them.

Hanni already knows her way around their house. They don't have a dog, and they don't have kids, so I know they'll give her their undivided attention. Because that's one thing she's always been used to: getting attention.

After all these years of side-by-side travel with Hanni, it is going to take a lot to convince me I'll ever love my next Seeing Eye dog as much as I love her. Blindness dictates practicality, however. For Hanni's sake and my own, I need to begin training with a new dog.

When I call The Seeing Eye to let them know Hanni is retiring, I tell them I want my next dog to look just like her. The instruction manager laughs. "You can't even see what she looks like!"

I try explaining my reasoning. Kids love the presentations I've been giving about *Hanni and Beth: Safe & Sound*. Won't they be disappointed if I show up without the star? "If the new dog looks even a teeny-bit like Hanni, I can get away with bringing an imposter."

The instruction manager chuckles again. "This is a first," he says. "I can't make any promises."

WITH A LUMP in my throat, I announce Hanni's upcoming retirement to my writers.

"What? How old is she?" Their voices ring out from under the table, so many of them ducking underneath to get a look. "Is she sick? What's wrong?"

They've come to consider Hanni as part of the class, and seem to regard her exit as seriously as that of other members we've lost.

"Look at her wag her tail! There's nothing wrong with her. Who says she has to retire?"

In the spirit of Hanni's retirement, I assign "Our Last Time Together."

Wanda shows up the next week with a letter to Hanni, reassuring me I'm doing the right thing, letting Hanni enjoy life without work. Her letter begins:

> *The announcement of your retiring and moving to another city came as a bit of a surprise. My first thought was how much I will miss you. How selfish of me. I have retired twice. Instead of expressing sadness I offer observations and bits of advice and say, "WELCOME TO RETIREMENT!"*

Wanda ends her letter like this:

> *... As I say Good-bye and God Speed, I raise my cup of Java and wish a Long and Happy Retirement to my friend and fellow author Hanni Finke Knezovich.*

After Wanda's reading, we break Seeing Eye protocol. Wanda hugs Hanni, and Hanni wags her approval.

WHEN IT'S TIME to go meet my new dog, I say goodbye to Hanni in our Chicago apartment.

"Mike will be right back," I assure her. She is used to Mike and me going out the door without her, and I want to keep our goodbye as low-key as possible for her sake, as well as mine.

Mike escorts me to O'Hare and gets a special pass to help me through security and right to the gate. When my flight to New Jersey is called, he kisses me goodbye, walks me to the jetway, and hands me over to a flight attendant to guide me on board.

Then he heads home to spend a few weeks alone with Hanni before delivering her to Nancy and Steven in Urbana.

Mike takes Hanni for a ceremonial walk through downtown Chicago when he gets home. When I call to say I made it to Newark, he tells me that when the two of them passed the building Easterseals is headquartered in, she pulled him to the entrance door.

"We stopped with a bunch of pedestrians at a light after that," he says, marveling at how a woman ahead of them bent down, looked Hanni in the face, and told her she was "one beautiful city dog."

That woman was absolutely right, but not anymore. Now Hanni's one beautiful college-town dog.

45

Meet Harper

IT'S BETTER THAN match.com.

The Seeing Eye school listens to our preferences – "I love German Shepherds" or "I'd really like another male" – but when it comes to matching us with our dogs, more important qualities take priority.

A yellow Labrador named Harper is the dog in class who best matches my strength, size, walking speed, energy level, lifestyle, and personality. It is just dumb luck that he looks like Hanni.

Harper and I spend our first day together just playing around and getting to know each other. I love his name, and it surprises me to discover how tickled I am to have a male for a change.

After that, our mornings go pretty much like this:

5:30 a.m.   Trainers choose songs to blast over intercom speakers to wake us up. One day it could be "Baby it's Cold Outside," and another maybe

Randy Newman's "You've Got a Friend in Me."

5:35 a.m.   Put bell on Harper's collar.

5:40 a.m.   Trainer arrives with bowl of food, Harper stays in assigned place as I answer door. I hear the bell on his collar if he moves off his place. He can't eat until he stays in his place.

5:45 a.m.   Harper inhales his food, I heel him to bathroom and measure two cups water. Harper only gets water when I give it to him, part of the bonding process.

5:47 a.m.   Empty out water he doesn't drink.

5:50 a.m.   Out to courtyard for "park time" – eighteen of us with dogs circling around us, all of us urging our dog to empty. Trainers shout when there's success: "#1 for Dilbert!" Dilbert's owner whoops it up to encourage him to always go on command. "Harry has a #2!" His owner squeals with delight. Once they do both, we command, "Inside!" Dog leads us back in.

6:00 a.m.   Set empty bowl in sink of nearest lounge for workers to pick up. I make myself tea to bring back to room (we've all been told to use lids).

6:15 a.m.   Shower.

6:30 a.m.   Harper leads me to nurse's office, sits quietly under my chair. Nurse checks my blood sugar level, I inject appropriate insulin.

6:45 a.m.   Announcement over intercom "First floor ladies, head down to the dining room," or "Men from upstairs, start heading to breakfast."

	We all parade to dining room, our dogs leading the way.
7:00 a.m.	Give dogs a series of commands to go "left," "forward," or "right" to get to assigned seat in dining room. Praise them when they achieve their goal.
7:15 a.m.	Breakfast. Dining room is lovely, white table-cloths and wait staff, all intended to help dogs learn how to act in restaurants.
8:00 a.m.	Van to training center in downtown Morristown.
8:15 a.m.	Dog guides us around Morristown with trainer.
9:30 a.m.	Shuttle back to The Seeing Eye school.
9:50 a.m.	Nurse's office for blood test. I don't usually test my blood sugar this often, but schedule here is different from home. Best to have it checked to make sure.
10:00 a.m.	Tea time. Optional, but I usually go. Another opportunity for Harper to learn to sit quietly under a table, plus I get to meet other Seeing Eye staff.
10:45 a.m.	Announcement over intercom: give dogs two cups of water again.
11:00 a.m.	Groom Harper, either outside or in basement.
11:15 a.m.	To nurse's office for blood test.
11:30 a.m.	Park time.
Noon	Lunch.

And that's just half the day.

Speedy Harper walks much faster than Hanni. While

training in downtown Morristown, I feel like a sulky in a harness race, Harper pulling us to the finish line and waiting until the very last millisecond to stop at the corner. I imagine us looking like characters in a Hanna-Barbera cartoon, sparks shooting from my heels at every curb.

Hanni had guided with a soft touch, intentionally brushing us into pedestrians waiting at intersections in hopes that her corner flirtations might encourage strangers there to reach down and pet her. Seeing Eye training taught me that interruptions like this could distract our dogs from their work. I had scolded Hanni, but to little avail.

Harper is different. He avoids other people at intersections, and I hold on tight to the harness while we wait at curbs. When it sounds safe to cross I command, "Harper, forward!" and pray we don't collide with pedestrians coming our way in the crosswalk. My prayers are answered. We never do.

Like Hanni, Harper turns out to be brilliant at traffic checks. After our first week, Seeing Eye staff starts heading out in vehicles to intentionally cut in front of us from time to time as we cross intersections. They want us to be ready for drivers who text, phone, and eat behind the wheel.

Harper routinely refuses to step into the street if he sees a vehicle barreling toward us, and if a car cuts in front of us in the intersection, he knows to pull me back from harm's way. "Good boy, Harper! Good boy!"

As my time in New Jersey ends, I start readying myself for life back in Chicago, where I'll have to be less friendly and more focused for a while. All worth it, to keep us, you guessed it: safe & sound.

46

Don't Ask, Don't Tell

A NICE SCHOOL mom meets us at the train for Harper's first school visit.

"Hanni can sit back here," she says, sliding her van door open. I don't tell her it isn't Hanni.

Second-graders squeal in delight as we enter the school.

"There's Hanni!" I keep my mouth shut.

During the presentation, I refer to the dog at my side as "my Seeing Eye dog," and suggest we come up with a fake name. This isn't a bluff. Asking kids to come up with a fake name for my dog is a good way to explain that calling out a Seeing Eye dog's real name while they're working can distract them. "If you use a fake name, my dog will think you're talking to someone else."

I ask the kids what their principal's name is. They respond with her formal name. "Does anyone know Dr. Miller's first name?"

"Adrianne!" they chorus.

"How about we call my Seeing Eye dog 'Adrianne' today?" The kids eat it up.

Students ask:

Does Adrianne like other dogs?

Does Adrianne ever slip on the ice?

Can Adrianne go on escalators?

They want to know about blindness, too. How do you shop, how do you eat, how do you cook?

"Can you use a cell phone?" one girl asks. I tell them about the iPhone I'm planning on buying soon. They are intrigued.

The hour flies by, and we leave the room to a chorus of cheers and goodbyes to Adrianne. Phew. We pulled it off.

Until we get to the train station. "Adrianne" needs to empty. Hanni would have squatted to pee. Harper will be lifting his leg, revealing our ruse.

I try to distract the nice school mom by asking about her family, their decision to live in this suburb over some others, what she thinks of the school system, the school board.

I'm not sure if she is looking at me or my Seeing Eye dog as we talk, but at one point she gets awfully quiet. Just then, *ding, ding, ding!* The train signal rings out like the Hallelujah chorus. "There's our train!" I smile, picking up my Seeing Eye dog's harness. "Forward!"

47

Grandma Lula Votes

THE WRITERS IN my downtown class don't just share themselves – they share their people, too.

We feel like we know Audrey's daughter, Lala; Gwen's husband, Lethell; Minerva's great-grandson, Jabril; Susan's husband, Ben; Doretha's son, Gregory; and Wanda's daughter, Wanda Jr.

Wanda brings us a cast of characters and stories from her upbringing that would "make the hair curl on a bald man's head."

Her grandparents, Grandma and Grandpa Johnson, settled in Columbus, Mississippi, in 1888, and raised their family under what Wanda calls a "caste system" that clung to the old thought of bluebloods. "Looks and family were of great importance – even if your family was poor as church mice," she says, explaining that to her southern family, color and texture of skin was important. "Our family fit the mold of 'bright, light, and damn near white.'"

Grandma and Grandpa Johnson raised five sons in Columbus, known to all as "We Boys." Hallie B., the youngest, was Wanda's favorite uncle. She lives by his words: "People who sit and mope with their head in their hands, they never see the good things coming their way."

In the late 1940s, Wanda was summoned to Mississippi to retrieve Grandma Lula, who had taken ill. We Boys instructed Wanda to change to the Jim Crow car when the train stopped in St. Louis on its way south. "I ate lunch in the station and when the call 'All Aboard' echoed through the station, I headed for the front car per instructions. The conductor stopped me and said I was to sit in the lounge car. I boarded the train, sat in a lounge chair and enjoyed the view as the train journeyed from St. Louis to Columbus, Mississippi."

Grandma Lula Moves to Chicago
By Wanda Bridgeforth

Mrs. Green called my Uncle Hallie B. and told him Grandma Lula had been in sick bed since before Christmas past. He immediately called a meeting of all the boys and me. They agreed to finance the trip to bring her to Chicago and I was appointed the task. I had not been to Mississippi since I was about seven and had no idea what I would encounter.

When I arrived the first thing Grandma and Mrs. Green did was to tell me how I was to act when I went to town. In fact they said it would be best if Mrs. Green accompanied me to town. I smiled and nodded.

All went well until a day I had to go to town alone. My first

191

stop was the parcel post office to arrange for shipping boxes to Chicago. I raised a few eyebrows before finishing my mission. Next stop the Woolworth store for souvenirs. After I placed my selection on the counter the young clerk asked "Did you find everything you wanted?" I replied "Yes, thank you."

She gasped and asked "Will that be all?"

Again I replied "Yes, thank you."

She went to the other end of the counter and called "Miss Millie!"

While they talked they looked at me. Then Miss Millie sashayed into the counter and asked "Did you find everything?"

Again I said "Yes, thank you."

Miss Millie said "You're visiting in our city?"

"Yes, I came to get my grandmother to take her to Chicago."

"O-O-H-H You must be Miz Lula's granddaughter?"

"Yes, I am."

"OOOHHH, Maryann, this is Miz Lula's granddaughter, take good care of her. So nice to meet you and be sure to tell Miz Lula Miss Millie said hello."

"Thank you, I will."

When I told Mrs. Green about the conversation, she let out a sigh of relief and said they had been on nettles until I returned.

The week before I arrived a lady didn't say "Yes, sir" to the man at the parcel post office and he slapped her for being discourteous and "forgetting her place."

At last all of the boxes were taken to the parcel post office and Grandma and I were safely on the train on our way out of the Southland never to return.

In her next essay, Wanda tells us more about their trip north and how the station master had hoped to get Miz Lula a first-class ticket for her ride to her new home in Chicago. "But then the ticket agent in Mississippi told us we'd have to ride in the Jim Crow car behind the engine," Wanda reads. "Mr. Miles, the conductor, asked Grandma where she was going. She told him she was moving to Chicago, and he took our tickets and went inside the station."

After a discussion with the station master, a porter was summoned to escort Wanda and Miz Lula to their own roomette, complete with room service, beds, and a bathroom.

"All of the train staff knew Grandma Lula and they gave us the royal treatment."

The family gathered at Wanda's house the night after she and Miz Lula arrived in Chicago, and the roomette was the main topic of discussion. "Grandma Lula said after more than 50 years of traveling back and forth in the Jim Crow car, she left Columbus, Mississippi riding FIRST CLASS."

Grandma Lula moved north just in time to vote in the 1948 election, a privilege she did not have in Mississippi. Wanda's essay describes the event.

Election – Village Style
By Wanda Bridgeforth

Today was Election Day in our village of Phoenix, Illinois. Our population of about 250 was located just north of South Holland, Illinois. Its size was 7 blocks from east to west and four blocks from north to south.

Election Day was always eventful, but this one was extra special. Our 80-year-old grandmother was "going to the voting" for the first time. A privilege she did not have in her home state of Mississippi. Her "Sunday suit" and blouse were pressed, Enna-Jettick shoes polished, bosom ruffle starched and ironed, white gloves washed and placed beside her hat and purse on the hall table.

The second important event was Mr. C. J. Berry had announced this would be his last campaign. He had been in office for many years and now wanted time to go fishing. He was a very tall, very lean man whose arms and hands always dangled below his sleeves. He walked with a slow determined step. All the young people said he looked like Ichabod Crane from "Sleepy Hollow."

Elections in our village were truly democratic. There were no appointed officials. All candidates had to go through the election process, even if there was only one name on the ballot. The ruling was: if a candidate did not receive a majority of yes votes he lost the election and search was on for a new candidate. However, in all of my years of residency I don't recall a losing candidate.

The Ballot Box was on the mayor's front porch in the summer and on his enclosed back porch in winter. The volunteer election judges worked in three hour shifts during the 12 hours the polls were open. The polls closed at 6 p.m. and by 7 or 7:30 we had our results.

When the day ended we celebrated Grandma's entry into the voting world and Mr. C. J. Berry's pre-retirement re-election as Village Dog Catcher.

48

Lincoln Park Village

THE WRITERS IN my class grew up on Chicago's south side, in the Philippines, on farms, as military brats, in plush Chicago suburbs. They are Catholic, Jewish, agnostic. One thing these seniors all have in common? They're resourceful.

Take Myrna. When her name isn't drawn in the lottery for our spring session, she goes to an organization in her Lincoln Park neighborhood to see if they'll sponsor a writing class there.

Lincoln Park is one of the wealthiest neighborhoods in Chicago, and Myrna is a member of Lincoln Park Village, a non-profit organized by older adults there who want to age at home. Many of the classes they offer meet in Village members' living rooms.

The programming committee agrees to offer a memoir-writing class at Lincoln Park Village, but they aren't about to hire me sight unseen. To get hired, I have to give a free introductory class first.

Our downtown class has been meeting for seven years now.

I have references. Other organizations pay good money for me to give memoir-writing workshops. Audition? The nerve! Who does Lincoln Park Village think it is? I'm tempted to refuse.

But then I get a call from Susan, a retired nurse practitioner in my downtown class. I like Susan. She'd grown up in Central Illinois, and she is who she is: open and playful, friendly yet frank. I connect with her essays, most of them contrasting the small-town life of her youth with her big-city experiences in Chicago.

It's only when Susan calls to tell me she understands my reluctance to audition for the new class that I learn she lives in Lincoln park, too.

"I'll have the thing at my house," she offers in a voice full of light. "C'mon, Beth. I'll even get a volunteer from the Village to come pick you up."

I come down from my high horse. "Okay, okay, I'll do it!" I laugh. At the very least I'll enjoy a five-mile drive over to Susan's free of charge to check out her fancy digs.

THE FREE CLASS at Susan's is open to anyone, and I encourage writers from the downtown class to venture over to Lincoln Park and support my effort. A haven for wealthy, educated progressive liberals, the housing in Lincoln Park ranges from historic row homes to courtyard apartment buildings to upscale condominiums. I'd been to restaurants and music clubs in Lincoln Park, and I'd visited the Lincoln Park Zoo, but this is the first time I've been invited to someone's home there.

When the big day arrives, Susan's husband stands as sentry outside their row house to assure me I'm at the right place. "I'm

Ben Squires," he says, and when I extend my hand to shake, he holds on and guides me up the stairs to their front door.

I breathe in the earth, grass, and flowers outside as Ben fiddles with the doorknob. Once inside, I am greeted with a welcome reminiscent of visits to Flo and her friends.

"Come in, come in! Welcome. Sit down. Can I take your coat? Would you like a snack? A cup of tea?"

A chorus of familiar voices calls out a hello from the living room. The downtown writers really did show up to cheer me on.

One of them, a semi-retired social worker named Jeff, had lost his sight in his thirties. He'd never been to Susan's house before, and he and his Seeing Eye dog Randy came by bus. Talk about resourceful! The work he and Randy put into being at my audition inspires me to do well with my own little challenge today.

The old-wood fragrance of Susan's living room takes me back to my Grandma Moos' house in Elmhurst. Susan leads me to her favorite overstuffed chair, and surprise, surprise: I feel right at home.

Once everyone has introduced themselves, I stand up and tell the SRO crowd more than they probably want to know about writing my own memoir. I describe my class at the Cultural Center. I list some of the topics I've assigned in the past. I take questions from the audience. Susan, Myrna, Jeff, and other writers from my Wednesday class chime in from time to time, and the crowd in Susan's living room seems impressed. I leave with a smile on my face and my head held high, confident I passed the audition.

49

Compare and Contrast

THE LINCOLN PARK class is lively from the start. Writers bond quickly and sign up to repeat the class. There is little to no turnover.

My downtown class attracts writers from all over. Some repeat the class, but because of the lottery, every eight-week session has new students, too.

The Lincoln Park class meets in people's homes. A few writers drive to class, but most live close enough to walk. I live miles away from Lincoln Park, so every Thursday, a thoughtful, reliable, no-nonsense man named Jim Zartman picks me up. In his eighties, Jim is always the gentleman and insists on escorting me to the door when we arrive. Once inside, I'm led by the host or hostess to an upholstered living room chair and offered a cup of hot tea.

Downtown writers swipe a card before entering our classroom, and we sit in hard plastic chairs around a long multi-purpose folding table.

Every week, six or seven of my downtown writers email me their essays for my editing suggestions. When I offer the same service to the Lincoln Park class, one of them dismisses me airily, "We don't need edits. We know how to write." Either way is okay by me.

Susan appreciates the difference between the two classes and decides to attend them both. Her work as a nurse practitioner at Cook County Hospital left her with a respect and understanding of some of the stories she hears from the downtown writers. She doesn't want to give that up. Occasionally she reads the same essay in both classes.

When I assign "The One That Got Away" for Valentine's Day, Susan writes about an object that got away rather than writing about a lost love. Her teenage daughters had a clandestine party when she and her husband were away for a weekend. "They snuck my grandmother's wedding ring from my jewelry box to show it off," Susan reads aloud. "Someone stole it."

When she gets to the part where she says the ring had been appraised at $2000, the downtown writers gasp. In Lincoln Park, no one makes a peep.

I'm grateful for the differences between the two classes. Each class boasts talented writers, and members of both classes encourage hesitant writers and cheer on those who lack confidence. Empathy is the common element.

I'm particularly fond of my downtown class for its geographic and socioeconomic diversity, and, especially, because they are the writers who trusted me to lead this class when I wasn't sure what I was doing. But the Lincoln Park writers are warm and welcoming, too, and hey, who can argue with a comfy chair and a cup of tea?

50

Wounded Warrior

STANDING AT A busy intersection with Harper, I hear cars going straight at our parallel. We must have the green light. "Harper, forward!"

The woman driving the van doesn't see us. She turns the corner in front of us, and Harper pulls us back with such force that I fall and crack the back of my head on the concrete. He saves our lives.

Mike inspects the harness later and discovers it is bent. We suspect Harper was clipped by the car.

After a near-miss like this, guide dogs will do one of three things:

- brush it off as if to say, "Hey, we almost got hit!" and just keep working
- need a little retraining before they get their confidence back
- never feel confident again and have to retire

Harper starts showing fear around traffic after the near-miss. He trembles on city sidewalks, his head down, his tail between his legs. City life has become too much for him.

Three Seeing Eye trainers come, one after the other, to help retrain him. But nothing works. Harper will have to retire.

Our friends Larry and Chris live in a quiet Chicago suburb. They offer to keep Harper while we take a long-planned trip to see our friend Sheelagh in Europe. I'll go back to The Seeing Eye to get matched with a new partner when we return from overseas.

While Mike and I are in Europe, Seeing Eye staff have one last meeting about Harper. Could they bring him back to The Seeing Eye for retraining? Place him with some other blind person, one who lived in a calmer environment?

The head of training phones when we return. Harper will not be retrained. He won't be placed with another person who can't see, either. I can go ahead and find friends to adopt him. "He took a bullet for you," he says. "And for that, he's earned an early retirement."

When we share the news with Larry and Chris, they offer to give Harper a permanent home. Larry suffers from PTSD from his time in the military. He and Harper form a bond that is healing for both of them.

Chicago neighbors generously take time away from their own busy schedules to walk me to places while I wait a month to return to The Seeing Eye for a new dog. I feel grateful for the assistance, but hate needing the help. The decision to retire Harper from guide work shakes me up.

HARPER'S REPLACEMENT IS a two-year-old Golden Retriever. When I bring Whitney home to Chicago, she memorizes my routes so quickly that she doesn't go all the way to the curb to wait for my directions. This is a Seeing Eye no-no, but it is fine with me. If she turns when she wants, we will avoid facing a rush of traffic at the edge of each curb. That helps me feel safe.

Until Whitney crosses a downtown Chicago intersection diagonally.

"We'll be crossing left once we get across this one, so, Hey, why not go kitty-corner?" she must have been thinking. Halfway across, the rush of vehicles swooshing behind, in front, and on both sides of us leaves me shrinking in fear. I keep my grip on Whitney's harness and brace for the impact.

Do you believe in miracles? We never get hit. Somehow, someway, Whitney leads us safely to a curb. Once on the sidewalk, I hug, thank, and forgive her. We all make mistakes.

Days later, she goes kitty-corner at a different intersection. We make it across again, but I can't risk a third time.

I phone The Seeing Eye.

The training department tells me the problem is consistency. Or, on my part, inconsistency. I expect Whitney to take me right to the edge of a curb if I want to go straight, or if we are on our way somewhere new and I need to know we are at an intersection. On a familiar route? I let Whitney decide for us.

A Seeing Eye trainer flies to Chicago to give me commands to use to drive Whitney all the way to the edge of the curb – the way she'd been taught at The Seeing Eye school. He shows me how to use the leash to encourage her to the edge. "Heap on the praise when you get there," he urges. "Then stand still a few seconds before giving her the command. Make sure she knows you're the boss, that you want her to stop and wait for your command at every single intersection."

When sighted friends witness us going all the way to the curb before backing up to turn, they think I'm correcting a mistake Whitney made. But who cares what it looks like? And it's much easier to count the streets we've crossed and keep track of where we are when we stop at every curb.

Ever since that Seeing Eye tune-up, Whitney no longer veers right and left at intersections. She knows what I expect of her. Consistency works – for both of us.

51

Guilty

ONE LITTLE WORD can inspire a surprisingly powerful essay.

On the week I assign the writing prompt "Guilty," 90-year-old Hannelore's piece leaves us uncharacteristically speechless. Hannelore's essay is haunting.

Hannelore's father died when she was a child, and her Jewish mother went on to run the family butcher shop in Germany. Then Adolf Hitler won the election, and things began to change. From Hannelore's essay:

> *Our delivery van was parked on the street, and Heini was responsible for its upkeep. He had been with us for at least 25 to 30 years, had started as a butcher apprentice and sausage maker. His wife Rosa had been with us for about 15 years. She arrived from the countryside the day I was born and worked as a sales lady. Rosa and Heini had met and got married in our house.*
>
> *The atmosphere is tense. The problem is that Heini is sitting in our van every afternoon making a show of reading*

The Sturmer, *the most anti-Semitic newspaper published in Germany. My mother and brother are very upset about this, and my brother tries to talk about it and suggests that if Heini wants to read the paper in our van, he should read the local paper, not The Sturmer. Heini is responding that the paper is an official publication, and he can read it wherever.*

"We are Jewish," my brother says.

"It is not against you. It is about the other Jews." He keeps on reading it in front of our shop.

After escaping Germany when she is 19, Hannelore and her husband Eugene return in 1965.

I simply had to confront my past and verify that it really happened to me. We had heard from Heini and Rosa shortly after the war. They wanted me to send them coffee, nylon stockings, and other goodies. After all, they had worked for us for 20 and 30 years, helped bring me up, we lived in wealth in America and had not suffered the terrible bombings and losses. I tore up the letter.

My brother had found out that they had started a restaurant after the business had been taken from my mother by force. This restaurant had been bombed out and they now have a newly established bierstube and restaurant. I had to now confront them.

Eugene and I are sitting in a booth by a window. We are the only customers, and we had ordered. Heini is waiting on us. He brings the beer.

"Heini, don't you remember me? I am Hannelore."

Long silence. He calls Rosa to announce that I am there.

He does not quite believe that it is the girl that he remembers. Rosa is crying.

We make small talk, they produce an album with pictures of my family in it. I asked them if I could have some of the pictures of my parents. They refused because these pictures represented their past.

They will invite all the butchers that had worked for my mother to a party, dinner the next day. We sat around a big table, Heini at one end, at the head of the table. We talk about our lives. Rosa tells that she visits my father's grave regularly and that all is in good order. I will be visiting the Jewish cemetery tomorrow I reply.

Rosa had made my favorite meal – fresh asparagus and Schnitzel, a plum cake for dessert. I feel good, she remembered. We are talking, and Heini tells me that he had been in the German army and how much they all suffered during the war. He tells that they had sent him to the Russian front, which was brutal – the worst.

I am looking at him and hear him say, "The reason why I was sent to the Russian front is because I had worked for a Jew for 30 years. It was all your mother's fault." Rosa started to cry. The meal was finished in silence.

All I could think of: "It was your mother's fault."

52

What's in My Head

HANNELORE'S "GUILTY" ESSAY has a way of getting under our skin. I can't stop thinking about it, and when I publish an excerpt from it on my "Safe & Sound" blog, neither can my publisher, Francine Rich.

Francine, the wise and wonderful woman who runs Blue Marlin Publications and published *Hanni and Beth: Safe & Sound* back in 2007, is so taken by Hannelore's story that she volunteers to publish Hannelore's collected essays.

While raising three lively children and running her own business, Francine somehow finds time to start turning 83 of Hannelore's essays into a book. She edits them, but only for consistency. "I'm not revising her essays," she tells me. "There's no reason to."

Soon Francine's husband, Jude, starts adding photos to the project. Their son Dominick offers to design a cover. "Any chance we can get some photos from her childhood?"

How sad my response is. Hannelore didn't bring any family photos with her when she escaped on her own before World War II. "No chance," I write back. "There aren't any."

Francine titles the book *What's in My Head*, from an essay Hannelore wrote about being a young Jewish student in 1933 Nazi Germany:

> *I told my mother the trouble I had with my Algebra teacher, the one who started each class with a loud Hitler salute. He raises his arm and shouts in a loud voice, HEIL HITLER as he walks in the room. "Heil Hitler," he shouts, and everybody in the class stands up, raises their arm, and shouts Heil Hitler back. If it is not loud enough, we all repeat the routine. Then there are some comments about how the Jews are destroying Germany, that Jews should be banned, and sometimes he also mentions the Gypsies. Now I am telling her about the problem I had just yesterday with Herr Professor Buhl. I had not told my mother that I had gotten a "B" on that important test, and now I had to confess. "On that last test that he gave us, after his Heil Hitler, he handed out the papers, and I had a B instead of an A. All of my answers were correct. I raised my hand and got up, shouted Heil Hitler, and asked him why I had a B instead of an A.*
>
> *His reply: "I gave you a B because you did not follow the formula I taught. You followed a formula I had not taught as yet. Besides, you are a nervy Jew to challenge me. I will down-grade all of your papers."*
>
> *I said to my mother, "I didn't tell you about it, but I will never go back to that school. They don't want me there." I started crying again.*

> My mother said, "If you really don't want to go back, I won't make you. You know, Hitler will not last much longer. There will be a change in government, and Hitler will not last. In the meantime, even if you don't go to school, you will have to keep up with all your schoolwork and study French and English. I will arrange to get the assignments, and when Hither is gone, you can go back. You know, they can take everything away from you, except of what's in your head."

Francine finishes the book in time for Hannelore's children and grandchildren to surprise her with it when they are all here in Chicago for Yom Kippur. The note that Hannelore sends me afterwards describes her reaction best:

> When my daughter Rudy announced on Saturday night after the Holy Day dinner that she had an announcement to make, she made sure that I was listening. I expected her to probably announce that my Great Grandson Eli at 4 months was now able to sit in his high chair or slept through the night. The whole family and friends had assembled around the dining room table, standing room only. Rudy was next to me and reached into the bag that was hanging on the back of the chair.
> "Mom, you are the author of this book." Applause.
> I am looking at the book, not quite comprehending what I am looking at. The first thing I recognize is the picture of the Synagogue in Mannheim, I still don't realize, that this is the book of my stories. I am totally speechless, I am dreaming this, it cannot be true.

Francine had sent dozens of copies, and the note from the newly-published author describes the bundle she carries when her son's family drives her home that night:

> *I am not only carrying some delicious leftovers but also 10 copies of my very own book. I hardly slept that night thinking of all the many people that have helped me to make this dream a very sudden reality, and all the friends and few relatives who would want to have a copy sooner rather than later. Given my age and energy level nobody ever expected that this book ever will become a reality. I, Hannelore L. Bratman, have reinvented myself as the author of my memoirs, of a beautiful book. I am adjusting to this. The word THANK YOU does not adequately describe how I feel.*

A few weeks later, author Hannelore Bratman appears on Rick Kogan's *Sunday Papers* on WGN-AM 720. I meet her at the studio to cheer her on. We're not sure how many people have tuned in at 7 a.m., but she is happy to be interviewed and talk about her book and how it got published.

Hannelore's memoir is not available commercially, and the only thing she asks of the hundreds of people she's given copies to is that they donate to Blind Service Association in Chicago, an organization she loves.

53

You Never Know

I RECYCLE MY prompts sometimes. I'd love to say it's because I'm so fascinated by hearing two different classes tackle the same topic.

But if you want to know the truth, some days I just run out of ideas. That, or I have weeks where other things keep me so occupied that I forget to come up with something new.

When I assign "1968" to the Lincoln Park writers, I find out that some of them, like Judy Spock, didn't even live in Chicago back then.

Judy's essay opens a decade before 1968, when she was attending Antioch College in Yellow Springs, Ohio, and lobbying the local Board of Education to let her classmate Corrie Scott student-teach there. The board refused to reverse their decision, so Corrie taught at a private school instead.

Years later, Judy writes, she and her friend Corrie get together at an Antioch reunion. Corrie tells Judy that now, rather than say they barred her from teaching, officials from the Yellow Springs school have rewritten history and claim she left Antioch to "marry some preacher." Judy's essay describes the loving smile on Corrie's face when the two friends share the irony: "some preacher."

1968 was a sad year for Judy and her loved ones. "It was the year my friend Corrie's husband, Martin Luther King Jr., was assassinated," she writes, explaining that early in 1968 Martin Luther King had been mentioned as a possible third-party peace candidate for the presidential election. As she continues reading, I learn that Judy's father-in-law had been named as a likely vice-presidential candidate on the MLK ticket.

Most days I have trouble remembering where I set my coffee cup down last. But in class today I somehow recall, perhaps because I thought it such an odd choice at the time, that famous baby doctor Benjamin Spock was supposed to run as vice-president along with MLK in 1968.

Surely this woman in my midst is not talking about Benjamin Spock. That can't be right. But wait again. Judy's last name. It's Spock.

"Your father-in-law is Benjamin Spock?" I blurt out my question right there in class. Unprofessional, I know, but that doesn't stop me.

"Yeah," Judy says, sounding as if I'd just asked if she orders a scoop of ice cream on her apple pie when she orders at restaurants. "Mike's father was an anti-war activist."

I hear Judy gathering her coat once class is over, and I call after her. "Mind if I hold your arm and walk out with you?"

Once on the sidewalk, I wonder out loud how hard it must have been to raise children with a baby expert for a father-in-law. "Oh, it was easy," she says with a laugh and a shrug. "I know how crazy his kids are!"

54

John's Baby and Child Care

THE WRITERS WHO host the Thursday Lincoln Park Village class all live in historic row houses that are at least 100 years old. Some residences are bigger or wider or longer than others, but each has a similar feel. The doorknobs are weighty, the throw rugs are sturdy, the wainscoting I brush across in the hallways feels solid. Oak floors and built-in bookshelves leave each place smelling wooden and warm.

The other thing these row houses have in common? They all have stairs. Lots of them.

The first writer to leave our Thursday class does so to move to a one-story apartment in a nearby suburb. It is decided that John Craib-Cox will be a good fit to replace her.

John is the proud father of a son and two grandchildren in London and a daughter and granddaughter here in Chicago. He and Bruce Hunt are the only men in the group.

John is quiet in class, and at first I'm not quite sure what to make of him. Other writers tell me his wife has died recently. She was only 67; the death came unexpectedly. Aside from reading his essays, initially he doesn't say much in class.

BACK IN DOWNTOWN Chicago, Audrey suggests "Bringing Up Baby" as a possible writing prompt during our walk outside after class. "Good idea, but I don't think I can use it," I tell her. "Not everyone in class has kids."

She laughs that off. "It doesn't have to be about kids," she says. "It can be about pets, or flowers – I'd probably write about the lonely cherry tomato growing in the pot on my windowsill."

I assign "Bringing Up Baby" to all my classes that week, and when the essay John reads references Benjamin Spock's philosophy for childrearing, no one makes any effort to point out that the doctor's daughter-in-law is sitting right there in the living room with us. Old news, I guess.

Instead, John's fellow writers commend him for his writing and thank him for conjuring up memories of failed attempts to raise their own children the Dr. Spock way.

Bringing Up Baby
By John Craib-Cox

> We were the generation that knew everything. During the sixties we were self-proclaimed and self-taught experts. Typical was my sister-in-law's reception of her mother's suggestion that before her wedding she should talk to the Family Planning Group. Fiona responded she knew all about that sort of thing and there was utterly no need to talk to Family Planning. My future mother-in-law replied: "Darling, that is

exactly what I said to your grandmother. Nevertheless, all five of you appeared."

Knowing all, we had no qualms about our abilities to raise children. We knew in minute detail what we didn't like about how we had been brought up. Often, with friends, we would recount unpleasant childhood memories followed by the statement that we would never inflict the same upon any of our children when they arrived. We were so confident. We would, of course, not be sexist. We would not stress competition. Opposed to the Vietnam War, we made a pact that our children would not be allowed to play with toy weapons. Rigid structure was to be shunned and we would raise our children in a completely unstructured manner. We knew exactly how we did not want to raise our children. We just didn't know how to raise our children.

When our firstborn arrived we suddenly realized that we knew absolutely nothing about children. My wife noticed that our day-old son needed his fingernails trimmed. She mentioned this to the nurse. The nurse said she would get some scissors for my wife to trim his nails. When the nurse reappeared with what appeared to be garden shears we freaked. Luckily my mother was there to help when we returned from the hospital. What a welcome sight.

Suddenly we realized that we knew nothing and bombarded her with questions about how to do everything in relation to our firstborn. What a change.

After a week we were on our own, a frightening turn of events. Dr. Spock became our combined dictionary, encyclopedia, how to do it source, diet guide, medical guru, question answerer. For many months he was living in our otherwise conventional household operating as the third parent involved in bringing up Justin. Thanks to Dr. Spock, Justin, and later Susanna Jane, survived their infant years despite their inept and often ignorant parents.

By the time they were in nursery school we found that many of our pre-children mantras of what we were not going to do were discarded in favor of pragmatic solutions. Justin was in continual danger of accidentally putting his eyes out with the sticks he pretended were guns. We thought to solve the problem by giving him plastic child-size "authentic" replica Roman shields, armor and swords. The crack in the dam appeared and soon the dam collapsed and the house was filled with plastic weapons and armor: Roman, medieval, Colonial Period, Civil War, up through World War II. At least he was no longer in danger of poking his eyes out with sticks pretending that they were weapons when he had no-sharp-edges plastic child-size weapons in his bedroom arsenal.

Our stand against sexist games vanished when we realized that Susanna Jane and her friends preferred dress up and simulacrum tea parties for birthdays rather than climbing on military tanks at Cantigny.

But this is only the tip of the iceberg. More is to come.

55

Audrey

NEW SUPERVISOR, NEW system. Finding the who-gets-into-class lottery too chaotic, the new administration goes with a waiting list instead. On the day the writers can sign up for the next eight-week session, they morph into Bruce Springsteen fans looking for tickets to the upcoming concert. Some spend the morning dialing and redialing their phones. Others are willing to climb onto crowded city buses and 'L' trains alongside morning commuters just to pound on the Chicago Cultural Center's door in time to be first in line to sign up.

Audrey Mitchell started applying for my class while the lottery was still on, and years went by before she was chosen. Her luck finally turned in 2009, and she hasn't missed a session since.

Audrey expresses her appreciation for the class by offering to help me with my coat, passing the Scrabble tiles and attendance sheet around, and letting me know when it's 11:30 and time to get started. She's also the keeper of the timer. Audrey

sets it for each reader, and best of all, she rings it again if that
that reader won't stop.

New writers are warmly welcomed in my downtown
class, due in large part to Audrey's efforts. She collects their
email addresses and adds them to our current list, emailing the
updated lists to all of us so we can keep in touch.

Audrey is also the guardian of the popular "Chat & Chew"
that takes place after the final class of each eight-week session.
About the sixth week in, she emails everyone on the list – current and past members of the class – to tell them to save the
date for the Chat & Chew. Everyone brings a brown bag lunch
and a drink, and once our last class of the session is over they
relocate to a table in the Chicago Cultural Center lobby to
reconnect with writers from previous classes and just, well, chat
and chew. I never attend the get-together myself. I like that it's
something the writers do on their own.

From listening to Audrey's essays each week, we've learned
that she grew up in Bronzeville and went to high school there
for two years before transferring to the public high school in
Hyde Park, the neighborhood where Barack and Michelle Obama
would be raising their daughters decades later.

While studying at Chicago State, Audrey fell in love, got
married, and dropped out of college. Soon she was a divorced
single mom. Decades later, she took advantage of her employer's tuition reimbursement plan and, at age 60, graduated with
honors from Chicago's Roosevelt University.

Audrey's parents came to Chicago from Edgefield County,
South Carolina, during the Great Migration. Before signing up for
my class, Audrey had tracked a lot of genealogical information

about her family – pages of names, dates, and addresses. But no stories. All her family stories were oral. None of them were written down. Now Audrey is changing that.

The Waiting Game (or How They Met)
By Audrey Mitchell

Mom and Dad were very compatible. They probably had arguments, but we never heard them. He was stubborn sometimes and wanted to have his way. My mother was very charming and catered to him. But in the end, she got her way most of the time.

Their courtship was not a very exciting one; it was just a long one...12 years. Their friends and relatives had doubts that they would ever marry. My mother was very petite and cute and turned away many potential suitors waiting for this skinny guy who was a foot taller than she. In fact, an old family friend, Mr. Green, said he came to court 'Miss Leila" as he called my mother, and she responded, "I'm sorry, but I'm waiting for Mr. Goodwin."

My mother and father courted when they lived in South Carolina. Both of them came to Chicago during years of the great migration from the South, my father in 1927, and my mother in 1930. Their letters to each other were very endearing.

He sent greeting cards to her when both lived in Chicago in the 1930s. Though the cards have very caring messages, he only signed his initials.

When my mother moved to Chicago, she lived with two of her cousins. They were all very close and looked after each other. In the 1930 census, they were boarders renting rooms in someone's home. *My mother was 27 years old at the time.*

She waited, and waited, and waited for my father to marry her, and I'm told, was teased mercilessly by her cousins and friends. But she persisted. He was a quiet man and I don't think he had any wild oats to sow. In later years, he told stories about his friends at the time and some of them probably had an influence on him remaining single for so long.

But eventually my mother's charm won him over. Or was it that she put her foot down and told him "my way or the highway?" He loved her and knew they would have a wonderful life together. They got married when she was 35 and he was 38.

My sister was born 9 months and 8 days later. They got a lot of teasing about that too. And more teasing because of my mother having her first baby at that age. My sister, Marie, was a runner and my mother's cousins told stories on how Marie would get away and run down the street with my mother chasing after that little 2-year-old. But that did not deter her from having another child, me, at age 40.

My mother and father had a happy marriage that lasted 35 years until Leila passed away in 1973. And I'm sure my mother often thought it was all worth the wait.

56

You're Fired

THE EMAIL ARRIVES from Chicago Public Radio: "Thank you for all the essays you've recorded for us over the years."

Uh-oh. Seems anytime an employer goes out of their way to thank you, you can bet a pink slip is next.

WBEZ is reorganizing local programming to emphasize live shows, the note says. "Our new formatting will encourage listeners to comment on social media or phone in live and in person." Translation: they will no longer be airing pre-recorded essays like the ones I've been writing for them. And there will be no hope of getting my writers like Minerva, Hannelore, and Wanda on the air to read their essays, either.

Radio is the only medium that allows me to experience my finished work the same way my sighted peers do. Working for WBEZ boosted my self-confidence. Jumping into a cab and asking the driver to take me to Chicago Public Radio convinced me I was a professional. More often than not, the driver was listening to WBEZ. One of them even asked for my autograph.

The email says the decision is final, but contributors who feel a need to talk face-to-face with someone at WBEZ can call to set up an appointment.

I call.

When Whitney and I arrive for the meeting, I detect quiet discussion behind the reception desk about where they should "put" us. We are eventually escorted to an empty room with a big table, where we sit alone for a long fifteen minutes.

The woman who finally comes in to talk with me never introduces herself. In a flat tone, she tells me that the traditional WBEZ format, where experts in their field (or people like me, with unique life experiences) talk about their specialties, is over. Listener-generated content is less expensive, she says. They want audience participation now. Call-ins. Other contributors are being told the same thing. They hate to do this, but times are tough, and they are going in a different direction.

They respect my work, she says.

"You can still donate your writing to WBEZ," she tells me. "If you want to pitch a story or personal essay, email Cate Cahan."

I've worked with Cate before, and we had a good laugh with sound producer Matt Cunningham after the three of us won an award for my piece about touring White Sox Park. Cate is a news junkie who never reads the sports section, and Matt says he throws like a girl. I'm as blind as a bad baseball umpire, but thanks to those two, I'm the only blind woman in America to win an award in sports broadcasting.

I point this out to the nameless woman who just explained they'd no longer be paying me for my work at WBEZ.

"Yeah," she says, pushing her chair back to stand up. "Do you need help getting to the door?"

BUT REPORTS OF my radio-essay death have been greatly exaggerated.

I schedule a meeting with the Managing Editor of Public Affairs to explore my options. She tells me that, new format aside, they will be covering topics in depth from time to time. Examples? Right now, Aurora Aguilar is producing pieces on literacy, and Cate Cahan is focusing on race issues. I've worked with both women before, and the managing editor suggests I pitch ideas to them now.

I pitch. Cate responds. I write. We record. On July 30, 2012, my essay is aired as part of Cate's "Race: Out Loud" series.

Ahead of the Race
By Beth Finke

I lost my sight when I was 26 years old.

I didn't see the planes going into the twin towers. I don't know what Barack Obama looks like. Mitt Romney, either, come to think of it.

Blindness doesn't bring a whole lot of advantages. So I relish the ones I have. I walk arm in arm with people all the time. My dog goes with me everywhere. And when friends drive me? We park in handicapped parking.

Best of all, I can't judge people by the way they look. Fat, skinny, beautiful, homely, young, old, white, black – it's all the same to me. Without being able to see them, I'm left to judge people "not by the color of their skin, but by the content of their character."

From what I'm told, my friends these days have many different skin colors. I don't always realize this when I first meet them. I'd been swimming at our Chicago health club two years before I found out there were two different men named Rich working there. I thought it was always the same guy. Baseball season cleared this up. Rich would walk me over to the lap pool and we'd talk about his favorite team, the Twins. The next day he'd settle Whitney behind the desk and marvel about the pitching staff on his favorite team, the White Sox.

They both laughed when I confessed my confusion. Baseball wasn't the only thing differentiating these two. The Twins fan was single and in his 20s. The Sox fan was married, had a few kids, and was in his thirties. Twins fan was White, Sox fan was Black. It wasn't until both of them were together explaining this to me that I noticed a difference in their voices.

Twins fan Rich left soon after that for a job in L.A. Sox fan Rich stayed on at the club. None of us knew that Sox fan Rich had been one of the thousands of African-Americans who had taken the Chicago Fire Department's entrance exam in the 1990s. He passed all the requirements, but because of the way the exam was scored, he and most of the other African-Americans were passed over for the fire department jobs.

After a 2011 court ruling in a class action lawsuit, Rich left the health club to train to become a firefighter. As much as we all miss him, it sure is comforting to know that a man as caring, kind, and smart as Rich is someone we can count on at the Chicago Fire Department now.

I don't hear people discussing race when I eavesdrop at coffee shops. I don't feel racism in the streets when I'm out and about.

Even when people tell me what color they are, it can be hard to remember. I lose track.

I listen to the radio, though, and my talking computer reads newspaper articles out loud. I know about the 17-year-old who was shot and killed in Sanford, Florida. I hear about the murders in Chicago. But unless something happens to someone near me, like Rich, I don't always, well, see it.

People work a lifetime to overcome visual prejudices, and while I'm not always sure blindness has given me an advantage, I try to use it as a handicap.

I like to think I'm ahead of the race.

57

What Hannelore Lost

HERE'S AN UNDERSTATEMENT: I learn a lot about history by listening to my writers' essays.

When I ask them to write about a treasured object they'd lost, broken, or destroyed, and then explain why that object had meant so much to them, Hannelore recalls something she hasn't thought of in years.

The Time of Loss
By Hannelore Bratman

Probably in 1936 or 1937, Hitler's need to finance the Army and the National Socialist Party had decreed that Jews could no longer own jewels, precious metal items, gold, silver, diamonds, or precious stones. I well remember the day my mother carried a bag of things to the police station. Upon her return she no longer wore her beautiful diamond earrings or the ring on her finger. They just always had been a part of her attire. I had never before seen her without them.

In return, to make this transaction official she received a detailed receipt from the police department.

We never talked about it.

I think it became about this time that my mother realized that Jews were indeed in for a difficult time in her Fatherland. Her belief, which she had often told, and I had heard time and time again, was this: "I was born in Germany, my husband, a pacifist in World War I, died for the Fatherland. He even got a medal for serving. What are they going to do to me?"

All our relatives and friends packed huge container boxes that we called "Lifts." These were to be shipped through Holland on the Atlantic Ocean to America for storage, as there were no more German boats allowed to go to the United States. We packed newly purchased furniture, bedding, household goods, clothing, anything you might need to start a new life in another country. We packed under the watchful eye of an official. Several Leica brand cameras were the favorite item to be included. They could be sold for needed cash.

Some of my clothes and personal things found their way into the Lift, some books, my tennis racket, ski pants, and jacket. I was especially watchful that the ski jacket was in a safe drawer, for it contained my secret: I had hidden my gold bracelet in it.

I could not bring myself to turn in my cherished gold bracelet that my mother had given to me for a birthday present. It rarely left my left arm.

This charm bracelet had been converted from my father's gold watch chain. I had seen him wear it before he died. The only charm it sported was the watch fob, about the size of a quarter, with my father's initials, M.S., in fancy script. Hitler was not going to get it to melt it down. This was mine. Hidden in my ski jacket.

I had sewn my bracelet between the quilted lining into the seams of the left sleeve, and the fob had found its way into the quilting. I was happy that it would escape Hitler's clutches.

In 1941, we made a claim to Lloyd's of London Insurance Company when they informed us that the container had been shipped on a container ship. The ship had been attacked and sunk by a German U boat. This was an act of war and the insurance did not cover war losses.

Years later the rumor had it that these Lifts never made it even to Holland. They were plundered by the Germans before they got to the safe border.

I often have wondered if someone found my father's watch chain, MY bracelet. Over the years I have gotten several new bracelets, but I have never worn any of them.

58

Floey

MY GREAT-NIECE ANNMARIE Florence Czerwinski is the only offspring in our entire family to be blessed with my mom's beautiful name. When she was younger, I referred to her as "Baby Flo." Now I just call her Floey.

Floey was born with radar. Her matter-of-fact sense of when someone needs help has rescued me on more than one occasion. She likes to stay overnight with me when her Uncle Mike is out of town, and in-between throwing toys to Whitney and describing characters she spies on in our lobby via the security station on the television in our living room, she regularly asks, "Wanna do a blood test?"

After popping a strip into my talking glucometer and handing me the lancet, I poke my fingertip. Floey is not afraid of blood. She gently places my bloody fingertip onto the test strip and waits patiently with me to hear the machine call out the result. She thinks this is fun, and I know it helps keep my blood sugar levels in control.

Floey's a good listener, too. Even in the middle of a chaotic Finke Christmas, she doesn't miss a thing.

When we're all together for the big event, I always make a point of sitting next to my mom so we can help each other in the holiday hubbub. Flo can't hear well, I can't see – we make a great team. I lean on her shoulder and clue her in on the conversations swirling around us. She describes each homemade gift as it is unveiled.

Head-to-head, Flo and I are speaking about her good friend Dorothy who had died just the day before.

"You're going to miss her," I say. Flo nods, then reaches out to hold my hand. I tell her I'm not sure I can attend Dorothy's funeral. She squeezes my hand, understanding.

Presents are opened. Babies cry. Wrapping paper is collected. Teenagers call out NBA scores from downstairs. Flo stays where she is, squeezing my hand.

Until six-year-old Floey taps my arm to interrupt the moment.

"Floey!" I jump. "I didn't know you were there."

"I was eavesdropping."

"Eavesdropping. That's a pretty big word."

"I learned it in school. You think it's a compound word?"

"Well, it's a useful one. So what did you learn?"

"You were talking about funerals."

And with that, Floey leaves. The chaos continues, but I am left with two lessons: we learn far more by listening than we do by talking, and it is a joy to feel close to those we love.

FOR FLOEY'S SEVENTH birthday, Whitney and I make a visit to her school. She volunteers to accompany us to all three first-grade classrooms. "I have to," she reasons. "You won't be able to tell if they have their hands up for questions." She is right, of course, so it is the birthday girl's job to stand in front of the class and choose who gets to go next.

The first-graders have all read *Hanni and Beth: Safe & Sound* before we arrive. Which means they have had time to come up with some pretty thoughtful questions.

What happens if you go to the library and the book you want isn't there in Braille?

Why do you need a dog instead of a white stick?

What if you go to the library and they told you no dogs allowed?

What if you ate food and it wasn't what you wanted and you asked for your money back?

What if the dog is blind and the person can see?

How do you know what your dog looks like?

Whitney is as spirited as the kids, sneaking out from under me to lick a first-grader in the front row, and somehow managing to roll over – even with her harness on – to beg the kids for a belly rub.

Floey's assessment of her day with Aunt Beth? Best birthday gift ever.

59

In-Laws

WHEN I ASSIGN "In-Laws" as a prompt in Lincoln Park, Myrna lets the class know that the essay she's reading is an updated version of something she'd read to the downtown class four years ago, in 2008.

No one in class seems to mind, and I sure don't. Listening to Myrna read this story of courage and understanding one more time is a privilege.

Myrna's husband, Henry, was only 16 when he said goodbye to his mother and father in Vienna and boarded the Kindertransport, the effort that saved 10,000 Jewish children from the Holocaust. Henry's father died in the Auschwitz concentration camp. His mother, Hedwig, survived by hiding in an unheated cabin in the Vienna woods. Hedwig would not reunite with Henry, her only child, until he was 24 years old.

Myrna married Henry a decade after the mother-and-son reunion. That's when she came to know Hedwig Knepler. From Myrna's essay:

Although she had proved both mental and physical sturdiness, she was thin and bent in a way that made her seem fragile and untouchable. Certainly her life experience was beyond anything I knew, in some ways so terrible I was afraid to touch it.

Moreover, I sensed the tension between her and my husband, her son. I, his new, much younger wife, wanted above all to please him. He loved his mother, but was troubled by what seemed to be her almost obsessive concern for him, a concern more appropriate to the mother of a young boy than to a balding assistant professor in his late thirties.

Myrna writes that her conversations with her mother-in-law were awkward until Myrna and Henry had their first daughter, Elizabeth.

Then for the six months between Liz's birth and Hedwig's death, talk was easier, focused on our mutual love for and wonder at this new creature, the grandchild she never expected to have.

Hedwig died in 1962, leaving Myrna and Henry to sort through a box of letters Hedwig and Henry had exchanged before and after the war. The letters were written in German and stored in their attic for years. The only time Myrna and Henry opened the cardboard box together, they closed it up right away and put it back on the shelf. The material inside was too painful for Henry to read.

Henry died in 1999, and before his death, when he was too ill to deal with the letters himself, Myrna realized that they were now her responsibility.

Myrna unpacked nearly one thousand pages of letters – all typed single-spaced and to the edge of the page – and started sorting them by date to send to the United States Holocaust Memorial Museum in Washington, D.C. In exchange, the museum agreed to translate them and make copies for Myrna and her three daughters.

The letters were translated by a native German speaker and trickled back to Myrna over a span of six years. Myrna skimmed through them, noticed some English colloquialisms weren't quite right, and set them aside. Late in 2007, she took time away from the downtown memoir-writing class to read through all 1000 pages of translated letters one last time, correcting any faulty translations before donating them all to the Holocaust Memorial Museum.

Reading the translated letters carefully, Myrna pieces together stories of how her mother-in-law helped a brother emigrate safely to Argentina. She reads heartbreaking details of her mother-in-law's attempts to help her mother and aunt, already interned. They do not survive. Myrna reads about her mother-in-law's struggles to support herself. About how she starved. How she helped save others. About how, in the end, some of the people she saved ended up helping her.

Hedwig's original letters are now preserved in a vault outside of Washington, D.C., where scholars can access them. Myrna ends her essay with a question. "Could I ever be as brave, as self-reliant, as helpful to others as she was?"

I say yes, Myrna, you could. I just hope you are never, ever put to the test the way your mother-in-law was.

60

Secret Ballot

I LOST THE right to vote privately and anonymously when I lost my sight.

After that, I needed Mike to help me with a ballot.

We'd squeeze into a voting booth – Mike, me, and my Seeing Eye dog – and Mike would read the candidates aloud. I'd tell him who I wanted, he'd help me punch the right candidate, and everyone in the place knew who I was voting for.

Once when Mike was away on business, two judges – one Democrat, one Republican – crowded with my Seeing Eye dog and me into the tiny polling booth. Yes, I cast a ballot, but the experience was invasive and overheard by many.

The Help America Vote Act was supposed to change that. The 2002 statute mandated that voting systems provide some way for everyone, including those of us with disabilities, to vote independently and privately.

To prepare for the 2008 Presidential election, I went to a free class at the Chicago Public Library to learn how to use new assistive text-to-speech software and a special keypad to choose my candidates by touch. I sat at the library for hours to get a feel for the machine and practice pushing the big center button that would mark my electronic ballot.

Mike and I walked to the polling place together on that beautiful November day in 2008, and while he took his ballot to a booth to vote, I waited and listened to the poll workers scramble to accommodate me.

"Where are the headphones?"

"Anyone know how you make that computer talk?"

"Why isn't there any sound?"

"How's it supposed to work?"

A special poll worker was called to the scene. I was the first blind person she'd worked with at a polling place. After flipping through the troubleshooting handbook, she plunked it down on the table, announcing there was "nothing in this book about talking machines."

And that was that. Backwards in time we went. Mike signed an affidavit and guided Whitney and me to a traditional voting booth. He read the choices out loud and had me tell him – and anyone else near enough to eavesdrop – who I wanted to vote for. So much for the secret ballot.

I called the National Federation of the Blind voting hotline when we got home. The kind woman on the phone sounded surprised. The technology usually works, she said. I should call my State Board of Elections.

I had to spend a fair amount of time on hold before someone at the State Board finally listened to my story. "Were you able to vote in the end, then?"

"Yes," I said, "But not independently, and the Help America Vote Act of 2002 mandates...."

"You got assistance, then?" he asked. I explained how my husband had to step in and sign an affidavit to help me in the voting booth.

"So you were able to vote, then?"

"Yes."

"Okay, then, you's all set," he said, and hung up.

"Save yourself the trouble," some friends suggested. "Vote absentee." But I don't like voting that way. Absentee ballots have an uncanny tendency to get damaged or lost, or not even counted. This is Chicago, after all.

Fast forward to the 2012 Presidential election. I've researched the issues. I've studied the candidates. I'm ready to give it another try.

Mike has an errand to run, so Whitney and I show up at our precinct alone. The poll workers seem sincerely happy to see us. They help me fill out a paper form to register, and after I use a straight-edge to sign on the dotted line, one of the workers shows us to a computer in a special voting booth.

"You know how to work these?" the poll worker asks, placing a special handheld contraption the size of a cell phone in my hand. I nod yes, because I have practiced at the library. I put the headphones on, and the sound comes in loud and clear. Tactile buttons on the contraption allow me to take my time, scroll through the ballot, mark my choices, and...abracadabra! I vote.

All. By. Myself.

A small thing for some, but a huge victory for me. And for all of us who are blind and want to vote independently.

61

Old Broads, New Tricks

HANNELORE IS THE guest on a "Someone You Should Know" feature on a Chicago TV news station. CBS teases the story by asking viewers, "What do you want to be doing when you're 90? Hannelore Bratman of Chicago is going high-tech to make memories, and as CBS 2's Harry Porterfield reports, she's someone you should know."

We all love the TV personality for applauding Hannelore's grit and determination, and we don't mind at all that it reveals a secret weapon: technology.

Hannelore has macular degeneration and uses special software to enlarge print on-screen so she can write her essays. On days her eyes are behaving, she can read the large print herself in class. Other times, she asks Audrey to read them for her. Audrey doesn't even flinch when Hannelore interrupts to correct any mispronunciations, and she often ends the reading exclaiming, "I want to be like Hanna when I grow up!"

Wanda is hard of hearing, but like so many her age, it went undiagnosed when she was little. In school, she was punished for being rude or for not listening in class when she simply couldn't hear what was being said. Wanda is not a complainer, though. She sorted things out as an adult, got hearing aids, and used her experience to build a career testing public school kids for hearing loss. Wanda is the only writer in class I allow to read print copies of pieces while they are being read aloud. "I wear hearing aids," she reminds us. "Not hearing replacements." Without a print copy in front of her, she can't keep up. Other writers know to reserve the spot right next to me for Wanda so she can read my lips and hear my every word.

When I call Wanda at home, a fancy contraption connected to her phone prints out the words I speak right as I say them. Wanda reads along and responds without a hitch.

I couldn't see the low vision magnifying reading glasses Andrea wore to read her essays when she joined our class in 2006. A year later she read an essay about losing a job, and that's when I learned she'd been diagnosed with a progressive eye disease called uveitis in her twenties. Glaucoma started setting in in 2009, and now she uses an audio and magnifying computer program called ZoomText to write and edit her pieces at home. Wanda reads Andrea's pieces out loud in class for her: the deaf leading the blind.

I use speech software called JAWS on my laptop, and VoiceOver miraculously allows me to interact using the touchscreen on my new iPhone.

Mike is more excited about new technology than I am, and when he hears about Tap Tap See, a "camera for the blind," he downloads it onto my iPhone. Users take a photo of what's in front of them, wait a few seconds, then abracadabra! The app announces out loud what's in the photograph.

Grateful? Not me. I am petulant. "I'm not ready to learn new apps yet," I tell him. "I still haven't figured out how to listen to voicemail with that thing."

Mike not-so-calmly points out that I've already been using apps. "VoiceOver, you know, the thing that makes your iPhone talk?" he says. "That's an app. So is weather. And clock."

I thought apps were things you added to your phone.

"Well," I grumble. "I'm just not ready to learn how to use a new one, then."

A few weeks later he is away on a business trip, so I'm on my own. Getting ready to take a cab, I feel through my wallet to make sure I have the right fare. I usually have each denomination folded differently, but I'd been in such a rush at the store earlier that I'd shoved bills in there without folding them first.

How will I know what to give the cab driver?

I haven't tried my Tap Tap See app yet, but they claim it can identify paper currency. I straighten a bill on the counter, launch the app, and twist my finger around the iPhone screen. VoiceOver says, "Take picture."

Somehow I manage to hold steady, hover the iPhone over the bill, and double-tap. "Picture taken."

Seconds later, abracadabra! "Woman with long hair."

George Washington looks like a woman, I guess. Must be a single.

I pull out another bill, take a photo, wait a few seconds. "Woman with brown hair." Lincoln doesn't look like a woman. Washington's hair is white. Who else's face is on American currency?

Off to my talking computer to Google it. Alexander Hamilton is on the ten. Did Hamilton have brown hair?

Back to the kitchen counter. Tap Tap See identifies all my bills as women, some with short hair, some with brown hair, some with long hair. Not the clear-cut answer I am hoping for, but the app is fun to play with.

I was 26 when I lost my sight. I'm in my 50s now. Would Tap Tap See identify me as "Middle-aged woman?" "Woman with wrinkles?" Do I really want to know?

I can't resist.

Off to the bathroom mirror. I hold the phone up to my reflection, smile pretty, tap "Take picture" and feel my heart race as I wait for Tap Tap See's judgment. Finally it comes. "Woman with brown hair."

Woman with brown hair? Maybe I really do look like Alexander Hamilton. I snap another picture. "Woman with short hair."

And that's when it dawns on me. I've been using my iPhone backwards. The round hole on the back of the iPhone is not what people look through to snap a photo. Those photos I've taken? They're all selfies.

62

Montessori Method

WHEN I GET to talking before our Lincoln Park class one afternoon about the school visits Whitney and I do from time to time, the proverbial light bulb goes on over Judy Spock's head.

Judy's young neighbor Elizabeth Seebeck is the founder of Oglesby Montessori Foundation, a not-for-profit organization that supports and advocates for public Montessori programs within Chicago Public Schools.

"She's already opened one of them on the South Side, Judy says, her voice full of pride for this young neighbor. "Would you come?"

Judy's husband Mike was the director of the Boston Children's Museum before they moved to Chicago, and much of Judy's own deep interest in childhood education stems from her mother, who had a master's degree in childhood education from Columbia.

All the school visits I've made with my Seeing Eye dogs the past couple of decades have piqued my own interest in childhood education as well, and I'm eager to learn more about this public Montessori idea.

One thing, though: the school Judy wants me to visit is located in one of the most impoverished neighborhoods of Chicago's South Side, right where the Englewood, Auburn, and Gresham neighborhoods meet. I'll go, but I'm not willing to take public transportation. I'll need a ride there and back.

So on February 15, 2013, Whitney and I climb into the back of Elizabeth Seebeck's car for a ride to a South Side Chicago neighborhood that is the center of a national focus on violence and guns. That very day, President Obama is at a Chicago high school nearby giving a speech about his new antipoverty policy initiatives. Our mission at Oglesby Elementary is far less controversial: Whitney and I will be there to talk about writing, Seeing Eye dogs, and what it's like to be blind.

Judy is along for the ride and is absolutely effusive about her fondness for the Montessori Method. I can imagine the amused smile on her face when she confides that her famous in-laws thought she and Mike were too lenient and sloppy when bringing up their own three children: "They were nice about it, though."

Judy sits at my side while I talk to the kids, and as she rhythmically flips through *Hanni and Beth: Safe & Sound* to show off the beautiful illustrations, she notices a boy in the class with his hand up. I usually have the kids wait until my talk is over before I let them ask questions, but hey, this is a Montessori School, and I'm not about to counter the free-wheeling daughter-in-law of Benjamin Spock. Judy calls on the boy, and he asks, "Can you color?"

"I can," I say, "but I'm not very good at staying in the lines."

"Can you paint?" I have to consider this one a bit.

"I could get the paint on the brush," I tell them. "But whatever I painted would be kind of, well, abstract."

Next question: "What's a stract?" Hmm.

"I guess I meant it'd be a mess."

The class grows quiet. I don't have to be able to see to know their little minds are thinking, thinking, thinking. All of a sudden another hand shoots up.

"You could finger paint, couldn't you?" a little boy asks. "We made a wreath!"

And just like that, all of them start talking at once. "It's right there! Behind you! We painted it with our fingers."

I turn around to look. Don't ask me why.

"No, over there! Not there! Behind you! On the wall!" Judy to my rescue. She turns around, looks up at the wall behind us, and describes a huge piece of paper with a beautiful green circle of painted handprints: a holiday wreath.

The boy is right. I could do that.

"Maybe you and that dog could come next Christmas to try," one of them says, which leads to the next question.

"How does the dog know where to go?"

"I'm the one who tells Whitney what direction to go to get our errands done."

I explain how I listen very carefully for traffic when we have to cross a street. When I think it's safe, I command, "Forward!" Whitney looks both ways, and once she's made sure it's safe to go, she leads me across.

More questions follow:

How do you wash up?

If you can't see, how do you know where the doorknob is?

If you can't see, can you play any games?

Did that dog write the book by itself or did you help the
dog type it into the computer?

What if you got to a hole in the sidewalk and the dog
took you around and right then a big bus came by and
beeped really loud and you fell into the hole?

How do you know where to press your fingers on the piano
if you can't see the sheet of paper?

Why is your hair so blonde?

That last question gives me an opportunity to tell them
how I tap the lane marker to keep my place when I swim laps,
and how the chlorine in the pool makes my hair turn lighter.

"Do I look like Beyoncé?"

They chorus a joyful, "Yes!"

Just as it is getting time to leave, one girl asks, "How can
that dog keep you safe?"

She must not have been listening when I explained our
routine at the stoplight, or what Whitney does to prevent us
from falling into holes. I repeat my story about Whitney check-
ing both ways before we cross a street, and then Judy and her
neighbor lead Whitney and me out to the car.

We spend the entire drive home yammering about the
delightful and curious kids at Oglesby and how thoughtful
their questions were.

It's only when I get home and turn on the radio that I
realize that last question might have been about a different sort

of safety. The radio story says that in his remarks that afternoon, President Obama had paid tribute to 15-year-old Hadiya Pendleton, who had attended a high school near Oglesby.

"Too many of our children are being taken away from us," the President said.

"Last year there were 443 murders with a firearm on the streets of this city, and 65 of those victims were 18 and under. So that's the equivalent of a Newtown every four months."

63

Code Blue

MIKE IS AN imaginative worrier. When I'm out of his radar he can conjure up injuries and maladies so graphic they're scary. "And those are just the ones I tell you about!" he'll say with a weary laugh.

We've been married 28 years when I'm awarded a writing fellowship from the National Endowment for the Arts in 2013. By now we are so braided together that I know to enjoy the initial celebration, then expect Mike to tighten up as my Vermont residency draws nearer. He loves me, and he doesn't want anything bad to happen to me while we're apart.

Before leaving Chicago, I have lunch with a writer friend. Audrey Petty, by chance, had spent a couple of weeks at the Vermont Studio Center years earlier. Over slurps of soup and sushi, I confess my own apprehension about the four-week residency ahead of me.

"A month is a long time to be gone," I tell her. "And all

the material brags about how beautiful and tranquil the place is. It must be in the middle of nowhere!"

Will the Wi-Fi work? What if my talking computer stops working? Any tech people on staff? I wonder how far away any medical services are. What if something goes wrong with my diabetes? Are there sidewalks there, or just footpaths? Will Whitney will be able to guide me around?

I'd like to believe I'm prescient, but truth is, I can get nervous before relatively simple trips with Whitney, too. Even train travel to Chicago suburbs can make me fret, but I rarely share these sorts of concerns with friends. This lunch with Audrey is exposing my uneasiness.

Mike and I decide to quell our fears by padding the residency with a fun stop in Canada along the way. On March 28, we'll fly to Montreal and stay there a couple of days. Then Mike will rent a car to drive Whitney and me to Johnson, Vermont, where I'll be spending the entire month of April with 50 other poets, visual artists and writers at the Vermont Studio Center.

What can go wrong? I'll make some progress on a manuscript I've been working on and make new artist friends, too.

I get the perfect send-off the day before we leave when Chicago Public Radio airs a piece featuring the writers in my Wednesday class. WBEZ has been doing a special series on what was going on in people's lives the year they turned 25 – the last year I could see.

Listening to that radio piece solves a mystery. The dread Mike and I have been feeling about this month apart traces back to when I was 25 years old and started losing my sight. After eye surgeries failed, Mike dropped me off in Chicago at what was officially called the Illinois Visually Handicapped Institute (IVHI). I called it Braille Jail.

Three months at a residential school for adults who had lost their sight would teach me new skills to live without being able to see: Braille, daily living skills, orientation and mobility, using a white cane to navigate. I'd also learn adaptive tools and techniques to measure out insulin. That way I'd be able to give injections by myself again.

Mike drove the three hours from Urbana to Chicago to move me into my dorm room. We took a guided tour, we met the director, and when it came time for our teary goodbyes, I wanted to feel like Mike was dropping me off at college. But it felt more like prison. Braille Jail.

Mike told me later that he drove all the way back to Champaign-Urbana telling himself that it was silly to worry, that this was important, that I'd be fine.

But while he was heading home, I was heading to Cook County Hospital.

Until I learned how to do my own injections, a nurse was required to give me my shots. The IVHI nurse had been sent home for the day, and when I offered to explain to staff there how to measure an injection of insulin for me, they said they weren't allowed. "Rules are rules." I spent my first evening at Braille Jail sitting in a wheelchair in the hallway outside of Cook County Hospital's emergency room, waiting for a shot of insulin. It was a bad start to my three-month sentence.

No wonder Mike and I share an odd sense of dread during any long period of time away from each other.

Mike helps me get situated in the room I'll be sleeping in at the Vermont residency, as well as my sweet office in another building. I open the office window, hear a stream, and Mike describes the nearby mountains. "That water you hear? It's coming down from there." He says the room is nothing fancy, but I don't care. I love my office already.

We head outside, and I sense Mike's anxiety returning as he sizes up the busy street Whitney will need to guide me across to get to the dining hall. "Eyebrows up!" I say with a smile. It might take days, but given time, I'll figure it out. Good thing I'm staying an entire month.

A week later I feel a strange sensation in my chest and contact a home health nurse to check on me. Blood pressure? Fine. No signs of angina. No swelling in the ankles, no lightheadedness, no pain in my arms or back.

When she asks me to describe the feeling, the only sensation I can think of to compare it with is what it felt like when I was a teenager working in restaurants, feeling hot and sweaty and going into an ice-cold walk-in freezer.

The nurse is stumped. "How about I come back tomorrow and take a walk with you?" She says she'll bring her equipment along on the walk. "If it happens, I can check you right then." She does. It happens. She tests. Blood pressure is fine. No sign of a heart attack.

After making arrangements for her to come every afternoon, I stick it out for another week and try to convince myself it's the cold Vermont weather. Anyone who's had diabetes 50 years knows better, though. Heart attacks are common among people with type 1.

Giving up my once-in-a-lifetime grant isn't easy. Writing a long thank-you letter to the National Endowment for the Arts helps me work through it.

> *April 19, 2013*
>
> *Dear National Endowment for the Arts,*
>
> *I am writing from the Vermont Studio Center to thank you for awarding me a Creative Access fellowship. It is a privilege to devote time to my writing in such a quiet studio space and share lovely meals with the 50 other poets, writers and visual artists who have come here from all over the world to work on their own projects...I am composing this note from my usual perch here: a cozy chair right by the window. From time to time I take a break, turn off my talking computer and open the window so my Seeing Eye dog and I can stick our noses out and enjoy the fresh air and listen to the river rush by outside. I'm black and blue from pinching myself so much....*

BACK IN CHICAGO, my first order of business is to take a stress test and echocardiogram. When I start feeling nauseous on the treadmill, Mike jumps up to catch me from falling. A nurse there calls an ambulance. I've had a heart attack.

After they stabilize me in the emergency room, I call 97-year-old Flo to explain that I'll be getting an angiogram to determine where the blockage is. Flo assures me I'll be okay.

"I love you, Mom."

"I love you, too, Beth," she says. "You're going to be fine."

I'm unconscious during the angiogram. When it's over, a young cardiologist comes to the waiting room to tell Mike that the angiogram showed my arteries are clear. He gives her a hug.

"Dude!" she exclaims. "I hope my pipes are that clean when I'm 54." It's a moment of respite.

And then, I code. That's slang for "cardiopulmonary arrest."

Suddenly, everything is quiet. Dead quiet.

Can a blind person see herself in a near-death experience?

Yes, but I'm not ready to talk about that now.

A defibrillator saves my life. "If you're going to code, the best place to do it is on an operating table," our young cardiologist tells me later. "Especially one surrounded by cardio experts and surgeons."

Those heart experts and surgeons in the operating room are stumped, though. Medical staff start frantically prepping me for emergency open-heart surgery. Mike is allowed to come in, and as they wheel me away the anesthesiologist tells Mike I am unstable. "We're going to do the best we can do."

I am awake in my hospital room. I lay there and listen a long, long time before opening my eyes. Before I'd gone in for the angiogram Mike and I had been given a few minutes to talk alone. I had assured him what a wonderful man he is, what an extraordinary life we've had together, how much I love him and how important it is to me that he'd go on living a full life if I didn't make it. We squeezed hands and he gave me a kiss before they rolled me away. I'd experienced very little pain during the operation, peace overwhelmed me at the beginning of my near-death experience, and I couldn't think of a better way to die.

But here I am.

I'm alive. And I can't move. Am I paralyzed? Probably. If I open my eyes, someone there will tell me what had happened during surgery. I'll learn how the ordeal I've just been through has put new limitations on my life, what new things I'll need to put on my "can't do this anymore" list, how much stricter my diet will be now. I don't want to know. I keep my eyes closed.

I hear murmurs. Visitors? Nurses? And then Mike.

"Beth, you're tied to the bed," he says. "That's why you can't move." Apparently I've been trying. Jig's up. He knows I'm conscious. I open my eyes.

"Hello, Gigi," he says. He had nicknamed me Gigi after I'd received the NEA writing fellowship. G.G. for "Grant Girl."

When the young cardiologist Mike hugged in the waiting room stops in for a visit I ask when the nutritionist will be coming in. "Don't I have to give up meat or something?"

She tells me no. "Whatever you're doing, keep doing it."

She doesn't know I follow a Judy Garland diet. I don't eat sweets at all, but I drink lots of coffee (uppers) all day, green salad and bites of cheese throughout the day, then wine or beer (downers) before bed. Uppers, downers, and lots of cheese in-between.

I throw out a laugh and a tease. "But you don't know what I eat!"

The heart surgeon comes to my room later to introduce himself and see the "miracle girl" sitting up and talking. Dr. Patrick McCarthy had come to Northwestern from the Cleveland Clinic. He tells me the heart attack I'd had on the treadmill was a mild one, and had nothing to do with my type 1 diabetes. Benign tumors on the aortic valve are rare. Doctors don't know the cause, but sure enough, that's what I had. The surgeons snipped the tumor away, and Dr. McCarthy assures me it will not return. He's done over ten thousand heart surgeries, but he's only seen benign tumors on an aortic valve a few times. "Never this big," he marvels. "Yours was like a marble. It really is very exciting." Considering the outcome, I have to agree.

I have to wonder, too. What were the odds? A surgeon on staff who's seen a rare tumor like this before? One who knew exactly what to do?

"You think I should join a religious cult now?" I ask Dr. McCarthy. "Maybe move to an underdeveloped country to help people less fortunate?"

The cocky cardiologist doesn't skip a beat. "No," he says. "I think you should buy a lottery ticket."

64

Thank You, Sheelagh

I GET IT that they had to crack my sternum open for open heart surgery, but I don't like hearing how careful I'll have to be for a while now to give my breastbone time to heal.

The strain of Whitney's pull in harness could re-break my sternum. She'll have to wait three months before guiding me again. I'll have to wait that long before riding a CTA bus, too: being jarred could cause harm as well.

That poses two problems. First, I need someone to walk Whitney to keep her healthy. Second, I need someone to walk me or I'm going to be stuck in the house for three months. A wonderful army of friends and volunteers is marshaled to help fill in when Mike isn't available.

Those gallant friends get me to my memoir classes again in June. It'll be the end of July before Whitney can pull me again, so when the doctor says I'm well enough to travel with Mike over the Fourth of July, we find a dog-sitter and start planning. We'd had to postpone a trip in spring due to my heart emergency. Now we can rebook those flights to Northern Ireland to visit our dear friend Sheelagh.

When Gus was an infant, Sheelagh was studying at the University of Illinois as an exchange student from Belfast. She volunteered to come to our house and plow through bills, news-letters, and magazine and newspaper articles with me. We fed her dinner in exchange.

I hadn't trained with a Seeing Eye dog yet and was delighted to hear that Sheelagh liked to go for long walks. As a teenager, she'd pushed heavy wheelchairs over hills, through woods, and even to the oceanfront while volunteering at a camp in Cornwall for adults with physical and mental disabilities. Pushing Gus while I hung onto her arm was a piece of cake. She'd escape her dormitory room and come to our house three, sometimes four times a week to walk us to the grocery store, the post office, or medical appointments. Sometimes we'd just sit at a coffee shop over a cup of hot tea.

When Sheelagh reported news of her American volunteer work to her mother in Belfast, Mrs. Livingston was horrified. "Sheelagh!" she warned, "You don't know a thing about wee babies!" If Mrs. Livingston had seen how many times her daughter swore at the bloody cars who wouldn't stop when we'd try crossing a busy street with Gus in the pram, she might have hopped on the next plane to intervene.

Sheelagh was a terror on our bicycle built for two as well. With Gus on back in a bike seat, it was a bicycle for three. Sheelagh tended to forget that we were longer than the usual bike, and Gus got more joy rides than he bargained for.

Mike had hoped a volunteer might take some of the

bill-paying and reading burdens off his never-ending to-do list, so he wasn't exactly tickled when walks with Gus in the pram or visits to coffee shops replaced my reading sessions with Sheelagh. He'd regularly come home from work, ask how the reading went, and Sheelagh and I would both break into laughter. "Reading?"

One night Sheelagh asked if Mike might be willing to stay home with Gus after dinner. "I'd like to take your missus out for a wee drink." Mike wasn't at all surprised.

Sheelagh was small, but strong. A bluegrass band was jamming as we entered a nearby music club, and Sheelagh barreled through the crowd with me on her arm – much as she did on crowded sidewalks with Gus in the pram. After pressing my palm onto an empty barstool, she stood on her tiptoes to get near my ear. "What will you take to drink?"

"A Guinness!" I shouted over the cacophony. Sheelagh ordered a pint for herself, too, and when the bartender returned, we held our pints up for a "Cheers!" Sheelagh jiggled my thigh every once in a while to let me know she was still there, having a good time. I sat back, sipped my pint and enjoyed the music. Rather than struggling to recreate something I used to enjoy when I could see, I was doing something completely different with a new friend, someone who liked me even though I couldn't see her.

MIKE AND I managed to get together with Sheelagh, here or abroad, about every other year since she left the States. Our previous trip had been a few years earlier, soon after she'd been diagnosed...with cancer. Her brogue rang out when she met us at the airport during that last trip. "Oh, my lovely, give us a squeeze!" Her hug felt as strong as her voice. I cried with joy. And relief.

Sheelagh was, as she put it, "in good form." Some days we'd walk from our campsite to the beach, other days we'd hike arm-in-arm along mountainside trails. The only outward sign that Sheelagh had any illness at all was the PICC (Peripherally Inserted Central Catheter) cannula attached to her upper arm. "Ach! It's no bother," she assured me. She'd be starting a second round of chemotherapy right when they got home, and the PICC was there so she wouldn't have to have a needle inserted with every treatment.

Early scan reports showed tumors were shrinking – even disappearing. She'd "gone off the drink" after the cancer diagnosis and had become a connoisseur of alcohol-free beers and ciders from around the globe. We lifted our glasses many times to Sheelagh's good health that week, and she laughed at all the positive attention. "You'll not be rid of me yet, my dears," she assured us. "I'm going to be around a long, long time."

SHEELAGH WAITS UNTIL a month after my release from the hospital to phone us with her own medical news: the cancerous tumors are spreading. She is deteriorating physically. She won't undergo further treatment.

"We'll book our flights," I say.

Pre-cancer Sheelagh would have responded with an "Ach, no!" and insisted I stay home, rest, recuperate.

But Sheelagh doesn't argue. "Ah, that'd be grand," she says.

We find a dog sitter for Whitney and land in Northern

Ireland on the Fourth of July. I spend hours each morning alone with Sheelagh, her propped up in bed with pillows, enjoying tea and toast, and me in the chair next to her. We talk about our spouses, her family, our plans for the afternoon.

Sheelagh doesn't avoid talking about her cancer, but she doesn't want to dwell on it, either. So she asks after my own health instead. She is eager to learn what I remember from the operating room. I haven't told anyone about my near-death experience, and now I share it with her.

I'd been in a lot of discomfort before I coded. Suddenly, everything was quiet.

Dead quiet.

The first thing I saw was me, looking the way I picture myself on a relaxing vacation. I had a serene smile, and I recall wondering why humans waste so much time on earth afraid of dying.

Rustling against the newspapers on the mattress, Sheelagh sips on her tea as I continue my near-death saga, explaining how I'd just been settling into nothingness when I saw my mom's face.

Flo looked confused. And sad.

Next stop? The living room of our Chicago apartment at dusk. Mike was despondent, walking from window to window, looking outside. Whitney tracked his every step. She couldn't find me, either.

Anyone who knows me well – and Sheelagh is one of those people – knows I do not suffer from low self-esteem. My oversized ego followed me to death's dark door, for God's sake.

"You'd think I'd be considering world peace, but all I was

thinking was that I couldn't let this happen," I tell Sheelagh, setting my coffee down to place my palm dramatically on my heart. "You must go on, Beth. Their lives will be so awful without you!"

Sheelagh doesn't laugh. She grows quite serious instead. "You have that wrong, my dear." She says those visions simply show how much I love Flo, and how much I love Mike. "When you love people that much, you don't want to do anything to make them feel sad."

When we get the phone call at home a few weeks later, I remember Sheelagh's words. She doesn't want me to feel sad, so I try instead to focus on the bewildering circumstances that brought us together in the first place. How much I love her. "When you love people that much, you don't want to do anything to make them feel sad."

Such a simple revelation. Such a priceless gift.

65

The Hunts

BRUCE HUNT, JOHN Craib-Cox's male counterpart in the Thursday Lincoln Park Village class, has been with us since the start. By the time his wife, Anne, decides to write her stories, too, the Thursday class is full.

No matter. Anne prefers being in a separate class anyway. She joins the new Monday class when it starts.

Bruce's father was a partner in the family's law firm in Boston, and as an only child Bruce was expected to attend Harvard and follow suit. He opted for divinity school instead, fell in love, and married Anne while they were both students at University of Wooster. Bruce was eventually ordained, and while he never led any particular church, he makes good use of his sermon voice when reading out loud in class on Thursday afternoons.

Anne Hunt is in the second class I lead for Lincoln Park Village. That Monday class allows newcomers in and meets at a one-story apartment in a high-rise across from Lincoln Park that is more accessible than the row houses. Members of Lincoln Park Village who use wheelchairs or are recovering from hip or knee surgery and want to write their memoirs tend to sign up for the Monday class.

Anne has always liked to write, but she had an entrepreneurial side to her, too. When their three daughters were young, she joined other parents to start an innovative preschool in Chicago. Well-known for her cooking, baking, and gardening skills, Anne turned to writing for food businesses once the girls were in school. Retired now, she donates her writing skills to the non-profit organizations she's interested in and is a regular contributing writer for the Lincoln Park Village newsletter.

Anne often brings treats along to our class. Could that be why Monday classes boast the highest percentage of male writers? Each eight-week session boasts at least three men, sometimes more.

After all these years of marriage, the way that Anne and Bruce feel about each other shines through in their essays. It's like listening to love stories in stereo. The two of them print out copies of the essays they write for class and include them in scrapbooks they're working on. Each scrapbook will cover one year of their marriage, and this one Anne wrote about their honeymoon will be included in year one.

I Knew I Was in Trouble When...
By Anne Hunt

FLORENCE, ITALY, MAY 1959: The trip through the Alps on a celebrated Swiss train was to be one of the highlights of our six months of travel through Europe. After pushing our bikes up several steep inclines in southern France, we knew we couldn't make it over the Alps. So, after a month of camping in Florence, we bought the tickets. The bikes, with their one-cylinder motors, would get a routine check at the border.

Pictures in the brochure of the passenger car showed compartments, each with a drop-down table and large picture window to view the spectacular scenery. We checked the bikes, boarded the train, and laid out our lunch of bread, sausage, cheese, and wine on the table. The tickets were stamped and we settled in.

We'd barely started lunch when we arrived at the border and Bruce went to make sure the bikes made it through customs. I was not concerned when the train began to move. It backed onto a side rail, then pulled forward again. I assumed we were just switching tracks. I saw Bruce and the bikes on the platform. He was gesturing toward the train. I assumed the train would stop. But no! We were picking up speed! I asked the conductor what I should do, and he suggested I get off at the next station and ask the stationmaster to call the border office to see if they could find Bruce and let me talk with him.

So I got off at the first stop and tried to explain my dilemma. With no language common to both the agent and me, I watched my train – and our lunch and luggage – pull away. I realized then that I was in trouble – but it could have been worse. I did have my passport and train ticket but absolutely no money. The next train was due in about an hour, I was told. I walked around the town conjuring up scenarios of losing our bikes, our tent, our clothes, AND my husband! No cell phones in those days.

I came around the corner of a building and was greeted by the smiling figure of a Harlem Globetrotter on a huge poster.

If I was stranded here when they came to town, maybe they could help me, I thought.

I boarded the next train to Zurich. I found the bikes in the baggage car, but no Bruce! I was beside myself. The sight of a family enjoying a sumptuous picnic across the aisle added hunger to my angst.

We finally got to Zurich, and there on the platform was Bruce! We embraced like long-lost lovers!

He'd come in on the second section of the original train, on an alternate route, via Geneva. Our bikes had been put on the next direct train to Zurich, (the one on which I'd ended up). The lunch and baggage had traveled safely in our original compartment and awaited us in Lost and Found.

We collected our gear, packed up the bikes, and rode out to an edge-of-town campsite. We pitched the tent in the rain with minimal light, crawled in and spread out the lunch. We sat close together, finishing the wine and giving thanks that we had everything we'd started with that morning in addition to another adventure to remember for the rest of our lives.

Where do Babies Come From?
By Bruce Hunt

Where do babies come from?

For many years, actually more than 300, my family apparently believed that babies come from a ten-mile radius of Boston.

Enoch Hunt established the Hunt family beachhead in Weymouth Landing on the South Shore of Boston in 1630. The Hunts did not move.

For generations the family also determined that boy babies come with the first or middle name "Atherton." This tribal pattern is evident in that my father's name was Frederick Atherton, my uncles were Richard Atherton and Edward Atherton. I even had a cousin named Homer Atherton, and a grandfather Atherton Nash. Tucked away in a dusty old book is a list of boy babies who carry the name Ebenezer Atherton and that list dates back to 1802.

By 1962, pressure was building to produce a Hunt baby beyond the boundaries of New England. Anne and I were living in Chicago, we had been married for 5 years, and I was finishing graduate school, ready to begin my career.

The next predictable step was to produce a child. At least, that kind of orderly progression seemed natural to me. So we did the natural thing: Lamaze training, hands-on massage, breathing exercises, books to read, the whole curriculum.

When babies come is almost as significant as where they come from. This baby came on Friday afternoon, June 15. Still sweaty from work in the ditch, I finished up my summer job with the Peoples Gas Company at 4:00, the water broke at approximately the same time, and we rocketed to Lake Shore Drive in order to turn south for Michael Reese Hospital. In search of minimal comfort, Anne stuck her feet out the front window of our 1954 Ford.

On Friday, during rush hour, one does not rocket down Lake Shore Drive, no matter the level of urgency. After endless stopping and starting, we arrived at the entrance to the hospital, ready to begin our preparation in the labor room.

Dr. Sol DeLee, noted gynecologist and avid golfer, arrived almost immediately, though reluctantly, from the golf course, and announced that Anne should go directly to the delivery room.

I slumped in the heavy chair in the waiting area. I was disconsolate. I had practiced so diligently. I knew exactly how to support the sides of the tummy and to encourage rhythmic breathing. I was ready. And now, with no place to go.

Doctor DeLee, as he was putting on his gown, stuck his head in, saw my miserable demeanor and asked jauntily, "Didn't you just graduate from theological school?"

"Yes, a couple of weeks ago," I said.

"So that makes you a doctor, doesn't it?"

"Well, sort of, I guess."

"Good enough! Put on a gown and cap and some gloves and come with me."

(Ten years later this would not have been a big deal. By the 70s, the doors to the delivery room were open to men.)

So I got to observe where babies come from and yes, I got to observe how Elizabeth Anne came into the world, and it was then, and still is, miraculous!

Vision Forward

AFTER SIX MONTHS of cardiac rehab and visits to specialists, I'm finally given the green light to travel with Whitney. And off we go!

During one October week, we travel nearly 500 miles, visiting four different schools in four different cities. At times, I am tempted to join Whitney on the floor of the train or bus or van moving us from point to point, but who am I kidding? These visits are so stimulating I wouldn't be able to sleep.

The first presentation is a thank-you gift to one of the cardiac specialists who saved me in April, the one who Mike hugged in relief. At her daughter Carolyn's Montessori School in Chicago, I tell the preschoolers that even when I open my eyes, all I see is the color black. One of little Carolyn's schoolmates wonders out loud, "Then how do you know when you're tired?"

Wednesday, Whitney and I travel to downstate Champaign where I give a guest lecture to an animal sciences class at the University of Illinois.

Thursday, we're back in Chicago for a talk with students enrolled in a disability studies class at DePaul University.

Finally, on Friday we board another Amtrak train, this one heading north to Milwaukee. I'm giving the keynote speech and leading a workshop for an organization called Vision Forward.

The temperature outside in Milwaukee is below normal, but the people we meet here are so warm we hardly notice. The thoughtful teacher who picks us up at the train station has a cup of hot coffee waiting for me in her warm car, and the blind and visually impaired students we meet when we arrive at the conference are bright, curious, and thoughtful. One of them even greets me with something I can read on my own. "I stayed up late last night," she says, and when I feel the card I know why: she'd painstakingly glued beads onto a sheet to create a note in Braille. It all warms my heart.

Vision Forward is all about kids in the public schools who are blind. Many of their parents, some grandparents, and teachers and other staff members who work with them attend the writing workshop I give after my keynote. These folks have a lot to say, and I hope the workshop encourages them to get some of their thoughts down on paper. It's amazing how therapeutic writing can be.

I end the keynote with my seven-minute "What It's Like to Go Blind" video from Good Stuff. A mother in the audience raises her hand afterwards to compliment the visuals and ask for the YouTube address. "We have such trouble explaining what our daughter's vision is like," she says. "Those missing puzzle pieces, that's a perfect way to describe it."

I sign books after my keynote and workshop is over, and it comes as no surprise when we sell more copies of the Braille version of *Hanni and Beth: Safe & Sound* than the print one. As he is patiently waiting in line for me to Braille my name into his book, a little boy who is blind asks me a question about Whitney's harness. I unbuckle it, lift it off over her head, and pass it over to let him check out the leather straps firsthand. He returns it when he's done, but before I buckle it back onto Whitney's back I ask if he wants to pet her. "Sure!" he exclaims. Whitney wriggles and wags and kisses her new friend in return. Don't look now, but I think we have a future guide dog user on our hands.

Whitney and I have a ball and make lots of new friends in Milwaukee, and you know what? Somehow, someway, even without being able to see, once we're on the train riding back home, I know we're both tired.

67

Introducing Bennett

October 30, 2013

Dear Beth,

I met you at the Vision Forward conference in Milwaukee this past weekend. I purchased your book, Safe & Sound, *for my blind 5½-year old-son, Bennett.*

My husband read it with him tonight, while I worked on homework with my 9-year-old. Bennett was so excited about the book. He told me, "I loved that book you got me. It's a true story, Mom. And no one ever writes true stories for kids about people who are blind like me."

Thank you for writing this story and reaching out to children who cannot see. Bennett has a Children's Companion Dog and he said when the story started, he thought for sure it was about his dog, Journey.

Thanks again. And it was a pleasure meeting you. Keep writing and we will keep reading :).

272

I swear, anytime I'm feeling blue, all I gotta do is read this note. It always makes me smile.

Hanni and Beth: Safe & Sound is available in a print-and-Braille format. The Braille and print match line for line, with the print just above the Braille (no pictures). I can tell you first hand, so to speak, that it's "good Braille," meaning the dots are stiff, they stand up straight, they're easy to read. Only problem? The Braille version of *Hanni and Beth: Safe & Sound* was produced in contracted (or grade two) Braille. I've never mastered contracted Braille, but I learned enough of it to be able to read *Safe & Sound* aloud at school presentations. Sighted kids like seeing what Braille looks like and how it works. They view it as a secret code.

Contracted Braille is an advanced form of the code that has a bunch of shorthand symbols (contractions) for commonly used words and parts of words. For example, one Braille cell means "th," another one means "ar." There's a cell for the word "and," another for the word "the," and so on. Most of the letters of the alphabet are also used as shorthand for common words, such as "c" for "can" and "l" for "like." Kind of like texting, only you can't make as many mistakes.

When I write Bennett's mom back to thank her for her note, I apologize that my book is only available in contracted Braille, making it harder for poor five-year-old Bennett to read it. No problem, she says. Bennett started learning Braille this past summer. "He knows the whole alphabet, all of the "secret" words for the letters when they are alone, and he just started the words that have two Braille letters together, like bc for because," she says. "Not to brag, but this little guy is a genius!"

I say she should go ahead and brag. Not only about Bennett, but about herself and her husband, too, and the family they are raising, all of them supporting Bennett's love for reading.

So let's talk about Braille. Here's a little-known fact: less than 20% of the 50,000 blind children in the United States are proficient in Braille. The American Foundation for the Blind reports a severe shortage of certified teachers of the visually impaired (TVIs), especially in rural areas or in small school districts. Without qualified teachers around, it can be a lot easier for parents of children who are blind to just let their kids listen to books on audio or hear words on a talking computer.

You might think that's no big deal. Isn't it a good thing that technology is doing all the heavy lifting for these kids? But think about it. If children who are blind never learn Braille, how will they ever learn to spell correctly? How will they know where to put commas, quotation marks, paragraph breaks, and so on? How will they be able to write clear communications for sighted people?

And what if they want to be writers?

68

Why Audrey Stays in Chicago

THIS JUST IN: winters can be cold in Chicago. Icy, too. But whether they be age 60, 72, 83, or 95, whether they travel on foot, via walker, CTA bus, or 'L', my memoir writers make it to class.

I tune into Chicago's all-news radio station on Wednesday, April 2, 2014, just in time to hear an announcement from the National Weather Service: "Chicago has just experienced its coldest four-month period on record."

Eyebrows up! The news gives me a good idea for a writing prompt.

Safe and warm inside the Chicago Cultural Center, I wait until we've all unzipped our down jackets and unraveled our layers and settled into our seats before introducing the assignment.

"Friends and relatives from warmer places are calling you, right?" I ask. "They're bragging about how high the temperature is today where they are. They're wondering why you don't move closer to them."

A chorus of "uh-huhs" tells me their heads are nodding. Quick as a slip on the ice, chatter erupts with details of phone calls from cousins in Arizona, old neighbors in Texas, a brother-in-law in Florida.

Ding! Ding Ding! It's Audrey on the kitchen timer. A few loud rings reel everyone in, and they quiet down again to hear the writing prompt for next week: "Here's Why I Haven't Moved to ___."

"It's up to you to fill in the blank," I say, encouraging them to toy with different forms for this assignment. "Think about writing it as a letter to the people who are calling, or maybe even a poem."

When Audrey joined our memoir-writing class in 2009, she told us her decision to write was due in large part to the time and travel she'd put into unearthing data about her relatives. She'd spent hours at her computer, and even more time at the South Carolina Archives, the Old Edgefield District Genealogical Society, the Great Lakes Regional Archives, and Chicago's Newberry Library.

Audrey can tell how intrigued I am by all her research. Over a cup of coffee at a local coffee shop, she tells me more of what she's learned.

The 1870 Census was the first U.S. census to list all persons, including former slaves, as individuals. "I don't have their slave records, but I do know my great-grandparents lived in Edgefield County in 1870," she says, reasoning that they'd stayed there after the Emancipation Proclamation. "I have oral history and written data to back that up, but what I'm missing is the voice of my older relatives, what they were thinking, what they were feeling and like that. That's why I keep taking your class. So my stories don't get lost like theirs are."

She then reveals that she's pretty sure she's figured out who owned her great-grandparents as slaves.

I've heard this genealogy stuff can get addictive, but does she really want to know who the slave owners are? Audrey doesn't skip a beat. "Oh, yeah!" she says.

I drum up the courage to ask an even more awkward question: Why?

Her answer is obvious. I'm embarrassed I had to ask.

"Most people do want to know who the slave owners were," she says. "In most cases, they're an ancestor, too."

BACK IN CLASS the next week, we learn many reasons my writers are entrenched Chicagoans: grandchildren, friends, public transportation, culture, independence, Lake Michigan, too hard to pack, the change of seasons, resistance to change, you name it.

From Audrey's essay, we learn that she had seriously considered moving back to Edgefield County, South Carolina. But it's no longer the place of her childhood. So, to my great fortune, Audrey stayed in Chicago. Every Wednesday now she stops at the front office to pick up the key to our classroom, hands out her handmade name tags to writers, and passes around the Scrabble tiles and attendance sheet. Audrey claims she is bossy. I say she has strong leadership skills. "I'm nice about it," she acknowledges. "It's in my nature."

Once class is over, Audrey walks outside with us to make sure Whitney finds a spot to "empty." We usually talk about her daughter Lala, the crocheting classes she volunteers to lead at her local library on Chicago's Southwest side, what books we're reading. Then one day she starts wondering out loud about leading a memoir-writing class like ours at her library.

"I won't get paid, and like that, and I won't take away any of your students," she promises. "And I'll keep coming to our class, don't you worry."

The only thing I worry about is that I might miss her cheek when I plant a kiss.

"Do it!" I exclaim, opting to hug her instead. I'm flattered, and curious, too. If her class is successful, it will help confirm a theory I've been working on: the unconventional method I've come up with to lead classes without being able to see might work well for teachers who can see, too.

Why I Have Not Moved to South Carolina
By Audrey Mitchell

I used to think I would move to South Carolina after I retired. Both my folks migrated separately from a small town in Edgefield County, South Carolina, in the 1920s. My mother made annual visits home when she was single. Those visits continued after she and my father married. My father only returned twice, when his mother passed and again on a visit in 1972. He wasn't too keen on the place.

When we were small children, my mother took my sister and me with her on visits. We found it kind of rustic and not very pleasant...you know, outhouses and well water. But we endured. *Fresh country air and all that running space helped.*

As we got older, my mother made the visits by herself. I had bonded with cousins and other family members I'd met in South Carolina, and kept in contact through letters and phone calls. A few of my aunts and uncles saved my letters and when they passed away, these letters were returned to me. Knowing that they kept my letters all that time only tightened the bond.

In the late 1980s I started making annual trips to South Carolina to visit relatives. I wanted to regain that closeness I had as a child, especially since both my parents now were gone. The warm and pleasant sentiments from my aunts and uncles were so comforting. It was enticing and alluring. All I could think about was this would be a pleasant place to live. It was not as rustic as I remembered – indoor plumbing everywhere and even the shanties shacks had air conditioning.

The mall was within an hour's drive. You wanted to buy everything in sight because the prices were so low. The country was quiet and peaceful. I liked getting up early take a walk up the roads.

I'd see a lot of relatives on my visits. One of my older cousins coined the phrase "door poppers." It's short visits to as many people as you can in a period of time. I think our top count was 15 in one area. No matter how short the visit, the people were glad to see you. Most of the people we visited were the elderly aunts, uncles, and cousins.

Things were so quaint. Several of my visits were noted in the local newspaper, The Edgefield Advertiser. *Within the last 10 years or so, the roads have been given names in place of route numbers. A few roads were named for some of my* relatives – "Anna's Lane" or "Adams Way." I must make this my retirement home, I thought.

As years passed, my dreams of going there dimmed. Things began to change. First, many of the relatives that provided the welcome comfort passed away. The next generations were nice enough, but not as thoughtful and caring. They were busy with their jobs and lives, some even moving away on their retirements. My thoughts had been that I would come to a place that would remain a quiet country town, but it was getting quite busy. The next generations were unlike their elders. A home-cooked meal became take-out. No "door poppers" with them. They are hardly home.

I thought I knew the traditions and behavior of the people in the area, but as generations change, so does the culture. It was great that the mall was close, but maybe I would have managed if it weren't so close.

I'll continue visits as long as I can, but I think I will stay in sweet home Chicago.

69

When the Saints Go Marching In

AFTER CHRISTMAS LAST year, Cheryl went to pick Flo up for a doctor's appointment and found our mom sitting in her nightgown, unable to move her legs. An ambulance took Flo to the hospital.

If you've been through this with a grandparent or mother or father, you know how the story goes. Hospitalization, one malady leads to another, frustration, weeks or months of rehab, hope, ups and downs, ups and downs.

Our sensational sister Cheryl lives in Elmhurst, the town where we grew up and where Flo's condo is. Cheryl is retired, and had been stopping in to check on Flo every single day. That routine continued when Flo was in the hospital, and then in a rehab facility.

Cheryl would stop at Flo's condo first to pick up Flo's mail – Flo always, always loved getting cards and letters in the mail. She did Flo's laundry and brought clean clothes along to rehab, attended meetings with doctors, nurses, therapists, and social workers. She translated the medical jargon into wording that Flo could understand.

Once Flo agreed to move to assisted living rather than return to her condo, Cheryl helped figure out what Flo should bring to the new digs, and what to leave behind. Cheryl packed boxes and filled out paperwork for Flo. She and her children moved select pieces of furniture and other belongings to the new place bit by bit, until it was all set for Flo's move there. Cheryl did all that without complaint, shrugging off our gratitude with a that's-what-you-do attitude that I know she inherited from you-know-who: Flo. "I'm lucky to be the one who lives closest to Mom – it means I get to be the one who's able to help."

Flo had already started asking us way back in her 70s and 80s to let her know which of her things we'd like to have some-day. She never said the words "when I die." We knew what she meant, though. Marilee had chosen an oak table, Bev requested a rocking chair. Flo would write each name on a piece of paper and Scotch-tape it to the bottom of our selection.

I chose her cedar chest. Flo called it her "hope chest" and only opened it on special occasions, when she'd be dressing up a kitchen or dining room table with fancy linens. Flo's bottles and powders had always perched in groups on doilies atop the lid. One of us – don't ask me who – spilled an entire bottle of her perfume once. The stain is still there.

The new apartment was significantly smaller than Flo's condo, so she told Cheryl not to bother moving the cedar chest there. Mike and I took it home with us and installed it in our front hallway. "I folded a quilt that Grandma Moos made on top of it," I told Flo during our next visit. "It's perfect, Mom!" When I leaned down to kiss her cheek and thank her, I hit the top of her head instead. Flo laughed, and I did, too. We were both tickled.

FLO CELEBRATED HER 98th birthday on April 20th at the rehab facility, where she'd made a lot of progress. When Mike and I celebrated Mother's Day with her there, she was in great spirits, full of news about her new apartment and eager to show off the new place.

Flo's new apartment was connected physically to the rehab facility. She loved parades, so it seemed perfectly natural for Whitney and me to follow behind Mike pushing her in her wheelchair to see her new digs.

Flo cooed once we were over the threshold. "Look at that!" she said. "Cheryl even put my mother and dad's wedding picture up. It's right there above my bed." She pointed the photo out to Mike and described the old oversized oval frame so I could, you know, picture it.

On our drive back to Chicago that night, Mike said, "The place looks like...Flo's!" Cheryl had already hung a lot of other pictures on the walls. Flo's own pull-out couch and kitchen table were already set up there. "Even the Bose radio," he laughed. "I can hear *Prairie Home Companion* already."

And then, another setback. Flo wouldn't be able to move to her new place the week after Mother's Day as planned.

Physical therapists, occupational therapists, and speech

therapists weighed in. Flo tried her best to please them. She worked hard, and she continued to light up with every visitor who came to see her. She commented on the beautiful spring weather. She told everyone who visited how good they looked and how much she loved them.

I always held Flo's hand during my visits, but one day when Mike and I walked in she told me to be careful. "I just got my nails done," she announced. She didn't think they were wet, though. I rubbed my hands over her fingertips to admire the shine. "How long did it take them to do this?" I asked. "98 years!" she said with a laugh. It was her first mani.

And then another setback. And another. And another. We, all of us, were worried. Concerned. Anxious. She'd bounced back many times, but maybe now her 98 years were finally catching up with her.

Mike was having an especially hard time with this. His mother and father had died 25 years earlier. Flo was the only one left. She was a big Gus fan, and was Mike's champion, too. Through all of the tribulations Mike and I faced, people would always ask him how I, Beth, was doing. Every time Flo saw Mike, though, she'd ask, "How are you, Mike?" She worried out loud that Mike looked tired (he often did), he drove too much (he did), and that he needed to rest (he did).

I knew she was worried about me, too, but she didn't have to say it. Not only did I have Mike, but she'd also provided me with six older brothers and sisters to look out for me. She knew I was in good hands. Sometimes when she looked at Mike, though, she saw someone who was in over his head. She'd been in a similar spot 50 years earlier. She knew how it felt, and she made sure Mike knew she was in his corner.

FLO WASN'T BOUNCING back. Not this time.

You communicate differently when you are alongside someone while they are lying down. When I visited Flo those last days, I could hold her hand, but even when sitting alongside her, the bedrails and IV poles and tubes made it difficult to get close enough to cuddle and talk right into her ear. Like we'd always done at Christmas. I'd slept in a double bed with Flo for four years after my dad died. I was seven years old before being moved to a bunkbed to share a room with Bev. Even then I'd sneak out to cuddle with Flo. She never kicked me out.

I considered sliding into the hospital bed and getting under the sheets with Flo. But when she was still talking some, she'd complained of back pain. Might my crawling in bed add to her pain? And what would the staff think of the blind woman leashing her Seeing Eye dog to the bedpost, just to make the 98-year-old patient scoot over in the bed? Just to talk right into her ear? I talked to her from the side of the bed instead.

The family contacted hospice. Cheryl encouraged each of us to look around the little apartment. "She won't be moving there now," Cheryl said. "Why don't you see if there's anything in the apartment that you might want."

Mike walked me over. He opened and closed drawers. "Here's her box of greeting cards," he said. Flo never missed a birthday or a wedding anniversary. He described utensils in kitchen drawers, fitted sheets folded perfectly in the linen closet.

I unbuckled Whitney's harness and let her nose around while I rubbed my palm across the kitchen table Cheryl's kids had moved over from Spa Flo. I brushed my hand across Flo's dresser, and ran across a book I recognized by its size and slick cover: a copy of *Safe & Sound*, right there by her jewelry box. When I turned away from the dresser, I bumped into the bed, felt across the covers for the pillows, lay down and cried.

We left with a small cutting board, the copy of the book I'd signed for Flo, and her Bose radio.

Jazz music was playing softly in her hospital room when we stopped to say goodbye and tell her we loved her. "We're going to be alright," I said, squeezing her hand one last time. "But we're sure going to miss you."

We sisters got together at Flo's condo to begin planning the funeral and made some thoughtful, good decisions. One of them was asking Doug to put together a traditional jazz combo for the service.

Flo died on Friday, June 20, 2014. She had slept through the entire day, and Cheryl was there at her side with her kids and grandchildren until dinnertime, when Bev would be coming in from Michigan. Cheryl whispered her goodbyes and love yous to Flo when she left and added one last thing. "Beverle will be here with you any minute. She's on her way."

Bev arrived ten minutes later. "A nurse in the hallway told me she was sorry, but I thought she just meant about Mom not being able to move to her apartment." Bev wasn't aware our mother had just died until she walked into the room and saw for herself. Flo had died in the short interim between Cheryl and Bev's visit. I believe she chose to die alone. She didn't like being a burden.

MIKE AND WHITNEY and I arrive at the church for the funeral and find the musicians warming up in the church kitchen. Many of them had played with Doug 50 years ago when he was in his twenties. I knew them, and they knew Flo. Greeting them is a wonderful start to a beautiful celebration.

The combo plays for an hour-long visitation before the funeral starts. Any time Flo heard traditional jazz like this, she'd clap her hands, do a little dance and say, "This is my kind of music!" Friends and family are surprised – and delighted – to hear jazz when they walk into the church foyer. The live music makes us smile and think of Flo. Exactly what she would have wanted.

Flo had requested an open casket. At the wake, I walk up there with Mike to pay my respects, but I don't touch her. I am afraid she'll feel hard and cold. I want to remember her soft and warm.

I do not want to speak at the funeral – I'm not confident I can memorize or recite a speech. I agree to be the emcee, though.

As it comes close to starting time, I have Whitney lead me to the front pew. People come to say hello, I accept their condolences, thank them for coming, and ask them to tell me who else is there that they know. It is one way for me to sort out who to make sure to talk with later, and just how many people have come.

I spend some minutes alone in the front pew, too, and use that time to talk with Flo.

"What a good party, Mom," I say. "This is your kind of music."

My job introducing the speakers is easy. None of them are her blood relatives. They are four people who especially loved her. Mike is one of two sons-in law to give a talk. At the luncheon afterwards a friend points out that having men stand in front of an audience and tear up about the death of their mother-in-law speaks volumes about Flo.

In the middle of the service, Doug opens a rendition of "Just a Closer Walk with Thee" with a trombone solo. He fluffs the first note a bit, a poignant symbol of our family in mourning. The rest of the tune is perfect, and when I get up to emcee and thank Doug, it takes me a while before I can go on.

The ceremony is a mix of biblical reading, prayer, and music, ending with a rousing rendition of "When the Saints Go Marching in," – one of Flo's all-time favorites.

Later I learn that two of Flo's grandsons who'd been chosen as pallbearers broke into tears as they carried her out of the church. The casket was heavy. They couldn't reach into their pocket for a tissue or handkerchief, so the tears just flowed. These were forty-plus-year-old tough working men who I've never known to cry. Someone later said it was the most touching moment of the entire ceremony. I wish I could have seen it.

ALL OF IT, everything, my life with Flo, that she really has died, it all comes together at the burial. Eight-year-old Floey must see it in my face. "Are you alright?" she asks, modeling her behavior on the grown-ups she's been watching all week. Her little voice is so sincere and caring that I finally let go and cry.

We have each been given a flower at the cemetery, and after some Bible verses and such, we are told to bring our flower up and place it on the casket. How will I find it? What if I fall into the hole with Flo?

"Need help?" It is that sincere little girl again. Floey leads me to the casket, holds my hand with the flower in it, lifts it over the casket.

"You can drop it now."

70

Together

THE DAY AFTER Flo's burial, I go with Floey and her family to visit the grave. Floey has me sit down alongside her near the grave marker and guides my fingers over Flo's name.

The grass under me feels cool and inviting. I slip off my sandals, turn around, slide my bottom along the grass with my head near the headstone, stretch out my long legs, and lie on my back with the sun on my face. Next to Flo. Next to Ed Finke. Just the three of us.

Flo never talked about my dad when I was a little girl. She couldn't afford a gravestone back then, so during weekly visits to the cemetery we knew this spot by the round silver-dollar-sized cement marker at the head of his plot. That, and its proximity to the huge slab depicting the Lord's Supper.

We'd approach the plot, and after commenting on the weeds or whether the cemetery had mowed the grass lately, Flo would send us to the water pump to fill the glass juice bottle with water for the flowers she'd cut from the back yard. My sister Bev was very thin but all bone and muscle, a good athlete and proud of it. She'd push the pump lever up and down, up and down, while I held the juice bottle firmly underneath to catch the water. Marilee, our disciplined and dependable older sister, could be trusted to bring the bottle back to Flo without spilling a drop.

Maybe Flo talked with our dad while we were busy at the pump. Or maybe she talked with him while we ran around to look at the Lord's Supper. But she never talked to – or about – him in our house. While we were graveside, she'd just talk about the weeds that needed to be picked.

Flo never told me what my father thought of me, whether he'd played with me as a baby, whether he loved me. As a young girl, I thought I ought to love him, but truth is, I never missed him. At least not consciously.

As I grew into my teens and headed to college and started assessing my looks, I had to acknowledge that I looked more like the photos of my father than I did of my mother. Flo was blue-eyed, short, and curvaceous. My face is longer, I am tall and flat-chested. She and I can both be a bit mischievous; perhaps we have a similar look when we are cooking up something.

During college breaks I had a waitress job in a German restaurant in my hometown. I brought an order of sauerbraten to a middle-aged couple once and the husband asked if I was Ed Finke's daughter.

I had never heard those three words strung together in my entire life. Ed Finke's daughter.

I looked the man right in the eyes. He looked sincere. "Yes," I said. "I'm the youngest."

"You look just like him," he said. "He was a good man."

And Flo was a good woman. And I was a good daughter. And here we all are, together in the sunshine.

71

Staring Contest

NEVER DID MAKE it back to finger paint with the Montessori school kids on Chicago's South Side last Christmas, but on this September day, Whitney and I enjoy a magical morning with the fourth, fifth and sixth graders there. The students are writing essays for a book they'll publish in November, and their teacher has asked me to come talk about memoir-writing.

The kids want to talk about other stuff first, though. Like what it's like to be blind, whether I can blink or not, does my dog sleep with me in my bed, how come I open my eyes at all if I can't see. A thoughtful fifth-grader asks a sweet, caring question:

"Do your eyes hurt?"

"No," I say. "My eyes don't hurt at all."

That answer prompts a question I'd never been asked before. "When you're blind, can you still cry?"

For a quick moment I consider explaining what tear ducts are, telling the kids how they work, but then I think about Jamal, a sixth-grade boy who'd approached Whitney and me right when we'd walked into the classroom that morning. He wanted to describe the memorial t-shirt he was wearing – it had photos of a cousin who'd died on it. Another boy had chimed in then to tell me he gets angry sometimes because his father is in prison. I keep my answer simple.

"Yes, I can cry," I say. "And sometimes, I do."

I picture the kids nodding their heads, understanding. The class is still for a moment, but then a boy in back breaks the silence.

"Would you win in a staring contest?"

We all have fun with that one. His question sparks a heavy discussion of staring-contest rules. Do you have to look right into someone's eyes? What if you're close but not looking right in their eyes? Is it just all about who blinks first?

After the long Q&A comes the writing exercise, one I use with my memoir-writing classes from time to time.

We all take a minute to write a few sentences that define our lives, then we read our sentences out loud.

I had learned that Jamal is new to the Montessori class, but his little sister Shamiya has been at Oglesby Montessori for years. Jamal reads his writing out loud: "I seen too much drama in my life. I wish I had a dog for a best friend and happiness."

A fifth-grade girl writes: "I'm oldest. One brother, 1 sister. Mom raised. Grandma died. Auntie baby died when came out. Happy that I am happy."

We go through an editing process to strike through words we've written and cut our stories down to six words. Some of the kids read their six-word stories out loud, and then we strike through more words to cut our stories down to just three.

The fifth-grade girl decides on "I'm oldest. Happy." A boy in class ends up with "I am awesome." Jamal's three words are downright poetic: "Drama and happiness."

The classroom teacher had asked in advance if I could leave the students with a writing prompt they could work on after Whitney and I go home. I have them finally cut their piece down to one word.

"That one word is your writing prompt for today," I say, and as Whitney and I leave to go home, they are already squirreling away in different corners of the room to start writing on their topics:

twin
oldest
angry
grandma
youngest
awesome

A teacher's aide tells me later that Jamal settled on "drama" as his one word, but then found that topic difficult to write about with all his classmates there in the room with him.

"I asked if he thought he could work on writing his memoir at home, and he said he thought he could," the teacher's aide says, adding that she suggested that he could write about something happy while he was still there at school. "He and I thought he could write about what it has been like to experience Montessori class as a new kid."

72

Doretha's Gift

HANNELORE LEARNED ABOUT our class from staff members at Blind Service Association. Tom's kids were tired of hearing him tell the same stories over and over. "They made me come so I'd shut up and write 'em down." A retired elementary school teacher signed up so she could tell stories like the ones she'd read to her third-graders for all those years. Writing exercises in a book about bibliotherapy gave Regan relief from her chronic pain, so when she finished the book, she signed up for my class.

Writers sign up for my memoir classes for all sorts of reasons, but most simply want to get their stories down on paper to leave for their families. Those writers just need writing prompts and deadlines to get them started. Some start off writing their own stories, then keep coming just to listen to others.

Only one writer has ever enrolled in a writing class of mine because her therapist told her to. Then again, maybe she's the only one to admit it.

Doretha is a soft-spoken woman with a velvety tenor voice. When she first introduces herself to our downtown Chicago class in 2010, she comes right out and tells us why she'd signed up. "My psychiatrist told me to come."

We don't hear another word from Doretha for four or five weeks. She's so quiet, and she sits so far away from me at the table, some days I don't even know she's there.

After weeks of listening, Doretha takes Audrey aside after class and says she's ready to start writing now, too. She was afraid that she would be judged by other writers in class at first, but she eventually realized there were other people in class who wrote about hard lives, so maybe she could, too.

Audrey encourages her to give it a try, and Doretha returns with a simple essay introducing us to the members of her family tree – a kind of biblical "my sister Mary married Albert and begat three sons, Albert Jr., James, and John."

Not a memoir exactly, but I've learned to never discourage a new writer. When the timer finally, finally rings, I tell her she's got quite a family. "Can't wait to hear more about them next week."

Doretha is encouraged, and the essay she comes back with the next week sounds more like the Book of Job than the Book of Chronicles.

When Doretha was four years old, she used to hide behind the banister at the top of the stairs to watch the poker games her daddy hosted every night to supplement his low pay.

One night, her daddy got so angry at the man he was playing against that he reached under the table, found his gun, aimed at the man's head, and killed him.

Little Doretha saw the blood. She saw the police come. She saw them put handcuffs on her daddy, and she saw him whisper something just as they were leading him out the door. The police looked up, and when they saw Doretha hiding behind the banister they allowed the culprit one last word with his daughter.

"Don't you tell nobody what you saw tonight," he ordered his little girl. "Don't you tell nobody."

Little Doretha listened to her father. For four years, she didn't speak at all.

This week, when the kitchen timer rings, we all urge her to keep reading.

In subsequent stories we learn about Doretha's mother's inability to cope, Doretha's car trip with her little brother Bobby to live with a faraway aunt and uncle, their visits to see their mother in the Asylum for Colored Insane in North Carolina.

"They gave her a lobotomy," Doretha reads in class, her voice so steady and low. "I didn't know about that until I got older."

After she gets that far, her weekly stories switch to the present. We learn that she has a grown son and find out where her little brother Bobby is now. And is that a little smile I hear when she reads about the relatives she's found in the Carolinas, and her trips to visit them?

As weeks pass and Doretha continues writing and reading, she begins to establish friendships in class. She shares stories about her granddaughter, and before class one day I hear her rolling her eyes as she confesses to a writer across the table that she's learned how to send text messages. "It's the only way that girl will answer!"

When one writer moves to live with her family in California in 2011, Doretha's granddaughter drives her grandma to the goodbye party. Doretha settles in a comfy seat right next to me, and the two of us carry on like old girlfriends.

Doretha's attendance in class wavers after that, and when she misses too many classes in a row, Audrey gets on the phone to check on her. Doretha tells Audrey that she is battling cancer. "She's going to fight it, though," Audrey tells us. "And she gave her memoirs to her son. She wants him to read them."

As Doretha's end approaches, her son, Gregory, starts reading her memoirs and speaking with his mother about her stories. Just before she dies, Doretha gives him her friend Audrey's phone number.

Gregory calls Audrey when the time comes. We are all heartbroken when she tells us in class that Doretha has died at home.

Audrey doesn't like to drive much anymore, but she offers to get behind the wheel and drive to the funeral home to represent us all at Doretha's service.

"I'm glad I did," she tells me later. "People there didn't even know Doretha was a writer – it wasn't in her obituary."

Doretha might never have written a word if Audrey hadn't encouraged her, and we'd all be the lesser for it. Afterwards Audrey sends me her notes from the talk she gave at Doretha's funeral.

Doretha's Gift

By Audrey Mitchell

Doretha and I shared something very important to both of us. We both belong to a memoir writing group called "Me, Myself and I."

Our leader, Beth Finke, myself and all of the members of the writing group send our compassion and condolences to the family. We want you to know that we all have the highest esteem for Doretha.

We are a group of senior citizens that write stories about our lives for ourselves and our families. In our class, we share stories with each other by reading them out loud.

When Doretha first joined the group, she was very quiet. She only listened and did not read during the first few sessions. As a new member, we wondered if she had anything to say. Finally, Doretha decided to read her stories to the class and "boy" did she have something to say.

Doretha was a prolific writer. She was clear and concise in her words, sentences and phrases. When Doretha read, every one listened. She captivated the class of 16 or so senior citizens with her stories.

There are two ladies in class who have hearing difficulties and when Doretha read, they would move closer to where Doretha sat so they could hear every word she had to say. They did not want to miss anything...nor did any of the other class members.

She read her stories in a way that enticed you into listening. She shared the times in her life that were challenging and as you listened to her read you could feel the pain she went through.

But as she continued to read, we also knew that she fought hard to overcome those hardships to become the woman she was. She would also write about the better times in her life.

Doretha always said that writing was very therapeutic for her. She wrote to share her life events with her family and others to show life is not always grand but if you worked hard at it as she did, you can make it better.

You and your family have been given a wonderful gift from Doretha. She put her stories down on paper for you because she wanted you to know where she came from, what she went through, and how she survived. As you read what she wrote in her memoirs, it will give you a very true and thoughtful picture of Doretha.

May God Bless You and Your Family.

73

Underground

WHEN I WAS a kid I thought it was magical, the way snowfall muffled the sound around me. I still do. But the driving snowstorms of this winter aren't the magic I'm looking for.

I regularly use an underground subway stop to get safely across a four-lane highway near our apartment. Whitney guides me down the steps on the south side, we walk underneath the highway, climb the stairs at the north side exit, and, voila! We're across.

Every time we exit the north side stairway, a baritone-sandpaper voice rings out from the gaggle of homeless men hanging out there. "Nine o'clock!" he belts out when he thinks I should turn left. "Twelve o'clock!" when he's decided I should go straight.

I take this route often. I know where I'm going. It's important that Whitney follows my commands, and his shouts can make it difficult for her to hear me. "Three o'clock! Twelve o'clock! Seven o'clock!" It's not easy to fake a smile when you're gritting your teeth, but I do my best. He's only trying to help.

Once when Mike walked Whitney and me to the train station, we skipped the subway trick and walked right across the four-lane highway together. I could hear the good-hearted-yet-annoying-Tom-Waits voice above all the others in a heated conversation across the street. Oh no, I thought, tightening my grip on Mike's elbow. Here comes the time clock. But Tom Waits ignored me. He kept talking with his friends. I let go of Mike's elbow and picked up Whitney's harness, letting her take the lead again.

But now I'm on my way home from the train station in the midst of a snow squall. Snow pelts the back of my hooded jacket as Whitney weaves me around the suburbanites heading to the train station. No wonder commuters call these things "blinding snowstorms" – they're all trudging our way with their heads down, blinded by the icy bullets.

Snow has accumulated on the raised, circular bumps I rely on to tell me we're at the edge of a curb ramp. The further we get from the train station, the fewer pedestrians cross our path. Suddenly, we are alone. No footsteps in the snow, no sounds of shovels, nobody there. Lost in a snowstorm. Where are we?

My iPhone is in my bag. I could call Mike. But what would I say? How can you tell somebody where to rescue you when you don't know where you are?

And then I hear it. The voice of an angel, though I'm not sure smoking is allowed in heaven. "Twelve o'clock!" It's Tom Waits, my subway sentry. I pick up Whitney's harness, square my shoulders towards the foghorn, and command, "Whitney, forward!"

Wonderdog Whitney pulls me toward the voice in the wilderness. "Twelve o'clock!" he calls out, sounding like he ate cinders for breakfast. "Twelve o'clock! Twelve o'clock!" When we get close enough, Tom Waits reaches out to put his gloved hand in mine and lead Whitney and me to the subway stairs. Once there, he places my palm ever so gently onto the banister, then turns around and walks away without a word.

74

Anises

IT'S OUR FIRST Finke Christmas without Flo. Ever.

Every year at this time, Flo would have been getting out her ceramic Christmas bowl and filling it with ruby-red anise candy for the holidays. Smart woman, that Flo, knowing the spicy taste of the hard candy was not terribly appealing to us kids, which meant we didn't sneak pieces when she wasn't looking so it would last throughout the season.

Floey surprises us with a poem she has written in her great-grandmother's honor.

Anises
By AnnMarie Florence Czerwinski
4th grade

> *As the sweet taste of licorice*
> *Melts in my mouth,*
> *Memories come back to me.*
> *Ones of my great grandmother*

Who always smelled of flowers and bleach
With her silvery white hair
Neatly curling on top of her head.
Oh, the joyful memories anises can bring back,
Even if some are never
going to come back for real.
So I'll just have another anise.

75

Grace Place I

I'M LEADING MEMOIR-WRITING classes on Mondays, Wednesdays and Thursdays. My Tuesdays are devoted to the part-time work I do for Easterseals, and I keep Fridays open for visits to elementary schools. So when a call comes from Chicago's Center for Life and Learning (CLL) asking if I'm interested in leading a memoir-writing class there, I want to say no.

CLL is part of Fourth Presbyterian Church, a sanctuary nestled between skyscrapers and fancy stores on Chicago's Magnificent Mile. Known for its music and acoustics, Fourth Pres boasts the largest pipe organ in Chicago. The stained glass windows in the sanctuary are said to be beautiful. Same goes for the church's members.

"Our last memoir teacher was from Second City," the woman on the phone says. The class has been going on its own since that teacher left, but now enrollment is dwindling. "The class needs a leader," she continues. "We heard good things about your classes at Lincoln Park Village, and we were hoping you might take this one on, too."

Hearing my name mentioned with Chicago hallmarks like Second City and Fourth Presbyterian Church boosts my ego. I say yes.

This proves to be a mistake.

I INTRODUCE MY teaching method to the new class. They are pleased with the weekly writing prompt idea and the 500-word limit. They like knowing they can email their pieces ahead of time if they want editing, and they sound relieved when I tell them we won't be doing critiques during class. "Our last teacher made us do that," one of them mutters. "We don't like critiques."

That's not the only thing they don't like. I find out the next week that they don't like relying solely on their sense of hearing while fellow students read essays aloud.

"The Center gives us free photocopying," one says, passing copies of her assignment around the table. "We've always done it this way. We like reading along."

The cost of photocopying isn't the reason I ask people to listen, but with this free service at their fingertips, the class insists on continuing their routine. "That's how we do it. We've always done it that way."

During the third week one student asks if anyone wants two free tickets to hear Patti Smith. I still haven't learned everyone's name, but this Ticket Lady says, "She's giving a talk at the Chicago Humanities Festival."

No one speaks up.

"No one wants these?" Ticket lady is incredulous. "Did

you read *Just Kids*? Her memoir? It's fantastic."

Ugh. "You liked it?" I ask, equally incredulous.

"You didn't?"

"I hated it," I say. "All she did was namedrop."

Ticket Lady laughs. "You might namedrop, too, if you hung around with Jimi Hendrix and Allen Ginsberg."

It's my turn to laugh. "Touché!" Ticket Lady has spunk. I like that.

"No one else wants the tickets, then?" I ask, and when no one speaks up, I tell Ticket Lady I'll take them. "Maybe she talks better than she writes."

Ticket lady introduces herself after class and presses the passes into my palm. "I'm Regan," she says, pronouncing the first syllable with a long E. Right then and there I should have used my sixth sense to respond with something like "You mean, like the girl in *The Exorcist*?"

76

Grace Place II

MICHIGAN AVENUE PROVES too chaotic for me to plow through with a Seeing Eye dog, and taking a bus to and from the Center for Life and Learning on Thursday mornings makes the turn-around time too tight for me to get to my afternoon class in Lincoln Park on time.

Even worse, I'm the only one in class who can't read along while students recite their weekly assignments. That leaves the class leader at a disadvantage.

This isn't going to work.

Eyebrows up! Linda, a member of my fellow-writers group, just completed her MFA this year. She's pretty enthusiastic about all she's learned, and when I tell her I've decided to bow out of the CLL class, I ask if she might be interested in taking it over. She is.

Regan follows me out of class. "You live down there by Grace Place, don't you?"

I do. Grace Place is an urban community center run by

the Episcopal Church. The old four-story building sits right across the street from our apartment. They rent rooms out for everything from yoga classes to chamber music concerts. My polling place is there, and Printers Row Book Fair, now renamed Printers Row Lit Fest, holds sessions there every summer.

"Why don't you see if you can rent space there?" Regan asks. "You're good enough to start your own class."

How can I resist that kind of confidence? I negotiate the rent and set the class up to start in a month, meeting at the same time the CLL class meets: 10:00 a.m. Thursday mornings. The across-the-street commute with Whitney will be so short that I'll be able to get back home in plenty of time to catch my ride to the afternoon class in Lincoln Park, no problem.

Mike helps me set up online registration forms and produces flyers to promote the class. Whitney the gallant Seeing Eye dog guides me to local businesses to plaster those flyers on every bulletin board and store window I can find. Enough people sign up to make the class a go.

THREE MILES AWAY at the Center for Life and Learning, my writer-friend Linda is getting started with her class. Building on some advice and tips from me, she adopts my 500-word limit for her new class and gives weekly writing prompts. But her students pick playing cards instead of Scrabble tiles to determine who reads when.

Rather than offer to edit the essays her students write, Linda puts her time and MFA education to work creating weekly handouts with sample short stories, essays, or poems for students to read at home. "Notice how the writer makes shifts in time with small phrases," one handout might say. "Look closely at how the author uses simile and metaphor."

Linda and I communicate by phone and email for the first few weeks. Unlike me, she seems fine with letting each student pass copies of their work around the table. As her confidence grows, we share fewer emails and phone calls.

When she phones me out of the blue later that month, her "Hello" shakes with enthusiasm. No doubt she's calling to thank me again for giving her that CLL class. How silly! She doesn't need to do that.

I'm about to tell her so when she cuts me off. Her voice isn't shaking from happiness. It's shaking with distress.

She'd gotten word about the Grace Place class I was about to start. "It's great that you are starting your own class," she says. "But did you have to pick the same time mine meets?"

Truth is, I did. "Thursday morning is the only time slot I have open to lead a fourth class each week," I tell her.

She's miserable, sure that every student in the Thursday morning CLL memoir class will be defecting hers to join mine.

I concede that Regan might very well sign up for my new class. "But that's only because she's the one who suggested I start the new class in the first place."

Linda mutters something about losing one of her best writers.

Her list of concerns continues, and the conversation lasts far longer than it needs to. But she is indeed right about one thing: I could have told her I was starting a new memoir class that would be meeting the same time as hers. I apologize to her for the oversight. It was a selfish decision. I wanted to get my own class started in a way that worked best for me, and was worried that running it by Linda ahead of time would muddle up the works.

Linda is still irked when we hang up, and I am shaken, too. Welcome to the business world, I tell myself. The decisions Mizz Haughty President of Beth Finke, Inc. makes can hurt other people's feelings.

77

Bob and the Pranksters

NEARLY ALL OF the writers in my Grace Place class take me up on my offer to edit their essays each week. Writers in my downtown class send essays my way each week, too. Ditto the writers in my second class in Lincoln Park.

It all takes time, but editing these essays teaches me a lot about my own writing and helps me appreciate – and accept suggestions and comments from – those who edit my work.

And, hey, it's flattering to know so many writers trust me with their work now. Bob is in my Monday Lincoln Park Village class, and I get a kick out of hearing my talking computer bark out stories of his childhood escapades with his buddies Squeaky LaPort, Da Da Hernandez, Mario DeSandro, and Bobby Butts Eisenberg, a.k.a. the Pranksters.

The ladies in class tell me that Bob wears his long white hair in a ponytail. Sure isn't how I picture an 80-year-old man who makes his living cutting and styling hair. He's a student of the Vidal Sassoon method, and after 60 years in the business he has cut back to part-time and takes an afternoon off every week to join our Monday class. Bob drives Whitney and me home after class, too, and always walks me right to our building's door to give me a peck on the cheek when he says goodbye.

Bob grew up in Chicago's "Little Italy," a neighborhood full of Jews, Italians, and Mexicans. When I assign the prompt "What Are You Afraid Of?" we learn more of his story: "My mother died right after I was born. I moved in with my mother's mother until I was six. Then she died, too."

After finishing the school year in his grandmother's neighborhood, tiny seven-year-old Bob is sent to military school. Sundry other relatives take him in after that. "As I look back into my past I count six different grammar schools I attended and seven different families I lived with." As tough as that must have been, he is so grateful for his escape from military school that he writes about them all with a sense of joy and appreciation.

When I assign the prompt "Of Course It's Illegal," we get a taste of what life was like as a Prankster in 1940s Chicago:

Of Course It's Illegal
By Bob Eisenberg

"Of course it's illegal," I said to the judge. Before you decide whether we're guilty or innocent, please let me explain how we came to our decision on what is illegal and what isn't."

"OK, Son," he said. "I'll listen to your story."

I put my hands in my pockets and started.

"Well, Judge, because I'm in my adolescence, I spend a lot of my time on the streets."

The story went on from there. I told him I belong to a

neighborhood gang called "The Pranksters" and that we were always looking for an innocent way to make money to support our pinball habit.

"All of us love to play pinballs at the arcade," I told the judge. "It keeps us off the streets." He was trying to hide a smile as he listened.

"There are 5 or 6 of us in our little gang and we are always coming up with ways of how to make money without hurting anyone. So what we did was make our way to Union Station," I told the judge, continuing my story. "As you may know, there are more than 25 phone booths in Union Station and each of us was responsible for just 5 of them."

I told him how we each brought a pocket full of toilet paper along to stuff up the coin returns in the booths.

"We left our phone booths then and waited about 15 minutes in an out-of-the-way location," I explained. "You know, a place where we couldn't be seen, while people rushed in and out of the booths. They lost their dimes that were resting on the toilet paper in the coin returns. When you think about it judge, they only lost one dime each, and it kept us busy playing pinballs all day, and we were off the streets. Think about that, Judge, before you make your decision."

I added one last important fact.

"On Friday nights we all went to Holy Family Church to say confession. Now I want you to know, Judge, I'm Jewish, all my friends are Italian and Mexican, but I thought it was such a good idea that I went to confession too. After 12 Hail Marys each, we were forgiven for our sins. And of course we should have stopped right there and been happy that we had been forgiven for the sins that we committed, but we got greedy and it was so easy for us to do the whole process again.

"But that's when we got caught and now we are here in front of you, pleading for you to give us a break. If you do, I can speak for everyone and say that this will never happen again."

The judge went back to his chambers to talk to our lawyer. After a while he came back to the court and brought all of us to the bench. He let us know that we were each on six months' probation and that we would have to report to a probation officer on a weekly basis. We were happy to keep on the straight and narrow...for a short while anyways.

78

Mike & Gus – The Sequel

SHORT VERSION: MIKE is okay. Gus is okay. We're all okay. We've made it through.

Long version: Gus is almost 30 years old now. Not much has changed. When we visit him, he still greets us with laughter or a clap of his hands. Although we can't know for sure, we like to think it's his way of letting us know he recognizes us and is happy to see us.

The past few years we've taken to putting him in his wheel-chair and walking him to a picnic table in the park across the street from his group home. I say "we" here, but I mean Mike. Gus weighs as much as I do now, so his dad is always the one to muscle him into his chair and push it when we're outside.

On this particular day, a bunch of kids are playing kickball on the baseball field at the park. Their battles over in-bounds or out-of-bounds remind me of the arguments my sister Bev and I used to have with the neighbor kids playing kickball on the street. So I can't help but smile when a cheer goes up after someone kicks a good one at Gus' park. Gus enjoys it, too – feelings like that are contagious, whatever your I.Q.

So there we are, sitting and enjoying the breeze and the sunshine, when one of the kids approaches our table, points to Gus, and asks, "Did that guy break his knee?" After some back and forth, we figure out this little boy's grandma is using a wheelchair after having knee surgery. Our new buddy sticks around for a while, asks us where "that guy" lives, and tells us about some of his friends at school. Eventually we have to say goodbye and walk Gus back home.

BACK IN OUR Chicago apartment, Mike walks through the door one day sounding shaken. On his way home he's seen a boy in a wheelchair. "The guy with him must have been his dad," Mike says. Father and son were both wearing ball caps, and Mike surmises the pair had just come out of their car and were getting ready for a walk. "The chair the kid was in wasn't one he could push on his own," Mike tells me, explaining that the boy had substantial physical disabilities. "You know, it had a major headrest and footrest, even more straps than Gus' has."

Mike can't help himself, he has to point out that the handles on this guy's wheelchair were higher than normal to make it easier for an adult caregiver to push. Low handles on wheelchairs have long been one of my husband's major pet peeves.

Mike describes how the father carefully adjusted and double-checked the boy's seatbelt and straps to make sure he would be safe. It was precisely what Mike used to do when Gus lived with us, and the image haunts him.

I hear mixed feelings of regret and confusion as he tells

319

me he'd considered saying something to the stranger and his
son in the wheelchair. "But what would I say?" he wonders
aloud. "That everything would be alright? I can't know that,
how would I know that?" So he ducked into a sandwich shop
instead, and by the time he came out with his Italian beef, the
man and his son were long gone. "I'm not sure walking up to
him and breaking into tears would be the right thing to do
anyway," he says with an uneasy laugh.

"Probably not," I say wistfully. My curiosity prompts a
question of my own. "Any idea now what you might have
said, though?"

Mike thinks a while before answering. "Well," he finally
says. "I wish I'd have told the dad that he wasn't alone."

Thoughts like that come easily to Mike – and given the
right situation, he is remarkably willing to share his struggles
with the world, especially when he thinks they'll be of help.
For years I'd been trying to convince him to have a regular gig
on my Safe & Sound blog. By then Mike was already doing
occasional guest posts on it, and he marveled at the oodles
of positive comments he'd get online, and also out loud from
friends and neighbors who'd greet us by saying how much they
enjoyed reading his essays. I also knew from experience that
writing personal essays can be therapeutic, but every time I
asked him to consider having a regular gig on the Safe & Sound
blog, he stuck to his story: "That blog is your thing, not mine."

Until one frosty winter day in 2014. Mike, Whitney and
I got to O'Hare only to discover that our flight to Washington,
D.C., to visit our dear friends Pick and Hank had been cancelled.
While we waited for another flight, we talked about everything

under the sun – housekeeping, budgets, writing, work, Facebook, Flo, books, business ideas, and...blogs, until we ran out of things to say. So while sitting silently at Gate B19 with Seeing Eye dog Whitney lying patiently at my feet, I got to thinking. Mike's pretty spent right now. I can catch him while he's weak.

Hey, Mike!" He answered with a not-so-nice, "What?" You know, the kind of okay-what-do-you-want-me-to-get-for-you-now-Beth sort of "What?"

Perfect. My question would come as a sort of surprise. A compliment, not a demand. "How about you write a post once a week on my blog?" We talked about a good time for him to start, what sorts of topics he could write about, how political he could get. "We could call it Mondays with Mike."

He gave in. The decision was made. And now, ever since February 3, 2014, Safe & Sound blog readers look forward to hearing from Mike every Monday.

Mike's posts openly discuss how he manages depression, along with posts about politics, magazine articles, movie reviews, baseball talk, and day-in-the-life sort of stuff about his family – especially Gus.

Mike wrote a book review about *Boy in the Moon* (an account of author Ian Brown and his wife raising and trying to understand their physically and developmentally disabled son, Walker) for the Safe & Sound blog. The post ends with a description of our feelings for Gus that says it all:

> *Beth doesn't mention our son Gus very often in these blog posts of hers. Like other parents, we love our son. Think about him. Worry about him. But loving a child who has severe disabilities can be difficult to explain, so we tend not to try.*

As for me, I admit I wonder what people think of what it's like raising a son like Gus. I can get angry if I detect pity – or condescension – toward Gus, toward me and Beth, or the unspoken wonder that we could love a kid like Gus. And I can get hurt if people don't ask or don't know how to ask about our son. And then, when they do, sometimes they don't really want to hear the answer.

Over time, I have come to understand that Gus, and life with him, simply had to be a mystery to others. After all, our son's life has been – at least in real time – something of a mystery to me.

79

Zartman & Zartman

BETWEEN MY RIDES to Thursday classes with Jim, and hearing Kathy read her memoirs in class, I'm getting to know the Zartmans, one of the three couples who founded Lincoln Park Village.

Kathy Zartman's accent gives away her upbringing – she grew up in coal-mining towns in Kentucky. She wasn't poor, though. Her father was an executive with the company who owned and ran the coal mine. A smart little cookie, young Kathy was sent to an all-girls boarding school for high school and is rightly proud of the quality education she received at Randolph-Macon Woman's College in Virginia. A saver, Kathy will read an essay she wrote during her school years when it suits our writing assignment. She was a good writer back then, and she still is now.

Kathy moved to Chicago after college and met Jim in a Presbyterian Young Adult group. Most of Kathy's friends in

Lincoln Park were career women, but Kathy chose to stay at home and raise their four children.

Jim isn't a writer, but when he drives me to class on Thursdays, I have the privilege of hearing his stories, too. I learn about his upbringing in a small town in Illinois, the mother who gave him his first violin, and getting free room and board in exchange for working as a houseboy for John Kenneth Galbraith's family at Harvard. "They said they named their son Jamie after me," he blushes. "But I'm not sure that's true."

Jim had a long, successful law career before retiring. He served as chairman of the Chicago Bar Association committee that prepared an important law establishing powers of attorney for health care here in Illinois, and discussions of older adults in my writing classes who have benefited from that law are routine during our drives.

Kathy reads her essays out loud to Jim before reading them in class, and like so many other discerning spouses, Jim always has suggestions for Katherine. And like so many others who receive suggestions from their spouses, Katherine often ignores them.

When Kathy turned 80, she taught herself to use an online self-publishing platform to assemble her essays into a book. I am given a copy of *Life's River Flowing*, and beam when I hear our class mentioned in the preface:

> "...[W]riters on the waiting list [for the Thursday class] are out of luck. Participants have developed a rare esprit de corps and a spot in the class is jealously guarded. What began as an eight-week project continues month after month, year after year.

Jim's review? "Some of the essays in it are good," he says. Just when I'm about to scold him, he finishes his thought. "And most of them are very good."

Jim especially likes the way Katherine uses a rocking chair to symbolize the competitiveness between two very important women in their lives. The essay she wrote for my "In-Laws" prompt is included in her collection.

A Tale of Two Mothers
By Kathy Zartman

In 1959, Jim and I each acquired a second mother – a mother-in-law. Mother-in-law stories abound, but the relationship between co-mothers-in-law is less often addressed. Competitiveness, sometimes intense, simmers beneath the surface.

My mother, Inez, Appalachian born, was shy, educated at a state teacher's college, and courted by a talkative, gregarious husband. After a brief stint of teaching, she raised her family, a quiet housewife who enjoyed sewing, painting, and watercolors. She rarely entertained.

Jim's mother, Louvenia, Minnesota born, a powerhouse of driving ambition and musical accomplishment, was a proud Carleton College graduate. Lou's mother-in-law had picked her out as ideal for her self-effacing, reticent son and engineered the match. Lou dominated their marriage, maintained an impressive home, entertained royally and worked two jobs.

Jim and I married. Each of our mothers felt we could do no wrong. How could these two women, diametrically opposite in so many ways, share a beloved child with another mother? Destiny required it of them for 43 years.

Initially, geography ruled. Jim's mother, 100 miles away, made frequent visits to Chicago and absorbed our new family into her bustling home life and holiday traditions. Jim and I, with 4 young children, rarely undertook the 500-mile drive to Tennessee where there was no fanfare and very modest holidays. This imbalance undoubtedly was hurtful to Inez. Rivalry for the affection of the grandchildren was more balanced. They appreciated the attention and copious gifts from Grandma Zartman, but also loved their quiet Gran Gran, her little southern town and the notes she wrote to them, sometimes accompanied by her drawings.

Long widowhoods changed everything. Lou moved to Milwaukee where she lived with her daughter's family for 22 years. Inez, after 14 years alone in Tennessee, moved to Chicago where she spent her last 15 years with us.

Family events often brought them together. Interactions were strained. Lou told lengthy stories that emphasized her accomplishments. Inez listened uncomfortably, attempting to come up with some matching anecdote from time to time. She clearly wished to escape to her room, her crossword puzzles and her tapes of old movies.

At our Wisconsin farm, the dueling centered on a favorite rocking chair in the kitchen. Their attempts to commandeer it were carefully choreographed. If Lou succeeded, she innocently asked if Inez preferred the rocker. Mother politely declined. If Inez got there first, which she rarely did, she staked her claim unapologetically.

In their final months, both Inez and Lou lived at The Admiral. During the afternoon of February 11, 2002, Lou, age 101, died quietly in her room in Assisted Living. Inez, age 96, lay a floor below in the Nursing Center and had been in a semi-coma for several days. She died the following night. I was asked if Mother knew that Lou had died. We cannot know for sure, but I think it is a pretty good bet that she did. She may not have been able to outshine Lou, but she was able to outlast her.

80

Back to Bennett

REMEMBER THAT LOVELY thank-you note I received from Bennett's mom a few years ago? We've stayed in touch ever since, and now I'm going to meet her little Einstein face-to-face.

When Bennett was still a toddler, his parents took him to the Children's Hospital of Pittsburgh to see Dr. Ken Nischal, one of the world's foremost children's eye specialists. Bennett had two corneal transplants then, both with negative results.

The cornea (the clear tissue that's about the size of a dime and covers the front of the eye) is the only part of the eye that can be successfully transplanted. My eye condition, diabetic retinopathy, results from problems with the retina, and so far, there is no such thing as a retina transplant.

Bennett returned to the University of Pittsburgh for another try at a cornea transplant in 2014, and when I didn't hear from his mother afterward I assumed it hadn't worked.

It's a year later, and I've been invited to make a day-long visit to Bennett's school in Muskego, Wisconsin. He is a big second-grader now, and during our visit he tells me his vision improved in his right eye after the surgery. "But just for a little while." His teachers tell me later that Bennett will return to the University of Pittsburgh next week for more tests. His mom adds that Bennett approaches each challenge with "a strength we never knew could come from someone so small."

An older boy who has visual impairments comes in on a field trip from his middle school to join us for the first hour, and Michael and Bennett both have questions about Seeing Eye dogs. I encourage each of them to inspect Whitney's harness and take a few steps with her. After that, we're off to the first presentation.

Tess Corners is a happy school. The teachers there expect a lot from their students, and they enjoy their work – I hear smiles in their voices. Their principal taught first and second grades for decades before accepting an administrative position there, and she tells me she still misses teaching sometimes. The school librarian has read *Safe & Sound* out loud to every class before Whitney and I arrive, and with Bennett at their school, the kids there already know a lot about blindness.

They still have questions, though. Bennett and Michael are at my side for the presentation I give to all the second graders. During the Q&A, I answer each question first, then pass it on to my young assistants.

"Can you see at all?" one girl asks.

I give my usual answer: "When I open my eyes, all I see is the color black."

Michael says, "I can see some things if I hold them really close."

Bennett says, "I can kind of see light, but everything is blurry...like a cloud."

Another child asks, "How do you read if you can't see?" I describe audio books and my talking computer, Michael touches the screen on his iPad so we can hear VoiceOver, and Bennett shows off his Brailliant, an electronic device people who are blind use to read with their hands. The Brailliant transforms the words on a computer screen into small plastic or metal pins that move up and down on a flat panel attached to the computer.

Michael eventually has to return to middle school, but Bennett stays in front with me long enough to read aloud to his classmates from the Braille version of *Safe & Sound*. His composure and confidence is remarkable — a credit to his fellow students, his family, the teachers and staff at Tess Corners, and, especially, to Bennett himself.

Bennett leaves with his second-grade class after that, and Whitney leads me out the door to give presentations to the other grade levels at Tess Corners.

We meet up with Bennett again one last time during his lunch break – he wants to show me how to use his Brailliant. He explains how he places his fingers on the panel to read the Braille characters formed by the pins, and then demonstrates by reading a line of text out loud. I tell him I'd never seen – or should I say, felt – such a thing before.

Bennett uses the keys to tap out secret messages and passes the device my way so I can read them in Braille. He can't help but notice – and chuckle – when I struggle to decipher his big words. He finally relents and dumbs it down to shorter words. He places my hands on the keys to show me how to compose and send a Braille note back. The blind leading the blind for sure. We happily exchange "refreshable Braille notes" for the rest of the lunch hour.

Bennett uses VoiceOver to check his school assignments, and he listens to audiobooks sometimes, too. But he and his teachers know that if he doesn't learn to read Braille, he won't learn to spell correctly. He won't learn all the punctuation rules of our written language. Bennett has already tackled a lot of this stuff.

And while it's true I'm not proficient in Braille, the little I know sure comes in handy when I label CDs, file folders, ID cards, buttons on computers and other electronic devices. My Braille skills are useful on elevators, too, and it is rewarding to have known enough Braille to exchange short secret messages with that bright, curious, cute – and patient – second-grade boy I'd been hearing about all these years.

Bennett and Beth at Tess Corners Elementary School

81

A Message for Susan

I HAVE THE best job in Chicago. Four times a week an adorable dog leads me to a quiet room and falls asleep at my feet for an hour or so while I listen to older adults read the stories of their lives.

Only bad part of the job? Sometimes aging gets the best of my writers. It's inevitable.

Susan has been a writer in my memoir classes since 2009. She was in the downtown class with Wanda and Audrey and the others until 2011, when she added the Lincoln Park Village class. Some of the essays from her "Me, Myself, and I" class mention she is recovering from cancer, but I don't learn much more about that until she volunteers to drive me to Lincoln Park for a few Thursday classes while my regular chauffeur Jim Zartman is on vacation. She tells me she has chemo treatments every Thursday anyway, so it's no trouble.

Chemo every Thursday? No trouble?

"What cute shoes!" Susan says. My sneakers are pretty

cool, yes, but I read Susan's compliment as a plea to change the subject. So I do.

Susan has been living with Stage 4 Multiple Myeloma for about six years, and has already undergone chemo, radiation, and a stem cell transplant. She describes her Thursday doctor visits as "maintenance chemo" and seems to regard her Myeloma the same way I regard my type 1 diabetes. It's chronic, you have to keep track of it, you deal with it and try not to think about it much.

Until 2014, when her cancer takes a turn for the worse.

Back in December, Susan had shared a secret with me. She's compiling her memoirs to give as gifts to her daughters. I've never met Amy and Sarah, but feel I know them well from the essays Susan has written about them. I know they'll love reading their mom's essays.

Now Susan's health is declining. Her fellow writers visit her in the hospital and give us updates each week in class. I visit Susan by phone and get to know Amy and Sarah even better now via the thoughtful, caring email messages they send out regularly to keep friends and family abreast of Susan's progress. Or lack thereof.

An email message from Amy in March, 2015, brings news: "It is with heartbreaking news that I tell you of Mom's admittance into hospice.... She is pain-free at the moment and we hope her stay here is short and easy." Within a few days, Susan passes away.

Another message follows, this time from Susan's daughter Sarah. I learn that when the family gathered around after her mom's death, Sarah had read essays to them from Susan's memoir book. "So we all benefited from those, and will continue to do so. I will be forever grateful to you for this precious, precious gift." Later, she writes, "Her essays have given me new insight into so many parts of her life. And since she has passed, I read some of them every night, which helps me feel closer to her."

I am touched when Susan's daughters ask me to speak at their mom's memorial service. I come prepared to recite short quotes from Susan's memoir pieces.

Over 100 people show up to pay their respects, and the other presenters steal my thunder. Dorothy, one of her best friends; Sherill, a friend of 60 years who she met in nursing school; Dianne, a colleague from her days at Rush graduate school of nursing and Cook County Hospital; her brother Steve, her husband, Ben...all of them mention Susan's memoir class in their talks. All of them read from one of Susan's essays. A couple of them read an entire 500-word piece.

The presenters who have traveled from out of town repeat the same story: after mentioning them in an essay, Susan had taken the time to make a copy, write a note, slip the papers into an envelope and mail it to them.

Hearing each person say how grateful they are to Susan for writing these essays leaves me with a wonderful mixture of emotions. I want to laugh and cry at the same time.

But I can't. I have to give my presentation. What am I going to say?

I start with "Whitney, forward!" and my faithful dog leads me to the podium. Susan's daughter takes my hand, and when she places it on the microphone to show me where to talk, it

334

comes to me. I want to tell Susan about all this.

So I do.

I tap the microphone, and everyone quiets. That's nice and all, but they're not the ones I'm addressing here. I'm talking to Susan.

"Susan. Susan? It's me, Beth." I pause, then go on. "Do you believe this? Can you believe all these people are here?" I tell her I got here early enough to meet a lot of people before the service. "I knew a lot of them already, though," I tell her. "You wrote about them in your memoirs." I tell her I especially enjoyed meeting the neighbor kids who were there. "Those sweet boys you love so much? They're here, too." I name her faraway friends, her siblings, and her daughters Sarah and Amy, who I'd met face-to-face for the first time that day. "They put together a perfect gathering for you, Susan. No wonder you're so proud of them. You raised them well."

I don't talk long. I don't even say 500 words. "And I'm not going to tell you I wish you were here, because I know you are." I tell her what she already knows, that her story lives on through her family and friends. "And through all those stories you wrote, too."

I need to let Susan know it's time for me to take off. It's Susan's daughter Sarah's turn to talk. How to say goodbye? Keep it simple. And so, I do: "Talk to you later."

82

The Regan Era

IT'S BEEN OVER a year since I started teaching at Grace Place. Linda and I have made our peace and still meet from time to time to talk about writing and offer each other suggestions about leading our memoir classes.

My Grace Place class meets for six-week sessions, one session each quarter. Regan signs up for all of them, and in-between she goes to Linda's class.

Students in the memoir-writing class at the Center for Life and Learning love Linda. Her class is so popular now that it has a waiting list. She also leads another weekly memoir-writing class in a Chicago retirement-living community and has taught a fiction-writing course at Chicago's renowned Newberry Library. With my Grace Place class on break now, Linda sends an email and tells me, "I sure am enjoying having Regan every week."

A civil rights activist, Regan writes colorful life stories. She sparkles when she laughs – which means she sparkles a lot.

But I learn from listening to her essays that her early life provided little to smile about. Her father drank, her mother drank, and Regan attended 11 different schools by the time she entered seventh grade.

When I give "Wheels" as a writing prompt, Regan writes about falling in love as a teen with a co-worker at a bar called Avon-by-the-Sea.

> *Jim Kelly and I met on the back of a 250cc Honda Dream motorcycle when he gave me a lift home one night in the early New Jersey summer of 1966. Our mutual attraction accelerated on that motorcycle, on the Jersey Shore's raucous dance floors, and in the soft sand under the boardwalk.*

Regan and Kelly, as she refers to him, were married that December. Their son Joe was born the next year. In August of 1969, Regan left the baby with Kelly for a few days and took off for Woodstock.

Months after Woodstock, Toddler Joe stayed with babysitters so both parents could join friends driving to Washington, D.C., to march in the 1969 antiwar protest there. Eight years later she returned to D.C. with her school-age son for Jimmy Carter's 1977 Inauguration.

Fifteen years later? Regan moved to D.C. to work in Bill Clinton's administration. "In 1994 he passed a crime bill I thought went too far. Next he signed NAFTA, an agreement opposed by every Democrat I respected," she says, reading an essay about the Clinton years in class. "Dissatisfaction settled in the space between my bones and muscled me awake at 3 o'clock in the morning for the next seven years."

In 2016, musician Prince's death inspires me to ask writers

about "A Celebrity's Death that Made Me Really Sad." Regan's essay describes her turning on the radio in her DuPont Circle townhouse one morning in 1995 and learning that the Grateful Dead's Jerry Garcia had died overnight.

In the Attics of My Life with Jerry
By Regan Burke

In the still of an August morning in 1995, NPR told me Jerry Garcia died. I collapsed on the bathroom floor weeping over the death of something I couldn't put words to. At 49 years old my idealism had come to an end: my false world of everlasting good died with Jerry Garcia. Reality glared back at me in the mirror as I brushed my hair, seeing for the first time a wrinkled face and rubbery neck. I dressed in a soft yellow, flowery cotton frock and pinned a silk flower in my hair, ready for the grieving day.

My dog Voter squirmed away from my extra-long hug and I went out the door to my old friend Keith Lesnick waiting to drive us to work. As soon as I got in the car tears spilled out. He asked about the sadness, and I slobbered out a few words, "Jerry Garcia signed into rehab last night," I said. "He died in his sleep." Keith waited a few respectful minutes, and then, with one simple sentence, he opened a new, naked reality that included the unspoken caveat of don't take yourself too seriously.

He said, "Well, it's not as if it's Aretha Franklin."

REGAN AND I meet in the city from time to time when my Grace Place class is on break. Over coffee one morning I wonder out loud if she started pronouncing her name with a long E after President Reagan took office.

"No!" she laughs. "It's been pronounced this way my whole life."

"But that's the way the girl in *The Exorcist* pronounces it, isn't it? The one who was possessed?"

"The author named the character after me," Regan says, sounding as nonchalant as if she'd just let me know my shoe was untied.

"My family lived in Georgetown for a while after I was born," she says, reminding me that in *The Exorcist* the guy who gets killed falling from the townhouse window is named Burke. That's Regan's last name. Until that guy in the book falls out of the window, he'd been drinking too many martinis during visits to the possessed girl's mother.

"My father, William Burke?" Regan says. "He liked his martinis." Regan tells me she's never run across anyone else with the first name Regan. "The only other one I know of is King Lear's daughter."

Hmm. Regan in Shakespeare's *King Lear*. Isn't she the daughter involved in the eye-gouging scene?

Regan was 24 years old when she first read William Peter Blatty's book. "I asked my mother about it back then," she says. "Agnes hadn't read *The Exorcist*, but she said I might be right, that Blatty could have easily been one of the college kids who came to parties at our house in Georgetown."

A friend of Regan's ran into Blatty years later, and he confirmed Regan's supposition. "He told my friend that my parents always had the best parties," Regan tells me. "And he always wondered how anyone could name their baby after King Lear's daughter."

83

Bob Holds the Reins

I ASSIGN THE prompt "Sum up Your Life in Three Songs," and surprise, surprise, "Chicago (My Kind of Town)" ends up on many lists.

Bob is one of those writers, and his essay explains how the line "Chicago is why I grin like a clown, it's my kind of town" makes him think of his Uncle Morrie and Aunt Sylvia.

"Uncle Morrie worked as a circus clown at Riverview Park, where he roamed the park and entertained the crowds," he writes.

Bob's Aunt Sylvia worked there, too.

"She worked at an amusement stand where she wore a bathing suit and sat at the top of a long slick slide, waiting for people to pay their dime and throw three balls at a target. Whenever anyone hit the bullseye, it would release Aunt Sylvia, and she'd slide down the sleek slide and hand you a box of candy."

And that's exactly how Bob's Uncle Morrie met his Aunt Sylvia. "Uncle Morrie walked up, played his dime, and hit the bullseye with the first ball. Aunt Sylvia slid down the slide, handed him a box of candy, and that was it. It was an immediate attraction for both of them."

Bob loved his years with Uncle Morrie and Aunt Sylvia. And when I assign the prompt "The Best Job I Ever Had," we learn that his uncle and aunt weren't the only ones in the family to hold down an unconventional job back then.

The Best Job I Ever Had
By Bob Eisenberg

The best job I ever had happened when I was 11 years old. I worked for Rubin Dunn. He was a short, thin man who always wore a leather vest, was in his late 60s, and emigrated here from Russia at about the same time my grandparents came to this country, somewhere around 1917.

Rubin had his own business pedaling fruit and junk items from his horse and wagon in our neighborhood during the summer and fall. Our neighborhood was the most exciting place to live in the city of Chicago. There was always so much activity going on. The knife sharpener would wheel his cart through the streets. Maxwell Street was only a few blocks from our house. On the weekends there was so much activity with the clothing stands, people shouting about their sales prices for socks and underwear. Our neighborhood was constantly busy with people selling their wares up and down the streets and through the alleys.

Mr. Dunn and his wife Bella lived across the hall from us

341

on the third floor in the apartment building that we lived in on Roosevelt Road.

One morning when I was on my way to school he stopped and asked if he could talk to me. He needed a helping hand on his wagon and asked if I knew anyone who wanted a job.

I jumped at the chance. I said, "Me." This was my very first real job. I was thrilled. I told all my friends and had a hard time sleeping at night thinking about it.

We were selling fruits and vegetables that were selling in grocery stores, and they didn't want us around. We did whatever we could to stay out of their way. We avoided the alleys behind the grocery stores whenever we could.

The start of my work day was the favorite part of my job. That's when I'd take the big brown workhorse out of his stall in Mush's barn and guide him into the alley. Then I'd get the empty wooden wagon and pull it out behind the horse and attach the long wooden wagon poles to the horse. I would climb up the wagon and wait while I sat on the driver's side, waiting for Mr. Dunn to climb up into the wagon and sit next to me.

Our journey to the South Water Market started with me driving, holding the reins, and Mr. Dunn sitting next to me guiding me all the way. I would look down at the car roofs and proudly wave to my friends as I drove the wagon down Roosevelt Road.

When we approach the stall at the South Water Market, Mr. Dunn took over the reins in order to guide the wagon into a stall so we could load our watermelons properly. When the watermelons were loaded and paid for we were off, back to our neighborhood.

As Mr. Dunn drove the horse and wagon through the alleys, I stood up in the back of the wagon, cupped my hands around my mouth and yelled "WATAMEELO." People ran down stairs to buy our watermelons. We talked and laughed with everybody and shared the news of the day as we heard it from people along the way. I got 20 cents for each watermelon sold. By the end of the day I felt like I was wealthy.

When our day ended we drove back to the barn. Putting the horse and wagon back in the barn was a lot trickier than taking it out. Mr. Dunn taught me all the steps in that process.

Mr. Dunn and I did this all summer. When the fall came around, we drove our horse and wagon through the same alleys and as the people came out to their porches, I stood in the back of the wagon and yelled "RAGSALION," which meant rags and old iron. People came running down from their porches with old clothes, old pots and pans, and all sorts of junk they wanted to get rid of. There were a good number of people that we sold watermelons to during the summer. Because we knew them and always told them our news of the day, they were especially nice to us and would feed us whatever they were cooking. When we were finished, everything we collected was taken to the junkyard and sold. At the end of the day I was exhausted but very happy. I felt like I was a contributing part of the environment that I was surrounded by.

My experience in my job with Rubin Dunn gave me the confidence to find many jobs in my adolescence. My first job gave me a feeling of self-worth and independence at a very young age.

84

Your Dog Is Too Skinny

I HAVE JUST finished tying Whitney's latest deposit into a pick-up bag and am leaning down to re-buckle her harness when a stranger approaches us. "Excuse me," she says. She can't wait for me to stand up before asking her question. "I'm not sure you notice, you know, not being able to see him and all, but do you know your dog is too skinny?"

My face breaks out into a huge smile. I even chuckle. And once I stand up, I look towards the sidewalk stranger's voice and thank her for her concern. "You know, it's funny," I say, explaining that the night before graduates leave for home with our new Seeing Eye dogs, a veterinarian from The Seeing Eye speaks at our "Going Home" presentation. "She warns us that once we get out and about with our guides at home, complete strangers will stop us to tell us our dogs are too thin...and here you are!"

During that lecture, the Seeing Eye vet told us our dogs are the perfect weight just as they are. "The vet said Americans feed their dogs too much food," I shrug. "Everyone gets used to seeing overweight dogs, and they end up thinking that's the way dogs are supposed to look." The sidewalk stranger is unmoved.

"I know they breed them special, I know that," she says. "But there's something wrong with yours. He's too skinny. I have three dogs, I know dogs. Bring him to a vet. Ask them, they'll tell you."

I consider telling her that I'd just had Whitney at the vet for a physical a couple of weeks earlier, and during that visit the doctor confirmed that Whitney is still the perfect weight. But then I think better of it.

During that same Going Home lecture at The Seeing Eye, another staff member had told us that when we're out and about with our Seeing Eye dogs it's normal to encounter questions, sometimes even interference, from people who do not intend to cause us difficulty. "Losing your temper can just make things worse," he said. "Giving a brief explanation will limit the interference, and educating these people will prevent more problems in the future."

And so, I don't lose my temper, even when the sidewalk stranger confesses she'd been following me for a while. "I was walking behind you and his back legs, you can't see him, but he's too skinny," she says. "The way he walks, there is something really wrong with him. You need to take him to a vet."

Time to go. I thank the sidewalk stranger again for her concern, and then I tell her I do have something she could — — help me with. "Without being able to see, you know, I can't tell where a nearby garbage can might be," I say. "Can you throw this out for me?" And with that, I hand her the bag of poop.

345

85

Anna's House in Prague

LOTS OF PEOPLE have interesting life stories to tell. The hard part? Getting those stories down on paper so that others can read – and reread – them.

As the writers in my classes master the art of writing about their lives, they find themselves with a new challenge: assembling finished stories into book form.

Anna Perlberg has been in the Thursday Lincoln Park Village class since it started in 2011, and it's been a treat to hear her unveil her stories one by one. She is a link to my downtown class, too, because she and Hannelore got to know each other through Anna's work at the Blind Service Association.

Anna has spent a lifetime listening to poetry – her late husband, Mark Perlberg, was a poet – and she reads her essays with exquisite rhythm and timing. You don't need to be able to see to know that everyone in class is at the edge of their seats, riveted by Anna's words.

When I assign "Feeling Homesick" as a topic, Anna shares an excerpt from a piece she'd written for the University of Nebraska's *Prairie Schooner* magazine.

Anna was born in Czechoslovakia. Her family, complete with maids, a cook, and a gardener, lived in a remarkable home in Prague's *Mala Strana* quarter. But their elegant life came to a swift end when Hitler invaded and World War II began. To escape Hitler's army, the family took a circuitous, and often hair-raising, route to New York City in 1939. Anna's story details countless friends and complete strangers who helped along the way. "I observed much, though I understood little, as we left one world for another in America."

Many essays later, Anna's literary agent has found a publisher interested in turning her stories into a book. Soon Anna becomes the first of my writers to be published by an independent book publisher and receive royalties for her work.

So here we are in the summer of 2016, Michael Knezovich and Beth Finke, at a book launch party in a beautiful forty-ninth floor apartment on the North Side of Chicago, all dressed up, snacking on canapés, celebrating the publication of *The House in Prague*, by Anna Nessy Perlberg.

The event is sponsored by Lincoln Park Village, and the fantastic space has been provided by one of the Village's generous members. Tonight this opulent Magnificent Mile apartment is overflowing with writers from both Lincoln Park classes, many of whom I now call friends.

One of those friends is Bruce Hunt, the man who has the great fortune of driving Anna to class each week. I know firsthand that car rides can spark friendships, and I am delighted to hear that Bruce will be introducing Anna's reading tonight.

Anna is comforted by Bruce's presence. She recites her clean prose in a strong voice, recollecting her nine-year-old self seeing familiar faces at Prague's cafés replaced by fierce-looking strangers in Nazi uniforms. She reads of kissing the family home goodbye, surviving brushes with the Gestapo, finally landing on Ellis Island and starting a new life in New York City. Her father, a distinguished attorney who'd worked for President Masaryk in Prague, never practices law again. Her mother, an accomplished opera singer, loses her career. And little Anna saves up for a radio to tuck under her covers and listen to *Your Hit Parade* at night, trying to become an American girl just as fast as she can.

Mike has graciously accompanied me to Lincoln Park Village events before, but none move him like this one. Mike is a news junkie. He follows politics. He reads far more on-line magazines and political blogs than I do and is far more introspective about what he reads than I am.

He talks about Anna all the way home.

Anna's 2016 book launch has come right smack dab in the middle of some especially volatile election-year rhetoric. "You know, we get lazy," he says, speaking of American culture and society. "We like to think the Holocaust, or even Rwanda, or our own history of slavery, we'd just like to think that's all behind us."

Mike is especially taken by a passage Anna read recalling sailing into the United States in 1939:

> *We stand together at the railing and watch as the harbor comes closer and closer. Mother lifts me up high to see the Statue of Liberty as clearly as possible. She says with a kind of fierceness, "Don't ever forget this."*

The House in Prague starts in present tense from Anna's nine-year-old point of view, and the voice is so strong that it inspires me to assign "Nine" as a writing prompt to my classes the next week.

Writers can do an essay about themselves as nine-year-olds, or use the number nine in any other way they choose.

Anna's success also motivates other writers in class to think about getting their memoirs published. Their questions inspire me to put together a memoir workshop for this summer's Northwestern University Summer Writers' Conference on Northwestern University's Chicago campus.

I plan "Getting Your Memoir Off the Ground" as a 90-minute workshop. I'll be giving a few in-class exercises and discussing techniques to get past whatever it is that's stopping writers from getting their work done, whether it be worries about writing as a victim, facing issues that come with writing about people we love, or figuring out strategies for organizing the raw material of our lives into book form. The overall emphasis will be on craft and on overcoming the barriers that keep us from writing and assembling our stories.

And I'll pass out a copy of *The House in Prague* as an example.

86

Winners All

MIKE KNEZOVICH LOVES baseball. But he doesn't love the Cubs.

Mike is a Chicago White Sox fan. He does not think the Wrigley Field ivy is cute. Crying is OK in baseball, shrubbery is not. He doesn't think naming a dog – or a child – Wrigley is clever.

He thinks the Cubs manager likes attention a little too much and is too fond of gimmickry. He finds grown men posing for photos in onesie pajamas a sign of weakness.

Mike Knezovich owns an "L" flag.

Earlier this month I came up with a plan. For Mike's sake – and the sake of Chicago citizens – I'd see to it that Mike was away from Cubs fans if the Cubs ended up playing at Wrigley in the World Series this year.

Cub fans are everywhere (they're like cockroaches, Mike says). Where on earth can we go to watch those games where Cub fans would be in a minority? The home of the American

League champions! So off to Cleveland we go to ride out the storm.

When the Cubs win the series, it's all anyone talks about – including Wanda. I assign "Winning" as a topic that week, and even Mike enjoys the essay she comes back with about her favorite Uncle Hallie B. celebrating the Cubs' win on Mount Eternity.

Winning
By Wanda Bridgeforth

My Dear Niece,

Greeting from Mount Eternity! Spunky (aka Bea) and I are hoarse from cheering our beloved Cubs, Winner of the World Series. Ernie Banks is running around yelling "NEXT YEAR IS HERE!"

I started thinking about other winners. Harry Truman holding the newspaper with the headline "Dewey Wins." I'm sure the editor had egg on his face.

I recalled the many folks who were winners against tremendous racial and economic odds.

Joe Louis crowned Heavyweight Boxing Champion of the World.

Jesse Owens, Wilma Rudolph, and Gail Devers, Olympic champions.

Your schoolmate John H. Johnson established a publishing empire with Ebony and Jet magazines.

Those are big winners.

The saying "May the best man win" is kind of iffy because the best man doesn't always win. This is proven by some of the duds the voting and non-voting public have elected.

351

Spunky and I polled the group and we say in some way we are all winners. Everyone has conquered the challenge of a mountain or maybe a hill.

I close with this thought: July 1776, our citizens were WINNERS with the signing of the Declaration of Independence.

July 1976, I arrived on Mt. Eternity in time to see you become a WINNER when you received your degree from Chicago State University.

So, Three Cheers for us, WINNERS ALL!

87

Simple Pleasures

SHORTLY AFTER THE Illinois State Lottery started in the 70s, psychologists from Northwestern University interviewed winners a few months after they'd won. They asked them to rate their happiness, and how much pleasure they were getting from mundane activities like reading a magazine or meeting friends for coffee.

Next they interviewed people who lived in the same neighborhoods as the winners, but hadn't won the lottery.

Results showed that the non-winners were nearly as happy as the lottery winners. In fact, the so-called losers were finding more pleasure in everyday activities than the winners.

The researchers also interviewed people who were paralyzed in accidents that same year. Their study, called "Lottery Winners and Accident Victims: Is Happiness Relative?" found that after initial sadness, people who were paralyzed rated their pleasure in everyday activities slightly higher than that of the lottery winners. Their life satisfaction was nearly the same.

That study makes a lot of sense to me.

It's Wednesday. I listen to NPR while I finish the cup of coffee Mike made for me this morning. Once I'm done, I flip on the stereo and load a CD. Something new – Chance the Rapper, maybe? Or old favorites like Ben Folds, Warren Zevon, Stevie Wonder. Or maybe a little piano jazz from Marcus Roberts.

I collect myself and my coat, buckle Whitney into her harness, and we head out to her favorite tree.

It's a sunny spring morning in Chicago. Maybe we'll take the long way home, listen for birds, smell the lilacs.

Back in the apartment, I spend a few hours on my job for Easterseals. Then time to shower, dress, check to make sure the Scrabble tiles and timer are in my bag, and head downtown to lead my memoir-writing class.

I'll feed Whitney when we get back, then maybe listen to a book while waiting for Mike to get home from work. I'm re-reading my favorite book from childhood, one my older brothers and sisters read aloud when they were teaching me to read: *The Adventures of Winnie-the-Pooh.*

After my trip to the 100 Acre Wood? Off to Costco! I'll hang on to the back of the shopping cart, eavesdrop on people from all walks of life, try to decipher the dozens of foreign languages I hear, all while Mike pulls us through the aisles. He'll stop periodically, say "Feel this!" and drop an enormous oversized jar of some unknown substance into my hands. "Miracle Whip!" he'll exclaim with glee. I always roll my eyes, but I can't help but laugh. And I can't help but relish the $1.50 hot dog and pop we enjoy before we leave. Free refills, too.

After unloading the Land of the Giants groceries at home, we might pad over to our friendly local tavern to share some wine with friends: bottles of wine are half-price on Wednesdays.

Who wouldn't think they'd won the lottery after a day like today?

And I didn't even have to buy a ticket.

356

Epilogue

LINCOLN PARK HAS outgrown its name – now it's The Village Chicago. Printers Row Book Fair is now called Printers Row Lit Fest. Hackney's, our favorite tavern, has closed and will reopen as Hax, a fast-casual spot aimed at a younger clientele. And our downtown class? It's still called "Me, Myself, and I," but it hasn't been the same since the weekly trek got to be too much for 97-year-old Hannelore.

"They have a writing class here that I could go to, but I'll tell you a secret, Beth," she says, scooting over on Speedo, her trusty walker, so she can whisper. "It's not the same."

Audrey visits Hannelore with Darlene and Sheila, two other writers from the downtown class. One Lutheran, one Baptist, and one Catholic, visiting their Jewish friend, chatting away and catching up on news of the other writers in their class.

Over the phone later, Darlene tells me that Hannelore and Speedo walked them all the way down to the parking garage when it was time to go. "She was still there at the door waving when we drove off," Darlene says. "And she was crying, too."

"And then she called the next day wondering where we were, what time we were coming," Darlene continues, starting to weep a bit herself. "She didn't remember we'd already been to see her."

The next time the trio visits Hannelore, she has news for them. "A staff member read some of my essays out loud," she says, rummaging through a bag strapped to Speedo until she feels the shiny cover of *What's in My Head*. "He read them from my book."

And that's when Sheila gets her idea. "How about I read some of these out loud now?" she asks.

The afternoon goes on from there, Sheila reading stories, Hannelore listening and answering questions about them, about her people, how she got here from Germany, her life since then.

Hannelore's voice is upbeat the next time I call. "Everyone here wants to know about my book!"

I tell her I have a book coming out soon, too. "You're one of the stars in it!" Hannelore laughs in pretend surprise.

"Me?" Her joy is contagious, and we chat away like happy chuckleheads. Just as I'm beginning to wonder what her visitors from class were worried about, Hannelore starts telling me about the writing class she takes, and the blind lady who teaches it.

She's lost track of who I am, but to my surprise that doesn't bother me. I like hearing about her book, and the conversation reminds me of ones I had with Flo when she was 97 years old.

Hannelore keeps talking about her book, how it's a part of her life now, how it's in its fourth printing.

"That book connects me, somehow, more than ever now. It connects me to the real world that I really lived through." She wants to tell me more, she says, she wants me to understand how important writing is.

I'm all ears.

ACKNOWLEDGMENTS

GOLDEN ALLEY PRESS took this project on sight unseen. I am grateful to my editor, Nancy Sayre, for your intelligence, tact, and above all, your grace in reshaping my rough draft into a book I can be proud of. And Michael Sayre, from all I hear, your design work has transformed *Writing Out Loud* into a work of art that stands out in the crowd. A huge thank you to both of you, and to Anna Perlberg, too, for sharing you with me.

This book might never have been written if not for Joyce Gallagher, Executive Director of the City of Chicago's Department of Family and Support Services. Thank you for seeing promise in me that I might have never noticed on my own. Thanks also to anyone who ever signed up for the "Me, Myself and I" class at the Chicago Cultural Center, and everyone else connected to Renaissance Court. You made it all happen.

Myrna Knepler and the late Susan Squires introduced me to their North Side neighbors, and Marjorie Freid, Kathy Zartman, and Judy Spock (three of the six founders of Lincoln Park Village) have been with me from the start. My thanks to you and to everyone connected with Lincoln Park Village, now known as The Village Chicago, as your enthusiasm for memoir writing has inspired me to keep working on this book.

My writers group read, reread, and edited the rough draft that eventually became *Writing Out Loud.* Thank you Linda Downing Miller, Cam Robbins, Lynn LaPlante Allaway, and Audrey Petty. You stuck with it right to the very end.

To anyone out there who ever read a post on our Safe & Sound blog, especially those of you who subscribe to the blog and leave comments there, thank you. The interest you take in our weekly writing encourages Mike Knezovich and me to keep working at it.

Thanks go out to the National Endowment for the Arts for awarding me a writing fellowship, and to Vermont Studio Center's Kate Westcott and my New England friends Greg Tillman, Siobhan Senier, and Sally Nelson for keeping me on my path while I was there.

To my brother and sisters, thank you for teaching me to read when I was a kid and inspiring me to write ever since. Cheers to you and the rest of the Flo Nation for your ongoing enthusiasm, humor, and encouragement.

I want to especially thank Carolyn Alessio, Pauline Alexander, Nancy Beskin, Benita Black, Cate Cahan, Jamie Ceaser, Matt Cunningham, Joe DeCeault, Jenny Fischer, Jill Foucré, Laura Gale, Lydia Gibson, Joe and Kate Hagen, Bill Healy, Colleen Keleher, Ann Lowry, Tom Morgan, Miriam Nelson, Jill Petty, Francine Rich, and Jean Thompson, all of whom provided and continue to provide ideas, information, help, encouragement, conversation, entertainment, and friendship. Same goes for my Printers Row neighbors. Whether it be at Sandmeyer's Bookstore or my office at Hackney's, you've been there for years listening to me yammer on and on about the writers in my classes. I hope this book helps explain why you, and they, mean so much to me.

And now, to Michael Knezovich, for, well, literally everything, including coming up with the title for this book. You keep me alert, amused, and alive, and I love you more than you know.

Thank you all.

CREDITS

Except as noted below, all images are courtesy of the author.

Grateful acknowledgement is made for permission to use the following photographs:

Front cover photograph of the author: Bill Healy

Back cover photograph of the author: Kaitlin McCall

ABOUT THE AUTHOR

Beth Finke is an award-winning author, teacher, journalist, NPR commentator, and recipient of a National Endowment for the Arts grant. She also happens to be blind.

Beth lives in the Printers Row neighborhood of Chicago with her husband, Mike, and her Seeing Eye dog, Whitney.

Beth loves hearing from her readers and
invites you to keep in touch.

Sign up for her newsletter: www.bethfinke.com/contact

Blog: www.bethfinke.com/blog

Facebook: www.fb.com/BethFinkeAuthor

Twitter: www.twitter.com/BethFinke

Email: bethfinke@goldenalleypress.com

63341786R00228

Made in the USA
Lexington, KY
04 May 2017